EVERYTHING MIX

MEMOIRS OF A CLERICAL LIFE

By

JAMES SCOTT MARSHALL

To Mary
whose courage, devotion and cheerfulness
have made me the good life

Contents

Prologue. PAGE 1

1. Making a Start. PAGE 5
Early childhood at Baronscourt Terrace up to the Armisitice 1918.

2. Leith 1919-1926. PAGE 17
School Days, holidays, hobbies and Scouts.

3. Baronscourt Again. PAGE 35
Leith Academy, family entertainment and music. Onset of epilepsy.

4. University 1932-38. PAGE 45
Agriculture or the Church? Meeting Mary Tough. New College.

5. On Probation 1938-39. PAGE 65
Trials, spiritual and physical. Marriage, hardship, and war again.

6. Twechar 1939-46. PAGE 76
First charge and manse. Miners and more fits. Experiences with animals, and digging for victory.

7. Kirkgate Church Phase 1. PAGE 96
Planning the childrens' education. Coming to terms with the Congregation. Music and drama groups. First writing of History and starting the Lunch Club.

8. Kirgate Church Phase 2. PAGE 121
The Claremont Park Manse. Morag marries. Friends in France. Research into Irregular Marriages and a trip to Norway. Politics and Ph.D. Civic Pride, Leith Civic Trust and Museum.

9. South Leith Kirk and Parish. PAGE 150
More travelling: Europe, Eire, Kirkwall, Palestine, Malta, Greece. Jack Kellet, and public speaking. National Bible Society, North Carr Lightship and The Cape Club Histories of Leith published. Canada and U.S.A. New Halls opened and a sort of retiral.

10. Last years in South Leith 1988-1990. PAGE 180
Roman Catholics in Leith and joint services. Mannheim conference with Andrew Doig. Leith versus Edinburgh again. Damascus and Cyprus Scots Language Society. Move to St.Andrews.

Epilogue. PAGE 200

Damascus Diary 1985. PAGE 204

APPRECIATION
by Lord Murray

The Rev. Dr. Marshall's autobiography spans over 90 years of contemporary life in Scotland, firmly centred in its capital city and Dr. Marshall's beloved Leith where he served before he retired as a distinguished associate minister of the historic South Leith Parish Church. The book is indeed a cameo of Scottish life and culture spiced with humour, a strong sense of history and a charming parochialism in some of its anecdotes. Through it Dr. Marshall's humanity shines brightly.

The book will be welcomed by all concerned with the story of Leith in its wider context of Edinburgh and Scotland. I first got to know the author when I was Member of Parliament for Leith in the 1970s. He worked with me and other activists for government funding to halt the decline and decay of Leith and to rehabilitate its very real community spirit.

The modern redevelopment of Leith and the new vigour it enjoys show that this effort has not been in vain. There has been less success, so far, in another objective dear to Dr. Marshall's heart - the establishment of a Leith museum. But there is general acceptance now that this is desirable and hopefully Dr. Marshall may yet see it realised. In the meantime we are fortunate to have this and Dr. Marshall's other writings on the story of Leith.

"Only God - and Uncle James - know everything!"
comment from nephew Duncan Marshall, aged five.

PREFACE

My mother, a great raconteur, always said she could write a book, and she certainly had plenty of material; but as she herself admitted, she had neither the time nor the patience for the job. I'd love to have had the reminiscences of one of my ancestors from some previous century, so this is my effort to supply material for life in the twentieth century. Granny was fond of proverbs, and in time of trouble or disappointment she would comment 'Everything is mixed with mercy' - probably derived from Paul's 'We know that all things work together for good to them that love God, to them who are the called according to his purpose.' (Rom. viii. 28.) Hence the title of the following rag-bag.

You will recognize this as a collection of trivia, and so perhaps completely boring; but our lives are largely made up of trivia which to future generations become surprisingly interesting. Historians today are very interested in the details of the lives of those socially or politically prominent in their generation. The lives of those not prominent or important might also throw up a good deal of interest, but those folk were mostly illiterate.

Trivial or not, this is my story. I have only mentioned things that happened to me, things I have been able to do, and not always done well - and my thoughts from time to time. Well, as we say hereabouts, you must just take it and 'make a kirk or a mill of it'.

And finally, I have been greatly indebted to Graham Wood, my grandson in Ireland, who has read through all this farrago, corrected my execrable typescript and produced a fair copy fit to be seen by the printer.

PROLOGUE

In Scotland there were no surnames until after the Norman Conquest in 1066. They are supposed to have been invented in France about the year 1000. Many Normans arrived in Scotland with the eleventh century invasion, and surnames became fashionable then. The French Marechal meant a groom or farrier. It may therefore be supposed that the first Scottish Marshalls were retainers of Norman knights. They were presumably the ancestors of the modern veterinary surgeon. From that same period many of the new surnames were descriptive of various trades and occupations, such as baker, tailor, (black)smith, webster.

In the course of time some of the Marshalls prospered, and a certain Philip Marescallus married a daughter of the Keiths of Humbie, who was heiress to the Keith estates; and as was common in such a succession to entailed estates, the husband added Keith to his name, and the Keith-Marshalls were established. The head of this family was raised to the honourable hereditary position of Earl Marshal in 1455. The Earl Marshal was a sort of chamberlain, who was also commander-in-chief of the cavalry. He ranked with the highest both at court and in the field; but the office of Earl Marshal came to an end in 1755.

According to the imaginary clan lore that is given to the public as commercial publicity, we are informed that the Marshalls are a sept of Clan Keith; but plainly it would be truer to say that the Keiths are a sept of Clan Marshall, since the male line of the Keiths failed when they intermarried with the Marshalls, but there is no point in pressing this since the entire history of clan organisation is full of doubts and difficulties, not to say fairy tales and fancies. The Marshalls, bearing an occupational name rather than a patronymic, appear to have owned no chief, enjoyed no clan organisation. They went their own way, lived their own lives, and were servile to no man. Our sole relationship to any chief was that of tenant to landlord . The association with the Keiths has no significance whatsoever for the great majority of Marshalls.

The earliest Marshalls in documented history lived near Torphichen in West Lothian in the eleventh century. Later a branch of the name appears in Galloway - gipsies alternately consorting with and fighting with the Faas and other wild clans. This group may have stemmed from a family of outlaws repudiated by the rest of the Marshalls.

Early records are scanty, but by the late seventeenth and early eighteenth century parish records bear witness to the presence of numerous Marshalls in the county of Perth. With few exceptions they worked on the land in the mediaeval infield and outfield system, as extended families, and in the parish of Auchtergaven, in the centre of the county the Marshalls wrought land on the south-eastern foot-hills of the Grampians. It is at this time that my five times great-grandfather appears in the parish records. He was James Marchel, born in the late seventeenth century, the son of Walter. He had an invalid son, David - not the eldest son, who would be Walter. Through the generations the father and eldest son were Walter and James alternately. News had reached Drumquhar, the holding in the parish of Auchtergaven where the Marshalls worked, that an infirmary had been opened in Edinburgh where something might be done for the invalid. James applied to the kirk session for help towards the expenses of the journey, and was granted eighteen shillings Scots (1s6d sterling). It was a major expedition. There were no roads, no wheeled traffic. Travelling had to be by walking or riding, so how the invalid was got to Edinburgh remains a mystery; but he did arrive seven months after the infirmary in Infirmary Street opened.

Whether David was left in Edinburgh then is not clear, but his father soon appealed to the kirk session again, reporting that the Infirmary had agreed to take David as a patient, and James would have to make the journey again, for which he received a somewhat larger contribution from the elders. David lingered for some months, but died in the Infirmary in 1743.

The '45 Rebellion brought out the political differences then deeply entrenched in the country. The landed proprietors and clan chiefs were all Episcopalians and Jacobites, but the working folk were strong Presbyterians. The chiefs could bring pressure to bear on their people to join the rebellion, but not many of the chiefs took up arms. There were two distinct cultures in Scotland. The folk working the land, as in Perthshire, hated the Highlanders north and west of the Grampians. They were savages, uncivilised caterans - marauders, who were lawless and work-shy. When they wanted food they raided south of the Grampians, stealing cattle and anything else they fancied. The failure of the Rebellion to a degree was inevitable due to their inability to agree among themselves and their complete lack of discipline.

After the Battle of Culloden there was a special service of thanksgiving in the kirk at Auchtergaven. The romantic tales and songs about the '45 Rebellion were all produced years later. At this period, too, pews seem to have been introduced to the church, and James Marshall of Drumquhar began paying seat rent - four 'bottom-rooms'. Other people just stood, or brought their own stools. The elderly in particular put their stools against the wall - a fact we are reminded of in the phrase 'the weakest to the wall.'

The Nairne family were the first to be granted lands in the Auchtergaven area in the early seventeenth century, and they were ardent supporters of the king in the Civil War. In the eighteenth century however, still loyal to the Stewarts, they lost their estates for their involvement in the '45 Rebellion. The Duke of Atholl became the Marshalls' new landlord, and he was one of the foremost agricultural 'improvers'. Scotland lagged far behind England in the business of land enclosure. The mediaeval infield and outfield system was still widespread in Scotland, but the Duke of Atholl was actively involved in creating fields with hedges or dry-stane dykes, building proper farm steadings and replacing the old extended families with one nuclear family occupying the house and working the land, and all the others cleared off the land and housed and provided for elsewhere.

This was the development known as 'the clearances' - a by-word for inhumanity and ruthless brutality, because of what went on in the Sutherland clearances. When it came to enclosing the land at Auchtergaven, the Duke of Atholl built the village of Stanley, to which my great-great-grandfather, John Marshall, moved at the turn of the nineteenth century. He married a cousin, Isabel Marshall, and the first child, Walter, my great-grandfather, was born in 1807. Stanley was a village of hand-loom weavers. In those days, weaving was the most prosperous of all the trades, meeting an insatiable demand for cotton and linen cloth. So Walter became a weaver, married in 1826, had five children in the next twelve years, and fell on hard times as the introduction of power-looms drove most hand-loom operators out of business. Walter left the weaving trade, moved some miles south to Fowlis Wester, and became a forester on the Abercairney estate.

By then, my grandfather, James, the youngest of three sons, was apprenticed as a joiner and cabinet-maker, and when his time was out moved to Edinburgh, no doubt following Ann Ross, whom he had first met at Fowlis.

As a teenager in the mid-1850s, Ann had experienced the brutal clearances in Sutherland when the house she was brought up in, in Clashmugach, was burnt over the head of her family, and her bed-ridden aunt died of exposure four days later. Ann moved to Fowlis Wester in domestic service, where she might learn some English, and then to Edinburgh, where she worked for a lecturer in Viewforth. James was a canny lad, and when he married Ann in 1870 he was able to buy a newly-built flat in Orchardfield, now part of Leith Walk. A few years later, with a growing family, he moved to another newly-built, larger flat in Montrose Terrace, and it was there that I knew him. He was in business for himself when, at the age of sixty, he broke his leg, which was never properly set, and he spent the last thirty years of his life in involuntary retirement.

1
MAKING A START

Before the first World War Edinburgh was a small city, looking back from almost a century on. Westward it ended at Murrayfield; to the south Liberton Brae led directly into open country, as did Comiston Road at Morningside. Northwards, Ferry Road was an unofficial boundary to the city, from which Newhaven could be seen over a wide belt of parkland, and beyond was the sea and the Lomond Hills of Fife. Eastward along Ferry Road was the Port of Leith - part of the city, as far as a visitor might see, but in fact, since 1833 Leith had been an independent burgh with its own culture and way of life. From the mid-nineteenth century, Edinburgh had been extending its boundary. Eastward the Portobello Road was gradually being built up, but apart from that road there was no built-up area beyond Jock's Lodge. Portobello itself was annexed to the city in 1901, and Leith's fate was already sealed, although no one in the port realized this, beyond a few of the Leith town councillors, who carefully kept their opinions to themselves.

My Mother.
Isabella Cameron Cormack Scott, looking very pleased with herself - just prior to her marriage.

In 1908, the site of what was to become Baronscourt Road and Terrace began to be developed. According to Stuart Harris, the city architect of half a century later, the name of Baronscourt came from Baronscourt in Co. Tyrone in Ireland, which was the seat of the Duke of Abercorn, the superior of the ground. In fact, no more than the west side of Baronscourt Terrace was built at that time, and it was here, at 38 Baronscourt Terrace, newly completed and bought by Walter Donald Marshall, that he brought his bride, Isabella Cameron Cormack Scott, on 18th June 1910. Three years later, on 23rd May 1913, I was born, and I am astonished, in 2001, to reflect on vivid memories that stem from my very early years. I cannot claim to share the detailed memory Compton Mackenzie enjoyed, or the photographic memory of Professor

Making a Start

John Baillie, but a swatch of thrilling (to me) incidents, dramatic situations, snatches of conversation have remained with me all my life, and surely they are worth mentioning, as contributing to a vignette of my life and the world around me - a world that has disappeared, and the recollection of those days has been largely blotted out by the changes the years have brought to daily life.

In my memory there was only sunshine at Baronscourt Terrace. Every morning, when I could not have been much over two years old, I clearly remember going to the Burnhouse Dairy, about two hundred yards from the house, for the breakfast milk. The dairy fascinated me. The front shop, on the Portobello Road, had a byre at the back, from which the kye had access to the field beyond, which later became the rugby ground for the Royal High School. I would go through the shop, where I seemed to be the only customer at that hour. I watched the milking and took home a pitcher of warm, frothing milk, long before there was any such thing as pasteurisation. Cream came from a cart which called round later in the day, and Mother would get a small can of cream, from which, next morning she would issue each of us with a dessertspoonful to go with our porridge.

A contrary experience came my way two or three times a week when the dustcart came round from Baronscourt Road into our terrace. It was pulled by a huge horse. It could hardly have been a Clydesdale, but it seemed gigantic to me. The horse seemed to know its way and the scaffy[1] walked behind, sweeping the gutter and throwing shovelfuls on to the cart. I always took to my heels at the sight of the scaffy and his horse.

The house was very modern, and the kitchen range was of gleaming, highly polished steel. There was a suite of four wooden chairs, a rocking chair and an armchair, and I am sitting in that same armchair now. There was also a wall clock of American manufacture, which had a wide sale at that time, and cost seven shillings and sixpence. Morag, my daughter, still has that clock, its large round face very plain to see, but alas, it no longer tells the time.

Mother was always a steering body - a dynamic force. She had a range of proverbs to cover all kinds of situations in daily life. 'Quick at meat, quick at work', she would say. On one occasion, after breakfast, when drying the dishes, at speed, she broke a cup - one of a set given as a wedding present. She burst into tears. Dad was just leaving for the office. He bestowed the usual farewell kiss and said, "Lay not up for yourselves treasure on earth", and made for the door. Years later Mother once said that that was the only time she remembered Dad ever quoting scripture.

---

[1] scaffy - scavenger

My Mother's family.
Bob, John, Sis, Bella and Aunty Bessie,
Granny's sister.

All the same, we were a religious family, although religion was not the subject of conversation. Father had been brought up in the Free Church, and Mother in the Established Church, but in each of them Christian Faith was so deeply ingrained that it did not need to be discussed - it simply underlay all their thinking. For Dad, Christian practice meant ordering your life, exercising self-discipline, bringing order out of chaos, bringing efficiency to bear in all he did. His handwriting was beautiful, and he never used a fountain pen at work. His account books were widely admired among his business associates. His personal habits followed suit; cleanliness and tidiness were ingrained habits, and he smoked six cigarettes a day - after breakfast, mid-morning, after lunch, mid-afternoon, after tea, and in the evening. Set out like this in writing, it adds up to a stiff, unbending self-centred personality. Nothing could be further from the truth. He lived out that pattern of behaviour because that is what he enjoyed. He laid down no rules for others, and was very easy to get on with. A bout of scarlet fever in his youth had left him with impaired hearing, and this gradually deteriorated throughout his life.

Making a Start

Father's parents James Marshall and Ann Ross, whose house was burnt over the head of her family during the Clearances.

My parents' marriage was a classic example of the attraction of opposites. For Mother, life was a gay adventure. She was an enthusiast, and her enthusiasm was directed to many and various ploys. She left school at the age of eleven, having reached the sixth standard and passed her final exam there. That was all that was deemed necessary in those days. As the youngest of a family of four, she was eager to get into the great world of opportunity, where her two brothers and a sister were already at work. Bella, as everyone knew her, tried many different jobs, apparently moving on when she saw something new and challenging elsewhere. In this peripatetic work pattern she picked up a variety of skills. She also learned to play the piano, and while no kind of soloist she became an acceptable accompanist.

Mother had an extensive repertoire of reminiscences from her youth, and often hinted she could write a book, but being pressed to do so, she claimed she hadn't the time or patience for that work. Dad, on the other hand, had nothing to say about his young days, and it was many years before I realized he had nothing to say about his forebears, because he knew nothing. His father, from Fowlis Wester, and his mother from

Clashmore, near Dornoch in Easter Ross, were Gaelic speakers in the central industrial belt of Scotland at that time. One result was that my grandparents conversed with one another in Gaelic while their children heard them but did not understand one word of what was being said. Another strand in the tapestry of the family history was the memory of the clearances. When Dad's mother was a girl of thirteen her family's thatched croft-house was burnt over their heads, and Ann's bed-ridden aunt died of exposure four days later. In the family the clearances were never mentioned unless it was unavoidable, for Ann was apt to dissolve into tears at the memory. My cousin Annie Denholm, born in 1901, told me that if the subject was likely to crop up, she was always sent out of the room. But Ann was a skilled shoemaker, and she taught her husband how to repair the family's boots and shoes. Her family had been the traditional shoemakers in Clashmugach, and later in Clashmore. John Prebble mentions them as '*Roaa alias Greusaich*' (Shoemaker). In remote communities then, while everyone worked on the land, different families took responsibility for different trades.

Fowlis Wester was the home of the Marshalls in the 19th century, and here my father spent all his summer holidays from school. As the only grandson from Edinburgh, he was a great favourite there. His father ('Pap' to my generation), always made for Fowlis when he had a holiday, and always took the 4.00 a.m. train from the Waverley Station to Crieff, and he covered the last five miles to Fowlis in time for breakfast. His father, Walter, worked as a forester on the Abercairney estate. After his retirement Walter Marshall came to his son's for a holiday each summer, and bathed at Seafield every morning, for everyone then believed that sea-bathing was a cure-all. He once brought my father a pet rabbit, and he died in 1896 just short of ninety.

Gaelic speakers who learned English spoke precisely and grammatically, and taught their children so. Dad never used a slang expression, but oddly, his sister Jane (or Jean) used English and Scots freely mixed together, though her sisters stuck more closely to English. Mother also used Scots as convenient, but that generation were all caught up in the tide of using English as 'proper' speech, to be deliberately used with strangers.

From my earliest years, and certainly before I understood all I was saying, or the implications of the words I was using, I said my prayers nightly, carefully supervised by Mother. Here are those prayers, as clear to my mind today as ever they were, to begin with,

> *This night as I lie down to sleep,*
> *I pray thee, Lord, my soul to keep.*
> *If I should die before I wake,*
> *Take me to heaven, for Jesus' sake.*

Making a Start

I was grown up before I learned that this was a children's prayer used all over Scotland, probably from long before my time. This was followed by the Lord's Prayer, and a final intercession - 'God bless Mammy and Daddy (and Sis and Terry, as that became appropriate) and all friends and relatives. And make me a good boy, for Jesus' sake. Amen'

I don't remember being told any bedtime stories. The classical tales of Red Riding Hood, Aladdin and the Forty Thieves, Jack and the Beanstalk and Cinderella I imbibed before bed. Bed was meant for sleeping rather than conversation, and I guess Mother was only too pleased to have got me into bed without postponing sleep unnecessarily. However, I did get some theological instruction at times, when, after prayers, I began to ask about what I had been saying, and Mother told me about heaven and 'The Burning Fire'. Neither she nor I were too much concerned over the dreadful prospect of burning for ever after death. If that was an unalterable situation in which we had to live our lives, we at least were well warned, and had 'better watch our step'. This conversation would end abruptly with the injunction, 'Now put your feet straight down, or you won't grow big.' I hated this command, for linen sheets were cold, especially in winter, but I consoled myself by studying the mountainous landscape created by the folds of sheet below my chin.

Our neighbour on one side was a French lady with whom Mother was very friendly, but on rather formal terms: on the other side two middle-aged spinsters, Minnie and Jenny Smith lived. They had a newsagent's shop in Wolseley Terrace and were members of our congregation. They had a Pomeranian dog I regarded as a friend. Our own family was completed by a black and white collie, and the twa dugs also got on well together.

We attended the Moray-Knox U.F. Church in the High Street, hard by John Knox's House. This had been the John Knox Free Church which in 1910 joined with Canongate U. P. Church and the Moray U.P. Kirk. My grandfather James 'Pap' Marshall had attended the Knox Kirk since first coming to Edinburgh in 1854, for he knew the minister, the Rev John MacEwen, who came from Crieff, where he and 'Pap' had been friends in their youth. Papa was an elder there, so Dada was brought up in the John Knox Free Kirk. It was about two miles from Baronscourt Terrace, but that was of small importance. We walked. Sabbatarianism was pretty strong then, and Free Kirk folk did not approve of public transport on Sundays, although this attitude was apt to be compromised, especially by the women in wet and windy weather. Even at that, very few Sundays drove us to try for a cable car. On such a day the inside seats would be occupied before we boarded the car, and as there was no roof on the upper deck, the journey was scarcely comfortable. Dad enjoyed walking and took it for granted that

Everything Mixed with Mercy

the rest of the family shared that enjoyment. I enjoyed the singing, and as our pew was at right angles to the rest of the congregation, I could see them all as I stood on our seat singing, double-forte 'Stand up, stand up for Jesus' and thinking how right and appropriate it was for everyone to be standing.

My sister Isobel ('Sis' to the family) was born two days after my second birthday, so she was at once enthroned in the pram, and twice a week Mother visited her mother in Barony Street for afternoon tea, pushing the pram with Sis enjoying the ride. I remember clearly protesting one day as we walked along by Meadowbank, that I never got a turn in the pram nowadays, and Mother telling me that big boys didn't need a shot in the pram. So I walked, and like my father, I quite enjoyed it.

The war was now bringing problems in daily life and work. Dad's eldest sister Johan had married Willie Ramsay - a master baker with a bakehouse and shop in Minto Street. He had lost skilled men to the Army, and was finding it more and more difficult to cope. Bakers made their own bread then, and the sponge[1] had to be set in the early hours for the batch to be ready when the shop opened. The Ramsays lived in Arden Street in the Marchmont district, so Uncle Willie had to rise at 4 o'clock to walk to the bakehouse, there being no public transport at that hour. He wanted a house nearer his business, but houses were hard to come by during the war. A house at 22 Fountainhall Road came on the market - a ten minute walk from Minto Street - but it was far too big. Willie then had the bright idea of asking us in Baronscourt Terrace to share Fountainhall Road with the Ramsays until the war was over, and housing might be easier. Dad agreed. There would be no difficulty renting our house, so we moved to Fountainhall Road at the May term 1916.

Our new house had a large garden and greenhouse, and I liked Uncle Willie, Auntie Johan and my two cousins George and Jimmy, who were aged 15 and 13, and attending George Heriot's School. Uncle Willie's father was a gardener, and Willie himself was knowledgeable about plants. He was also quite a skilful fiddler playing Scots songs and dances with the traditional 'spring'. His fiddle hung on the wall by the fireside. We also kept hens and were generally quite comfortable. I was consigned to the attic for a bedroom, and as there was no lighting or heating there, I went to bed with a candle.

Dad was then thirty-nine years old, and we had only been a few weeks at Fountainhall Road when his call-up papers came. There was silence at breakfast when he opened the recognisable envelope and announced that he was conscripted. Mother said, 'Will you go?' She realised the futility of the question, but of course it was the first thought she had, and it was something to say. The answer was brief: 'I'll have to go.' But

---

[1] sponge - leavened dough

Making a Start

he was rejected with his defective hearing. He was called up again a few months later and was again turned down, but he joined the Volunteers, and spent two or three nights a week fire-watching at Holyrood Palace. Putting on his puttees was quite a ceremony which I watched with interest. Those nights on duty made for an exhausting day, coming on top of his normal work with George Barclay & Son in Hunter Square.

That was the year of the Battle of the Somme, and the immense casualty lists were stunning. One Sunday afternoon the family was at Montrose Terrace for tea, and Jimmy Heron was there. He had been Dad's best man at the wedding in 1910. I loved him for he was irrepressible, with a ready wit and a great fund of tall stories. And that afternoon I also admired him in the uniform of the K.O.S.B. He had been on leave, but was due to join his train that evening at the Waverley Station. After tea we stood at the top of the stairs, and Mother, finding his unquenchable spirit hard to assess, said, 'Are ye no feart, Jimmy?' Silence, then, 'Aye, A'm feart, but A've got ti go.' That was the phrase on every soldier's lips. Then Dad and I went with him along Regent Road to the Waverley. About a week later we got word that he had been killed.

At my age there was no reflection on the past, or anticipation of the future. Immediate impressions were what counted, and on many days we joined the crowds in Princes Street to watch the columns of infantry marching off to war, with the pipes skirling, kilts swinging, and my heart nearly bursting out of my chest with pride and admiration. It was an infantryman's war, and the P.B.I.[1] marched everywhere, and everybody sang the marching songs which cheered the spectators as well as the troops.

At home too, the war loomed ever larger. George left school in the summer of 1918. He was seventeen, and had another year to go, but his father was desperate for help in the bakehouse. George was a big strong fellow, and his joining the business was a great relief to Uncle Willie. But in the autumn George announced that he was going to join up. He and his father had several long arguments about this in the kitchen. Uncle pointed out that he was not due for call-up until his eighteenth birthday next spring. But George was feeling the strain, as all his pals were joining up. This argument never ended, as the Armistice was signed that November.

By that time I was a schoolboy. After the Easter holidays of 1918 I began my schooling at Sciennes School in Sciennes Road, next to the Sick Children's Hospital. My teacher was Miss Walker, and I remember nothing of what she taught us except for Art. This one subject provided a memory that has never faded. In the autumn we were each handed a sycamore leaf, in its vivid autumnal glory, and told to paint it. My artistic effort deserved to be forgotten, but the sight of that leaf aroused in me

---

[1] P.B.I - Poor Bloody Infantry

Everything Mixed with Mercy

something like appreciation, and this seems to have been my response to visual beauty all my life - appreciation rather than performance.

Miss Walker, however, knew how to control her class of fifty boys and girls. Education was drilled into us. We chanted the multiplication tables, and mental arithmetic was a kind of competition. We read in turns round the class, and at the command we sat with our hands on our heads or behind our backs. We began to write and count by using slates and slate pencils, which produced blood-curdling squeaks. We cleaned our slates with damp rags, which in time stank rather strongly. When we were promoted to using pen and ink, our handwriting was practised in copy-books, where a proverb headed each page in copperplate.

Our classroom was separated from the next room by a moveable screen, so that if one of the two teachers was off work, the screen was folded back, and either Miss Walker or the teacher of the other class was left in charge of anything up to a hundred pupils. Yet both teachers and pupils accepted the inevitable.

I walked to and from school, but twice a week Mother met me at the school gate with a piece, and we walked down to Barony Street to visit Granny as usual.

Without any doubt, the highlight of each year was our summer holiday at Saltcoats, where Aunt Jessie and Uncle Willie Denholm lived with my cousins - Annie, who was ages with George Ramsay, and Eric, four years my senior. We made this trip every year during the war. Saltcoats was then a lovely, unspoilt seaside town with a splendid beach, and Eric was my hero. The holiday began with the appearance of Dad's Gladstone bag for the luggage. Then the horse cab, with straw on the floor and a strong ammoniac smell of horse, took us to Waverley Station, and the splendid adventure of the train journey. This became more exciting every year, as I was able to remember past years' journeys for comparison.

Eric and I went to a nearby farm for milk every morning. He was very knowledgeable about birds, showed me many I had never heard of, and took me bird-nesting. He had a large collection of eggs carefully arranged. On wet days I watched from a window freight trains running to and from Ardrossan, and I counted the wagons, impressed that just one engine could pull all these trucks.

Uncle Willie worked at Nobel's explosives company, and I'll have something to say about him in later years, for he was a lively character. On one memorable day he took me to Ardrossan to see a ship launched. It was quite a small ship, but this being the case, I found myself thrillingly near the slipway, and if the ship had been the Queen

Making a Start

Mary it could not have given me more satisfaction as it swooped by me and into the water.

Before the war Dad had been a keen photographer, and there were piles of quarter-plate glass negatives lying about the house. I don't think he ever took up that hobby again after the War, but those glass plates lay around for a long time. He also liked cycling, and had a bike with a green painted frame. In the summer months he tied a green cushion to the cross-bar and took me for runs before breakfast on Sunday mornings. This was about the only time such excursions could take place, as he only had a Saturday afternoon off from work, when he felt obliged to be company for Mother, and the rest of Sunday was fully occupied.

Both he and Willie Ramsay were elders in the Moray-Knox Church, and on one occasion, on the Saturday before Communion, when they were both on duty, Willie realised he ought to have been at the barber long ago, but being so busy he had kept putting off this vital service. Dress and general appearance at church were much stricter then, especially for elders, who had to appear in morning dress and white ties. Dad reassured Willie. He had a pair of hair clippers; so Willie sat down with a towel round his neck and Dad went to work. He had not had much practice beyond trimming my hair, and the result on Uncle Willie was quite dreadful as he made mistakes and tried to correct them, until Willie's head looked more and more like a draught-board, and I don't think he went to Communion after all.

As soon as the war was over Dad left George Barclay's, and set up in business for himself as a credit draper. That line of business doesn't exist now. In partnership with John Nairn, an ex-ploughman, Nairn and Marshall stocked all kinds of gents and ladies outfitting, household furnishings, bedding etc. These items were bought from the manufacturers who in this way made contact with the public. Originally operating from premises at 12 North St Andrew Street the firm later moved to 1 Albany Street and then to 12 Hill Place, near Surgeons' Hall. The bulk of the customers were from the mining areas around the Lothians and Fife, where John Nairn had extensive personal contacts. Customers either came to the Edinburgh warehouse for the items they wanted, or else ordered from the collector who called once a week. The goods went out on credit, and were paid for in weekly instalments. This method of shopping suited the miners, who were poorly paid and were able to adjust their weekly instalments to what they could afford. In the early years of the business, Dad went round several districts himself, covering many miles on foot. In this way he got to know and assess the customers.

In that same year, 1919, my maternal grandfather died. I didn't know him as well as my other grandfather 'Pap', for of course Papa was always at home, having been long retired with a broken leg which confined him to his chair; whereas in our twice-weekly visits to Barony Street my mother's father was at work as a compositor with Morrison and Gibb. When he retired he was blind and bedridden. The funeral from Barony Street to Rosebank cemetery, set off with all the trappings of a horse and two coaches - these all drawn by black horses sporting black plumes. The coaches were for the nearest relatives, followed by the other mourners on foot, two by two. I as a grandson was a near relative, but being only six years old I did not rate a seat in a coach, and walked in the procession. Looking back it seems rather bizarre that a child of six should have taken part as a mourner, but *autres temps, autres moeurs*. No women went to the cemetery, of course. They remained at the house to prepare cold meats for the return of the mourners, when there would be drinks all round, followed by refreshments that rated somewhere between afternoon tea and high tea.

This may have been the first time I met all my mother's family. She had two brothers and a sister - John, Elizabeth, (Sis to the family), and Robert (Bob). John was a tailor and married Joan Johnston from Inverness, whose family considered she had married beneath her, so had no more to do with her; but she was a kind and jolly woman. Bob started work with Houliston the grocer at the corner of Barony Street and Broughton Street. With his first week's wages in his hand he walked to the West End and ordered a cabbie to drive him home. The cabbie only consented when he saw the money. That was characteristic of Bob, who in this was very like his mother and younger sister, my mother. He married Mary Wattie from Stonehaven, who retained her Doric tongue all her life. After marriage both he and John lived in Stockbridge, and on their army call-up both were eagerly seized by the Army. John was sent to London where, he said, his army career consisted of sitting cross-legged, stitching kilts for the troops. Bob, on the other hand spent 1914-1918 at sea, where he served in the galleys of troopships sailing from Britain as far as Australia. Auntie Sis married John Cummings who worked as a bookbinder with Andrew White in Bothwell Street. He was also something of an athlete, and ran in the Powderhall Sprint.

The end of the war made little difference to a boy like me. Demobilisation took time. Men in uniform, with red wound stripes were still in the streets, as were convalescents in hospital blue suits, and before long disabled beggars appeared minus one or more limbs. And unemployment added its misery to the horrendous 'flu epidemic, which took a heavy toll of lives.

All that being the case, there were some who escaped unemployment

Making a Start

in unexpected ways. Men who had fought and survived, and faced with unemployment, were ready to turn their hand to anything. One old man in South Leith Church told me that before the war he had been quite good at football, and with that in mind he got a job playing for West Hartlepool. For this he received two pounds a week, with an extra pound for every goal he scored. He had a wife, and with the utmost economy they soon realised they could hardly raise a family on that income. In time he did get another job, but not in West Hartlepool.

Another man, a friend of Mary's father, Sandy Tough, came through the four years of fighting without a scratch. After being demobbed, he was on his way north from King's Cross. He was profoundly thankful to be alive, but thought, 'I'm so tired. I feel I could sleep for days. The first thing I need is a good holiday.' Before the war he had been a porter at Abbeyhill Station, and at Abbeyhill the train stopped and he got out with his kitbag. As he walked up the stairs from the platform, his old boss appeared coming down. 'Hullo! You're back?' 'Aye, juist back' 'Good, start on Monday' 'I thought about it. I thought about quitting and enjoying that holiday. Then I thought about unemployment, and the thousands trying to get jobs. So I turned up that Monday morning and spent the rest of my working life at Abbeyhill Station.'

For our family, as soon as the Armistice was signed we started house- hunting. It turned out to be a long-drawn out business, but the Ramsays found a very suitable house in St Albans Road, and we thought we might now get back to Baronscourt Terrace; but the Rent Restriction Act made it impossible to impel the tenants to leave until they had found another place to rent, and Fountainhall Road was much too big for the Marshalls alone. Dad at length found a large flat in Leith Walk, which he bought. It was almost opposite the flat where he had been born, and being on the corner of Leith Walk and Lorne Street, it was roomy and even afforded Dad a small room for an office - and as the Cummings lived in Lorne Street there was a kind of family feeling about the district.

2
LEITH 1919-1926

We arrived in Leith at a critical time in the history of the port. The amalgamation of Leith with the City of Edinburgh had just been confirmed, after a plebiscite had resulted in a massive vote against the union. Leithers were scandalized at this betrayal, this evidence of massive corruption in high places. Leith had only gained its independence in 1833, after over three centuries of unjust subjugation by Edinburgh. There was intense local pride in independence, but from the start the town council had had to struggle with debt, from which there seemed to be no escape. From the mid-nineteenth century Edinburgh had extended its boundaries through a series of Parliamentary Acts. The result was that by the end of the century the city possessed all the land adjacent to the port. Leith being an industrial town, there was much overcrowding and a pressing need for expansion. The town council had recognized the danger as the city bought up land over the years, but Leith had no money to spend on land. The Leith Improvement Scheme in the 1880s had seen the demolition of eighteenth century tenements and the erection of new tenements on the same area of land. In 1895 Edinburgh proposed amalgamation, but this was angrily rejected by the Leith town council, and the fact that this proposal had been made was not made public. No councillor who wished to retain his seat would have dared mention the proposed amalgamation in public, for the council knew that amalgamation in the long run was inevitable.

All this, of course, didn't worry us, as we did not expect to be long in the port; but the Higgins family, who were the tenants at Baronscourt Terrace, could not be pushed to find other living quarters. I was soon a pupil at Leith Academy. This was the old Grammar School of Leith, which since the Reformation had been managed by the Kirk Sessions of the Parish Church. Previously there had only been a 'sang schule' conducted by the canons of St Anthony. The Grammar School became the High School in 1806, when a new building on the Links replaced the old and decaying King James Hospital where the Grammar School had met. The 1872 Education Act brought a massive increase in the number of pupils, and the High School was demolished in 1896 and a new school erected in its place on the same site.

Under the 1872 Education Act the High School was taken from the management of the town council, and came under the aegis of the new School Board, and from then on was known as Leith Academy, although its academic record had sunk quite low. This was largely due to the fact that the town council, who were managers of the High

Leith 1919 - 1926

School, spent nothing on it, having no money to spare, and there were no endowments. When George Watson's in Edinburgh opened in 1870 many of the Leith High School pupils were sent there, and this was a severe blow to the High School. But to the ordinary Leither what mattered was not high academic standards, but that the High School, and later the Academy, belonged to Leith rather than Edinburgh. All the same, the fifty years under School Board management before I arrived had wrought a considerable change for the better. But the new Leith Academy was overcrowded from the day it opened, and at the end of the Great War an army hut was erected in the boys' playground, and half a dozen classes were accommodated there. The primary school, however, was accommodated in the main building, and in front of it, just over the road, on the Links, stood 'Julian the Tank'. This had been used as a centre from which war savings certificates could be purchased. It had been a kind of publicity stunt, but with the war at an end there was no more use for it, except to provide an exciting playground object for us boys.

My teacher was Miss Kathleen Large. She and her sister Monica were teaching at the Academy, and from time to time she would announce to us, 'I'm Irish but I'm Protestant.' We of course had no idea what she meant, but those were the days of the Black and Tans, and Irish revolt was filling the newspapers. On occasion she also expressed the desire to hear a pin drop, which certainly produced rather a puzzled silence. But it was Miss Large who noticed that I could only see the blackboard if I held my head sideways; so she had me taken to the centre in Links Place, where I was found to have an astigmatism, and I became the possessor of a pair of steel-rimmed spectacles, and this was my first mark of distinction. Those specs had some rough handling. When I was squaring up to some other boy for a fight he would urge me to remove my specs, as he had no wish to break them, although he certainly intended knocking me flat.. But the most vivid enduring memory of those specs was when the family paid a visit to the Zoo. The tramcar took us to Murrayfield, and from there a bus took us the rest of the way to the Zoo. I was duly thrilled at the lions' roar, and greatly amused at the monkeys. My amusement changed to horror when one of the monkeys suddenly stretched out and whipped my specs off and capered round the cage with them. To my surprise, after examining them, the monkey actually handed them back, but squeezed into a ball of wire and glass. I was further surprised to discover I was able to straighten them out again and hitch them back into position.

Back with Miss Large again, one of the big days at school was the visit of the inspector. We were warned the day before to arrive next morning tidy, and with clean faces and knees. I now realize the teacher was as nervous as we pupils were. The great man arrived as we were having a spell of writing in our copy-books. Miss Large took the inspector round each pupil, remarking on his work. I was a poor hand at writing, and was not looking forward to my turn. 'This is Marshall', said Miss Large, 'Quite an intelligent boy, but he only works by fits and starts.' 'Fits and starts, eh?' boomed the inspector, 'You won't get far by fits and starts, will you?' 'No sir', I mumbled, keeping my head well down. And to my great relief, that was all. They passed to the next desk.

Our first winter in Leith was an eventful one for me. November 1920 I was taken to the City Hospital at Colinton with scarlet fever. There was a discussion over whether I should be nursed at home. Until 1926 there was no hospital in Leith for infectious cases, and better-off people with accommodation usually opted for treatment at home. The matter was more serious in our home because my father had contracted scarlet fever as a boy. I don't know whether he was treated at home, but the fever left him with impaired hearing - a condition which gradually worsened throughout his life. Leith, however, had just become part of Edinburgh that year, so we were entitled to share in all the resources of the city, and in any case the doctor was adamant, and I was taken to the City Hospital.

Fever at that time was more virulent than in later years, and the normal period in hospital was six weeks. I, however, was not set free until February 1921, after fourteen weeks' confinement. That prolonged stay was the result of infection lingering in my ears. Little did I realize the anxiety of my parents. No visitors were allowed in the hospital. Mother came once or twice a week, but she was not allowed into the wards. I was only able to see her through the window which was rather upsetting. I didn't have much appetite, and I was served quarter slices of bread smeared with margarine with a revolting taste. Each patient had a number, and the numbers were published daily in the 'Edinburgh News', sorted into various categories as 'making progress', 'convalescent', or 'seriously ill'.

Once I had got over the fever after about a month, I was bored. The nurses let me give them a hand, pushing the floor polisher on the ward floor. My release came eventually, and on arrival home I found my Christmas present, kept in its packing for my return - a set of Meccano. I was completely taken aback, and burst into tears. I was astonished at myself. Why was I weeping? I was overjoyed. This was a mystery, but it was forgotten quickly enough. Later that year I had my first experience of paid employment. Auntie Johan asked if I would like a job. Saturday was a very busy day at the Minto Street bakery, and there was need for an extra message boy, who would be needed for only that one day in the week. Being eight years old, I took the job, and from then on every

19

Leith 1919 - 1926

Saturday morning I got on the No 7 tram, which ran from Leith to Liberton and arrived at the Minto Street shop at 10 o'clock.

Newington being an upper class district, customers almost all had their orders delivered, and the basket I would carry was being gradually filled. I knew the district fairly well from my time at Fountainhall Road, so I set off. The heavy basket grew lighter as the orders were delivered, and I learned more than the street names. The gates at the pavement in front of each house had two brass bell-pulls set one above the other. The upper bell was for visitors, the lower one for tradesmen. I, of course, had no idea of the significance of each bell, but I soon learned. When I pulled the top bell, a very clean and tidy maid appeared, and the sight of me with my basket would change her welcoming smile to a frown, and I was sharply told to ring the other bell.

The round with the basket occupied the forenoon, and I then got a welcome lunch in the back shop - generally a pie and some tea bread and a cake, all of which I enjoyed hugely. From the back shop a gallery ran along to a room where George Ramsay presided over the confectionary side of the business. I would linger there watching him icing French cakes and the like. The gallery looked down on the bakehouse, and here I watched the bakers at work, while I waited for my basket to be filled for the afternoon round. It was fascinating to see the dough being kneaded, preparing a fresh batch. Then the previous batch was brought out from the oven on a baker's peel[1]. Looking at the rapid, skilful manipulation of the peels was enchanting.

Tipping was then universal - a normal token of appreciation of good service. You tipped the barber, the taxi driver, the porters on the railway and at hotels, servants when visiting, chambermaids, and of course the postman, the milkman, and errand boys at Christmas/New Year. In my weekly job at the baker's I did not collect many tips. Customers were confused as to my standing. Obviously I did not rate as high as a daily errand boy, but I was a weekly part of the business, so I was modestly rewarded at the festive season. Before the advent of the safety razor many men visited the barber every morning for a shave, which cost twopence plus a tip. Men with a steadier hand, or more time, shaved at home, carefully stropping the blade on a leather strop. Some men had a set of seven open (cut-throat) razors, one for each day of the week.

In 1920 we had a different kind of holiday. Dad had a couple of friends, not close friends, but a young married couple. He was an amateur boxer, and I think he was probably unemployed and looking for a cheap holiday. They had a bell tent - army surplus which could be had cheaply then. Their difficulty was that neither of them had ever camped before, and they were inviting our family to join them. We had never camped either, and Dad and Mother had a long discussion on

---

[1] peel - wooden shovel

this. Mother was against it. She saw difficulties in two families strange to each other working together for a week, and living together in a tent. Dad thought it worth trying. With his business in its early stages, and having just bought the flat in Leith, money had to be watched very carefully. In fact, that week at Pomathorn was an unmitigated disaster. It rained all week, relentlessly, day after day. There were no modern camping facilities. Cooking had to be done on an open fire outside the tent. There was an oil stove which in itself was quite inadequate for us all. Added to that, Terry was only seven or eight months old, and the couple who owned the tent were quite useless. When they saw Mother was coping they left everything to her. With great relief we lasted for the week, and thankfully arrived home again, and had no more contact with that couple, whose name escapes me now.

After tea at home, my parents and I settled down to read, and Mother at the same time carried on knitting. Isobel my sister went to bed much earlier than I did, and Terry was hardly more than an infant. Dada recommended Scott although he didn't urge him on me at my age. Mother recommended Dickens, and at not more than ten years of age I did get around to the 'Pickwick Papers', and 'The Old Curiosity Shop'. Some of Dickens made me laugh, and other passages almost made me weep. I once said to Mother, 'Did these things really happen? Is it all true?' Nowadays she might have said, 'That's a good question.' and left it at that. She did better, 'It's all founded on fact.' So I discovered early on that fiction and fact are not opposed, and that good fiction can draw our attention to aspects of fact that had probably escaped us.

Every fortnight Mother took me with her to the public library in McDonald Road to hand in books we had on loan, and select the diet of reading for the next fortnight. But the lending library of those days would be quite unrecognisable now. No books were to be seen. Instead, the foyer was surrounded by screens with hundreds of numbers printed in white on a red or blue background; and at the top of each screen a notice said 'Red is out'. Several book catalogues were laid out, and the borrower looked through a catalogue for a book that seemed attractive. Each book had a number, and by looking over the lists on the screens the number of the wanted book could be identified. If the number wanted was on a red background, that book was not available; another borrower had it out; so the whole process had to be repeated until a desired book had a number on a blue background, when application was made to the librarian at her desk. This system ensured that a visit to the library could take a long time. There could be no browsing, and if more than one book were sought, a large part of the afternoon or evening might be spent.

Another ploy of my mother's was work in the allotment. At Baronscourt

Leith 1919 - 1926

Terrace and Fountainhall Road we had always had a garden, but the flat in Leith had no garden, and Mother was very keen to grow vegetables and flowers. She acquired an allotment in Dryden Street, about half a mile from our flat, and got Dad and me every Thursday afternoon (Dad's half day) to join her at the allotment. Neither Dad nor myself were very keen, but Mother's enthusiasm carried all before her. We had tools, but there was no toolshed on the allotment, so we had to carry the tools to and from Dryden Street until a suitable shed was erected, which took quite a long time. Dad's idea of gardening was to grow tomatoes in a greenhouse, and mow a small lawn. Mother had an extensive acquaintance among the customers of Nairn Marshall, and made a point of conversing with any gardeners among that clientele.

She had quite an outstanding memory for names and faces, and I well remember when I was about seven years old walking up Elm Row with Mother one day when she stopped a lady coming down the street, and addressed her by name. I saw the lady had no idea who Mother was, and I cringed in embarrassment and stared at the stranger's black and white striped skirt. Mother reminded the lady when and where they had last met - which was when they were both single - and the incident ended with mutual warm recognition. Over the years this kind of thing happened even into her old age. The last memorable example I remember was at the Newhaven fishmarket soon after the Second World War, when my parents were living in Park Road. Mother was very fond of fish, and knowledgeable about fish in the shops. She liked to go down to the fishmarket before breakfast to see what had come in. She returned one morning to say she had met an old acquaintance. Typically the old acquaintance had not recognized her, but as usual Mother was quite right. They had only met once, some thirty-odd years ago, when they were both guests at the wedding of a mutual friend.

On Leith Walk we boys were always on the lookout for the arrival of cargoes of locust beans (carob), which were transported from the docks up the Walk in a long line of horse-drawn lorries. These beans were sweet and we tried to finger them out of the sacks through any holes there might be. When they saw us behind their lorries the drivers would reach back with their whips, and if that didn't stop us they left their horses to carry on by themselves and walked behind to keep us at bay. It was common practice to hitch a ride on the back of a lorry if there was room and the driver couldn't see us. I was cured of this habit when one day I jumped on a lorry passing the tramway depot in Leith Walk, but found there was hardly room to scramble on board, so I swung my legs underneath and caught an ankle in one of the wheels. The pain was agonizing and the driver stopped at once. My ankle was badly swollen but was not broken; I never tried that ploy again.

Everything Mixed with Mercy

In 1921 we made our way north for a holiday with the Scotts, who ran a bakery in Fyvie. Uncle Bob and Aunt Mary had been asking us repeatedly to visit them. After the war, as soon as he was demobilized, Uncle Bob started looking for a place to start his own business, and when the Fyvie premises came on the market Mary urged him to go for it. Mary certainly yearned to get back north where everyone spoke proper Doric, unlike Edinburgh. So off they went. They had four children, three boys and a girl. Cameron (Cam) the eldest, was six months my junior; Gordon (Gordie) was two years younger; then came Lesley, and George.

Dad was keen to go by sea, and so one summer evening we boarded a cattle boat at Leith, appreciative of the 10s fare to Aberdeen. Mother didn't like it. She wasn't sick, but felt queasy, and I don't think she slept much. The smell of sheep in close confinement below deck was no help either, and we docked at Aberdeen at 5 a.m. Dad's idea was that we should have breakfast somewhere before taking the bus on to Fyvie, but at that hour there was no restaurant or eating-house open, so Dad recommended a brisk walk. It was perishing cold, and the brisk walk had to develop into a brisk run so far as I was concerned. Eventually we did get breakfast, and then on to the bus for Fyvie.

We got a very warm welcome. Uncle Bob was a jolly man, energetic and a hard worker, and Aunt Mary, too, was a splendid match for Mother. The Scotts were a steering couple, which suited Mother. We found the manner of life in Fyvie a stimulating change from Leith. The outside toilet was in a wooden shed at the far end of the garden, known to all the family as the 'stinkatorium'. Cam and Gordie and I hit if off together very quickly, and the first few days saw me quickly learning the Doric. Coming into the house one day for dinner, after playing outside, we found we had to wait a bit for the meal, and we wandered into the sitting-room, where I began fingering the piano keys, only to be stopped by Cam who said 'Ye'se nae ti titch the piannae wi thae fu hauns'. It was some time before I grasped what 'fu hauns' meant, but once learnt I didn't forget, and soon built up enough of the dialect to get on with the others.

We spent a lot of time in the burn, a tributary of the Ythan. They showed me how to guddle and how to fish for mennens (minnows) and brown trout. I managed to get a fish hook embedded in my palm. The doctor removed it but the v-shaped scar remained visible till I retired. About twice a week one of the van men would take me with him on his rounds. The horse-drawn baker's vans covered a large area of the surrounding countryside, calling at farmhouses and cottages. The weekly call by the baker's van was for many of these folk just about their only link with the outside world so that these calls could be quite lengthy, as news was

Leith 1919 - 1926

retailed and discussed and cups of tea relished. These men had a long day, starting at eight in the morning, after the horse had been fed and watered and harnessed. Their round finished around six in the evening, or later in winter, when the roads were often difficult. These trips with the van were great fun, and I got the chance of driving the horse from time to time. I don't remember seeing any motor cars or lorries in that countryside in those early twenties. We spent several holidays in Fyvie, but in 1928 the Scotts moved to Strichen, which turned out to be not as good a move as they had anticipated. They only stayed a year there before moving again to Kintore, where they prospered for thirty years before Uncle died.

Cam carried on the business for a while and became involved in local politics, eventually becoming provost of Kintore. But he began suffering fits of depression and became convinced he had cancer, although he was assured by the doctors who saw him that there was no trace of the disease. Nevertheless he died in his fifties. Uncle Bob and Aunt Mary visited us in Edinburgh several times. They never warned us beforehand, but simply rang the bell and walked in. They'd have been most welcome to stay, but had already booked in at a hotel before coming to us, and they always visited Uncle John (Mother's brother) and Aunt Joey. Their holidays were never planned beforehand as Uncle felt Cam was not quite up to taking charge. Gordie was an odd character. He was quite brilliant at Maths but could not settle to any steady job. He came to visit us in Leith one year, and invited Mary to go with him to the Empire Theatre. On arrival he found that he had forgotten to bring the tickets. Mary was appalled, but Gordie told her not to worry as he knew the ticket numbers. This was enough for the girl at the ticket office, who made no difficulty over letting the two of them in. But like Cam, Gordie had a streak of melancholy, and he took his own life, to the family's shocked astonishment.

Aunt Mary retired to Aberdeen with her daughter. When Lesley was young her mother thought it would be a good idea to send her to a boarding school, where, presumably, she would not only be taught the usual subjects, but would also learn to 'speak proper' and acquire social graces. So Lesley went off, but only lasted a few weeks there before coming home again determined to have no more to do with all that nonsense. She married Bob Riddel and remained in Aberdeen. George, the youngest of the Scotts, was a banker, and his wife had a hairdressing business. They have now retired and live in Huntly, but George never made any contact with us.

As we returned south again from our first holiday at Fyvie, Mother said to me, 'You'll have to stop using the language they have up there. Nobody in Leith will understand you.' I recognized the truth of that but was sorry to give up all the idioms and phrases I had relished so much. We collected cigarette cards. Almost every brand of cigarette had its own set of cards. We collected them avidly and swapped them till they became very tatty with much handling. For a couple of summers we collected motor car registration numbers, for which, rumour had it that the 'Edinburgh Evening News' would pay a fabulous amount for the first thousand numbers sent in - all different. This indicates the comparative scarcity of motorized transport in the twenties. That craze died a natural death when we had gathered a few hundred numbers and found it impossible to check through our list for numbers repeated.

As there was no radio (wireless) or television then, the most popular public entertainment was the cinema, rapidly overtaking the music hall, and there was quite a range of quality programmes offered. The Gaiety Theatre in the Kirkgate presented two-, three- and four-reel films, with music hall interludes while the projectionist took time to change reels. At the other end of the scale admission to the Laurie Street Picture House cost one penny, or an empty jam jar. My parents were not keen on my going to 'the pictures', as they never went, and suspected there was not much good likely to come from picture-going. Most parents regarded the Laurie Street venue as a flea-pit, but I did get there occasionally and it was always a hilarious experience. There were no music hall interludes as at the Gaiety, but a lady pianist produced suitable music both for the film and the interludes for reel-changing. We all looked forward to the film appearing upside down, or breaking, and these interruptions were hailed with vociferous cheering.

Two picture houses outside Leith I remember visiting. Pringle's Palace was in Elm Row - the building that later became the Gateway Theatre. I don't remember the programme there, but someone had given me a poke of San-Toy cashews, which I began eating as the picture started, but I had to rush outside again suddenly to be violently sick on the pavement. The other Edinburgh picture house I visited after a long struggle with my mother. This was the Salon in Baxter's Place. The picture was called 'Silent Joe', which all my pals said was a great picture. I have forgotten the story now. What I do remember is that having seen the show, I discovered it was to be continued the next week, and there were in fact six episodes to be seen. Having made the first concession, Mother made only token resistance to my seeing the rest of that film. But I never became an addict of the cinema.

The public library did not cater for children, and there were few children's comic books apart from 'Comic Cuts' and 'Funny Wonder', but throughout the inter-war years this gap in the market was gradually filled. 'The Rainbow' with Tiger Tim I read avidly, and when 'Adventure', aimed at an older age group, appeared at twopence weekly, Mother

Leith 1919 - 1926

declared it was too dear, but she relented and allowed me to buy the first number, and finally gave way, but stipulated that that was to be the only weekly paper. Other boys bought 'The Rover', 'Wizard', 'The Magnet' and so on, but I was happy enough with one paper, as it could be used to swap for other papers. We read these in class beneath our desks, but when detected by the teacher they were always confiscated. Dixon Hawke and Sexton Blake and other detective stories appeared in booklets priced 4d, so I only read what came from other boys.

People of my generation often complain of their boredom on Sundays long ago. I never found it so. Sunday School followed directly after church, and I came home to Leith with Gibby, or Gibson. (We never used Christian names then. The surname was all that mattered, and was all that was ever used. My Christian name was reserved for family use.) Gibby always talked non-stop about some mechanical marvel, of which he always seemed to know every detail. Oddly enough he grew up to go into insurance. Wet Sunday afternoons we often spent at the Museum in Chambers Street, which was usually crowded with youngsters like ourselves. On good days the West Pier at Leith was a popular walk with Leithers. We walked around the ships at anchor, from many countries - merchant ships. We gazed at the decks and the crews in admiration. Leith was then much more obviously a port than it is now. Lascar seamen with a few hours ashore would process up town to see something of Edinburgh. They walked, Indian file, one behind the other, from the west entrance to the docks, up Constitution Street and Leith Walk, then turned and came back, in complete silence. I never heard them conversing, but they were first class seamen.

In my teens I once looked round the classroom and realised that every second boy came from a family with maritime connections, and it was not uncommon for a boy to get a job on a trawler during the summer holidays. They could be useful as ship's boys and took their share of gutting fish as the nets were hauled aboard. But they came home with their hands raw and sore with the salt water, and I never knew one who went with the trawlers a second time. One lad, however, got a job with the Ben Line and sailed to the Far East, missing a year at school. He also had had enough, and went on to take a degree in Modern Languages.

The docks were obviously busy then. Six dockers and six stevedores would normally handle a cargo, loading or unloading. With the advent of automatic lifting gear and containerised cargoes the hundreds of dock labourers have disappeared. Dockers used to arrive at the dock gates in the morning. They were employed on a daily basis, and as many would be taken on as were needed for whatever ships were berthed. Those who failed to get a job congregated at the Foot of the Walk, and would try again for a job in the afternoon. Shipbuilding was greatly diminished after the Great War, but still carried on, employing many skilled workers, and these all added to the vibrant life of the docks. There were also several flour mills in the port, employing many men in real hard labour, shouldering two-hundredweight sacks of flour in a dust-laden atmosphere. Now the old mills have been replaced by two automatic mills which deal with the bulk carriers, lifting grain from the holds to the top floor of the mills and thence downward, being processed all the way till sacks of flour are delivered on to lorries and moved from the docks to their final destination - the whole supervised by half a dozen men with dusters. Today the docks at Leith are busier than ever before, but to the visitor the dock area appears almost deserted.

We frequently spent Sunday afternoon at Montrose Terrace, where we had tea and usually a sing-song of hymn tunes, for the family were all singers, able to sing parts. Auntie Jean, who kept house for Pap, and carried on her milliner's business from the sitting-room, bought the Sunday Post, which I always eagerly got hold of. We never bought a Sunday paper. The Free Church had always been against that, and Dad always stuck by that tradition. Auntie Jean usually sent me down to the ice-cream shop a few doors from the foot of the stairs for sliders all round the company. Dada was also against Sunday trading, but was not prepared to make an issue of it as he himself did not buy the ice-cream. Presumably this related to St Paul's advice to Christians not to ask questions as to whether the food they might be offered at a friend's house had been offered to idols.

I was quite a favourite with Auntie Jean, as I was always ready to pick up dozens and dozens of pins from her carpet. But I discovered it was folly to presume too much on her favour. She had a crystal cream jug which she valued, and one day I found it on the sideboard. She told me to put it down, but I still fidgeted with it, and she said, 'My certie, an a cum ower ti ye ma mannie, a'se warm yer lugs ti ye.' whereupon I dropped it and it broke. Not realising its value I was taken aback by her wrath, and it was a long time before we were reconciled.

Papa died in February 1925, and was buried in Piershill cemetery beside his wife. Oddly he always claimed to be two years younger than he really was. This only transpired two years later when I saw his death certificate and the census returns. He was born on New Year's Day 1836, so at his death he was eighty-nine years old. Very little attention was paid to personal anniversaries in those days. I only discovered the birthdays of my parents by direct questioning, for they never exchanged presents and didn't even refer to their birthdays when they came round. At Christmas time our stockings were filled, and in addition there was one present to signify Christmas as a special day.

Pap's funeral has remained in my mind because of the rather dramatic gathering of the family afterwards to hear his will read. I had only the vaguest idea of the proceedings, being only eleven years old. I had never thought of him as a moneyed man, and he was not wealthy, but he bought the newly-built house at Orchardfield (Leith Walk) where he brought his bride, and a few years later, with a growing family he moved to the newly-built larger flat in Montrose Terrace. His relatives in Fowlis Wester spoke ironically of James Marshall's 'mansion', and quite a number of legacies were left within the family. I heard that he had invented something new in window frames, but didn't have sufficient resources to market it, and the patent was bought from him.

I was able to join the Boy Scouts in 1924. I had already been to camp at Humbie the previous year as a cub. This was not allowed, but George Ramsay, who assisted the cubmaster, got me the privilege. The Scouts provided a big step forward in life for me. We had a very good scoutmaster in Mr. Ames, an analytical chemist at Cox's Glue Works. He had been in Egypt during the war, in a cavalry regiment, and he had ideas of his own. We were encouraged to work for the Tenderfoot, Second Class and First Class badges, but he took no interest in proficiency badges. As we grew older we saw members of other troops sporting armfuls of badges in various subjects and we tried to get Mr. Ames to start classes to prepare for various badges, but he would have none of it. He claimed these badges gave boys silly ideas about their proficiency. I did get a musician's badge on the strength of my violin-playing, which Mr. Ames was quite happy about, as I was practising steadily and might make something of it one day.

We went to camp every summer, and twice went to Cardrona, near Peebles. The day at camp was regulated by bugle calls. The assistant scoutmaster (ASM) had been a bugler in the army, and we were wakened by Reveille at 6.30 a.m. The various patrols took it in turns to spend a day on fatigue, which meant rising at 6 a.m., preparing breakfast, and thereafter washing the dishes, cleaning the dixies, going on expeditions for firewood, preparing mid-day dinner, then joining the others for afternoon jaunts or exercises, and then preparing tea for early evening. As breakfast was not due till 7.30, everyone not on fatigue went for a run, which was welcome as it was usually very cold at that hour, even in July. Another adult helper turned up each year at camp. We didn't see him during the rest of the year but he was an ex-Navy petty officer who taught us knots and lashings. These did not always agree with what we saw illustrated in books, but he assured us, 'That's the Navy way' and we let it rest at that.

When I became a patrol leader I was in charge on fatigue. The menus were ordered by Mr. Ames, so we knew what to do. The results were perhaps not what would have been acceptable at home, but everyone

Everything Mixed with Mercy

was generally 'starving', and cleared what was left on their plate without too much trouble. My one spectacular flop was rice pudding. It was cooked, but to my astonishment it swelled so much it practically filled the dixie. Everyone ate to bursting-point, and the cookhouse team were sentenced to eat all that was left - which we did not quite manage.

After mid-day dinner we all had to lie down for an hour. Scoutmaster's orders. That siesta was not popular, but Mr. Ames was strict about it. After high tea in the early evening the fire was built up and we had a 'campfire' - singing, chattering and so to bed with 'lights out' at ten. We slept in bell tents - army surplus, going cheap - and one 'Niger' tent for the officers. There were no sleeping bags then. We had groundsheets and blankets. There were no rucksacks. Each boy had a kit bag to hold everything needed for camp, including blankets. We had our share of wet weather, of course, but that was no great problem at twelve years of age.

At that time of life I was consumed by curiosity. I read everything that came my way, picking up all sorts of information. Baden-Powell's 'Scouting for Boys' became my *vade mecum*. It was from there that I got the set of five exercises which, with additions, have been with me over the years - the kind of daily routine one goes through almost without thinking. Many years later, in Virginia, at the entrance to a woodland popular for walking, a board had been erected, illustrating these same exercises, recommended as basic for keep-fit enthusiasts, presumably by the American Scout Association.

At home, about this period in summer, I found myself awake at six o'clock, and casting about for something to do till breakfast, I began, on the strength of 'Scouting for Boys', to experiment with cold baths. On fine summer mornings I found this a stimulating start to the day. On other mornings, with the weather not so fine, I occasionally took Mother a cup of tea in bed. This was my good deed for the day, which obligation as a Scout I took seriously, and was hopefully anxious to achieve and so be free of that duty for the rest of the day. Of necessity Mother also rose early, and she was not best pleased with the tea, but she accepted it with an admonition to me to go back to bed and get enough sleep. I did not realise that tea is usually not welcome to the early riser in the family anxious to get on with the urgent business of getting breakfast ready.

I remember lying in bed in Leith Walk, in pitch darkness, seeing a shooting star. This was repeated for several nights. I didn't know what it was but got enlightenment from a series of cigarette cards produced then under the title 'Do you know?' One of these dealt with shooting stars, with an illustration. I also recollect seeing the 'Northern Lights' from the North Bridge in Edinburgh - a remarkable and unusual sight.

Leith 1919 - 1926

It was probably in the summer following my spell in hospital that I spent a holiday with the Denholms for the first time since they had moved from Saltcoats to Nappyfaulds, a large house with several acres near Slamannan. Uncle Willie had been promoted and was now a manager at Nobel's. My cousins, Jimmy and Eric, were attending Airdrie Academy, and Annie, now nineteen years old, was at home, having finished school. Uncle had a pony and trap, and Annie drove him every morning into Slamannan Station, where he caught the train. In the evening Annie met him again and drove him home.

This was the first of several holidays I spent at Nappyfaulds, and I loved the place. One day Aunt Jessie asked if I'd like a cup of tea, but warned me I could not have sugar as they were still on war-time rationing. I had never had tea before, so I have never had sugar in my tea. Every time I went there Aunt Jessie got me to hoe the drive, which was a job no one else was willing to do. Every time I went there Uncle Willie had a new hobby. One year it was fruit bushes; another time it was poultry; he was an ardent fisherman; he was keen on growing vegetables. He had several beehives one year, and he spent much time on the wireless. It was a cat's whisker set. He would home in on Hilversum, and the whole family would listen intently for the words or music coming through. One year I arrived to find the parts of a motor-bike spread over the floor of a shed. This was another absorbing craze for a year or two. Annie's boyfriend (as he would be called nowadays), Tom Wilson, was a keen motor mechanic. His parents thought there was no future in that sort of job, and insisted on his going into a bank. He did so, but became manager of a country branch and refused to move into town, where he would not have had it so easy to keep up his passion for motor-bikes. He was for many years bank manager at Aberfoyle. Apart from all the hobbies at Nappyfaulds, the whole family were keen politicians. Uncle was a strong Tory, Jimmy a fierce Liberal, Eric chipped in on either side, and Auntie from time to time broke in to try to cool the temperatures. This was the daily table-talk at Nappy.

At home the effects of the war were obvious. Ex-servicemen sang in the streets and back greens, grateful for pennies thrown from the upper flats or tenements. Inflation was rife, and Mother lamented the price of coal, at five shillings a bag - the same bag as had cost ninepence before the war. Message boys and lads with paper rounds had bare feet summer and winter. I admired them in winter and envied them in summer. There were some warm summers then, and while Mother was adamant about our wearing our canvas sand shoes while playing, we often removed them after leaving the house, depositing them at the foot of the stairs. Summer rig consisted of grey flannel shirt, shorts and sand shoes.

Everything Mixed with Mercy

Early on I had a tricycle, which I soon outgrew, and to my pride and joy Dad got me a second-hand bicycle. Compared with modern bikes it was weighty and solid. There was a brake, which was unreliable. This didn't worry me as long as I was learning, but when I had mastered the art of staying upright on two wheels I became more venturesome, and while there was no free-wheel mechanism, I coasted down the brae from the Hibs football ground to Easter Road. Unfortunately there was a left turn near the foot of that brae, and I realised I was going too fast to manage that turn without the brake, which was not working that day. The bike and I crashed into a dyke. I was uninjured but the bike wheels were badly twisted. But they were straightened again, and the bike served me well, until I outgrew that eighteen-inch frame, and acquired an adult bike.

Dad was keen for me to learn the violin. Both he and Mother sang in the church choir as tenor and soprano, and there was both a piano and a harmonium at home. Mother played the piano but the organ was Dad's favourite. A half-sized violin appeared from nowhere, and it was arranged for me to begin lessons with Miss Sutherland in Pilrig Street. The first lesson was scheduled for four o'clock the next Tuesday afternoon, and Mother warned me again and again to come straight home from school that day. Normally I didn't go home after classes but stayed playing football in the playground until around five o'clock. Well, I forgot to go straight home that day, and when I did get back to the house Mother was very angry and promised me a thrashing from my father. Dad kept a long leather razor strop hanging on the kitchen door, although he never used it. But this time he was furious, and I got laldie. That was the only thrashing I ever had, and of course I duly remembered my music lesson the next week, and before long had mastered 'Home Sweet Home', which I had never heard before.

From then on violin practice became part of my daily routine. Half an hour daily on that half-sized fiddle kept me going until I could stretch to a full-sized instrument which was waiting for me. Willie Keir, a bachelor, had for years lodged with my grandparents in Barony Street. He had died there, and his violin was left. It was a James Hardy instrument, made in 1890. The Hardys were well known in Edinburgh, and the violin had a good tone, but over the years I realised the neck was thicker than it ought to have been. This affected the fingering and took away from the value of the instrument, but didn't worry a beginner like me. But with this real violin the daily practice was extended to one hour. This continued until we returned to Baronscourt Terrace in 1926, and I was then looking for another teacher. We heard of Jack McConnel, a local teacher much sought after. He accepted me as a pupil on condition that I practised for an hour and a half each day. He

Leith 1919 - 1926

normally insisted on two hours but we agreed on an hour and a half until we saw how I was progressing. Eventually I managed two hours, but in my later teens school homework became so demanding that I had to give up lessons altogether, and I continued playing for my own amusement.

After Mother's father's death, Granny came to stay with us and she, like my mother, was always on the go. She was a wee wifie, and although slower than she had been, she was still very useful to Mother, keeping the house when Mother was at the shop. She had begun taking an interest in Dad's business, and she soon began supervising in the afternoon at 12 Hill Place, where Nairn and Marshall had their warehouse and shop. Mother kept an eye on the shop girls, and familiarised herself with the stock in the warehouse. John Nairn had now quit the partnership. He was not a businessman. His contribution to the firm had been his wide acquaintance with the miners and farm labourers in Fife. Mother went to the shop two or three times a week, and got to know many of the customers and sized them up. She always felt Dada was apt to be gullible, and more interested in finding jobs for other people than in attending to his own interests. So she said, but that was gross exaggeration. Those were the years of industrial depression. Unemployed men on the dole received twenty-four shillings a week, and bringing up a family on that income afforded a very thin living. Dad made his own assessment of people's circumstances, and was well aware of what he was doing in not pressing too hard for payment.

The old age pension had been introduced just before the war, and as Granny reached the age of seventy shortly after she came to stay with us, she duly received her five shillings, and was completely mystified. Where did this money come from? Who was sending it ? Finally she went out with it and spent it on presents for the family. Every week the same thing happened. As soon as she laid hands on the pension Granny would make a bee-line for the door to search for quite unnecessary presents - until Mother got wise to this and insisted on going with her mother to prevent such a waste of money, as she saw it. But one day, when I had been with Mother shopping, we found Granny lying dead on the floor behind the front door. She had had angina, and was buried beside Grandad in Rosebank. That was in March 1926.

At school, Mr. Naughton, who took the Qualifying Class, was the first male teacher I had had, and I liked him very much. He had a resonant, bass voice, and was a patient, reasonable man with whom I felt at ease. In the secondary school the boys and girls were taught in separate classes and they had separate playgrounds, so there was no contact between the sexes until the fifth year. We now had only male teachers, and they were a mixed bunch. The Rector was John Tait, who had been with the school since the beginning of the century. I say little of him as he retired while I was still too young to have had contact with him. His successor, Dr. Peter Comrie, was a small man with a forceful personality, but fair-minded, and a good public speaker - an asset in any schoolmaster. Dr. Dall, a quiet man, taught geography, and we had no trouble with him. French was taught in one of the hut classrooms by 'Bulldog', who was only known by his nickname, derived from Bulldog Drummond, a popular fictional character of those days. 'Bulldog' had a 'down' on me, since he had once caught me having a nap at the back of the classroom. He developed a habit of pouncing on me whenever he thought my attention was wandering, so I was apt to close my eyes deliberately, while listening attentively to what he was saying. We developed a kind of armed neutrality. Mr. Anderson taught English in the main school building, to the fifth and sixth years. He was rather belittled by my classmates as it was rumoured that he only had a third-class honours degree; but many teachers returning from war service did not settle easily to student life. But I liked him very much. He had a relaxed manner, and chatted away about the poetry and prose writers we were reading. He even managed to make Shakespeare interesting, and he spent several Friday afternoons reading to us from J.B. Priestley's 'Good Companions', which had just been published. I owe Mr. Anderson a lot.

That was in my fifth year. Other classes for younger pupils were taught in Watt's Hospital. John Watt's Hospital was a home for old men dating from the mid-nineteenth century. At the end of that century it had ceased to be a home, and the funds, after the sale of the home, were used to pay pensions. The building had been taken by Leith Academy, which still needed to expand, and Watt's Hospital fulfilled this purpose until 1928, when it was demolished to make room for the new Leith Academy on the same site in 1931.

In Watt's Hospital I had Latin and English classes. Mr. Scott taught Latin. We all knew him as 'Watery Belly' from his habit of leaving the room every twenty minutes or so. Of course we didn't know, but he had a kidney complaint which gave him much pain, and sharpened his temper. When 'Watery Belly' appeared in the classroom doorway, we rose and said, '*Salve Magister*', to which he replied, '*Salvete pueri*', and the lesson always began in a relaxed atmosphere, which gradually became embittered as our mistakes and his pain began to take effect. Next door, James Paton taught English. We got on well with him, as he was a witty man, given to mild sarcasm, which we didn't mind so long as we were not personally involved. But Mr. Paton blotted his copy-book with me.

'Watery Belly' was off ill for some time, and a student, a country lassie with rather a broad accent filled in for him. She left the room on one occasion to consult Mr. Paton on some matter. As the meeting in the English room seemed to be taking quite a long time, a bit of a rammy developed in our room, with quite a bit of noise. I was not taking part in it, having something quieter to occupy me. Suddenly Mr. Paton appeared in the doorway and pointed a finger at me. 'Come to my room, Marshall.' 'Sir, I was not doing anything.' 'No argument. Come to my room.'

I went, and without another word from him I received six of the best. The belt, in a way, was a side issue. I was furious but helpless. That remained my lasting memory of James Paton. Many years later when I was taking a service in Junction Road Church, Leith, preaching for the vacancy in the Kirkgate Church, the Session Clerk came into the vestry before the service to bid me welcome. 'Good morning, Mr. Marshall, do you remember me?' The face was vaguely familiar but the name eluded me. 'Mr. Paton. You remember you were in my English class?' I remembered. He looked smaller than he had seemed, towering over me with his belt in hand, but he obviously had no recollection of our last meeting, so I avoided the subject, but it was disturbing, just as I was about to begin that important service.

One more teacher I have never forgotten was 'Daddy' McLaurin the art teacher. I was never anything of an artist, and he would never appear to anyone as inspirational. He was nearing the end of his career, and he was suffering from Parkinson's Disease, but he spoke about painting and architecture. I remember his showing us a slide depicting Dalmeny Street, off Leith Walk, and pouring scorn on the dull monotony of those tenements. From time to time he took us to visit the galleries in Edinburgh, and showed us what to look for in the paintings we saw. 'Daddy' McLaurin couldn't make me an artist, but he did teach me how to appreciate the work of others, and that has remained with me.

When I entered the secondary school some changes were taking place. The school had always played soccer in maroon and white jerseys, and the cap badge (we all wore caps) showed the Leith coat-of-arms in a shield, flanked by the initials L and A. Now it was decided to switch to rugby, like most other schools, and as Watson's already wore maroon and white, Leith Academy changed to blue and white. In the summer term we played cricket, and as practice for these sports took place on Saturday forenoons I gave up my job at Ramsay's bakery, where my wages had risen to 1s6d plus, of course, my kit of tea bread to take home. I was never much use at cricket, making no impression with bat or ball, and being more or less permanently relegated. I did better at rugby, but it was still early days.

3
BARONSCOURT AGAIN

In the spring of 1926 we got news that the Higgins family would be quitting our house in Baronscourt Terrace at the removal term in May. This was tremendous news for us. We had been away from that house for ten years, so that to me our original stay there seemed like ancient history. The move, I felt, would fulfil my fondest dream. Transferring from the Leith Walk flat to Baronscourt was like a move to a different country. There was only one side of the street built up. Facing our house was a field of potatoes, and I soon met up with a bunch of local lads making the most of the opportunities that field afforded us. As soon as the crop was cleared in late September we gleaned up the odd tatties missed, and soon had a roaring fire going from the withered shaws. We set about roasting our haul, but the roasting wasn't much of a success as in our impatience we retrieved the spuds from the fire before they were ready. Still, it was an interesting ploy.

Our garden backed on to the local bowling green, and Dad joined the club. He soon discovered, however, that he seldom got the chance of a game, as his half day was on Thursday when no one else seemed to be free, and as he generally had to bring work home with him in the evening he was not often free then. He got the idea of getting me to play with him, and I was quite thrilled. Normally the green was out of bounds for us lads, for the greenkeeper objected to youngsters playing around his sacred green; but Dad made it all right with him. At first the main attraction for me was the privilege of getting the run of the place. Then I got a set of bowls from somewhere or other, and I became interested in improving my game.

It had been decided that I should continue at Leith Academy as I was in the third year of the secondary school; so I walked down to school through Restalrig Village, and on through the new Lochend housing scheme. This had started in 1924 - the first of the Edinburgh post-war housing schemes. This development was part of the agreement between Edinburgh and Leith when the Amalgamation took place. The scheme provided for tenants from both Leith and the Canongate, and a good deal of building had yet to be completed. In the winter of 1926-7 I twice saw walls which had been erected the day before collapsed overnight in high winds.

I enjoyed walking, but it took too long - a good half hour - so I took to cycling. About half a dozen of us of the same age came to school from a distance, and we carried sandwiches for lunch. After sandwiches we went to an ice-cream shop in Duke Street for a "penny brun". This was a wafer about two inches square, twice as thick as an ordinary slider and topped with chocolate. This must have been a specialty of that shop, for I never came across bruns anywhere else. After a while school meals were introduced for lunch. We sampled them for a week, but agreed they had a peculiar flavour, so we reverted to our sandwiches.

While still living in Leith I acquired a dog - a messan (a mongrel), a cross between a collie and an Airedale, called Ranger. We had always had a dog and a cat, but Ranger was mine, and school-hours permitting, we went everywhere together, and while I was at school Ranger developed the habit of visiting houses we had visited together, on the off-chance of picking up something worth sampling. From Baronscourt Terrace we often went to the King's Park, and Ranger had great entertainment chasing rabbits, although he never caught one. He liked swimming and sampled all three lochs in the park. But one day, when I came home from school, I found him in the kitchen lying stiff on the floor, with Mother very agitated. Shortly after, Ranger died, and I was grief-stricken. We reckoned he was poisoned from something he had picked up.

The east side of Baronscourt was now to be built up, so there was no more direct access to the field, but while the building went on the site was a fine playground, though we had to keep our eyes open for the watchman. The area of the field beyond the building was still open ground, and soon became the rugby field for the Royal High School. My bike gave me access to a much wider area for recreation than had been possible in Leith, and from time to time on fine summer mornings I went bathing at Seafield, where the sands were beautiful and largely deserted at that hour. This came to an abrupt end when Mother found traces of raw sewage on my towel. Since then Seafield has gone from bad to worse.

Swimming and golf attracted many youngsters in Leith. In the Primary School we were taken every week from school to the baths at Dr. Bell's School in Great Junction Street, and there taught. This was compulsory, unless a medical certificate excused any boy. Golf on the other hand was entirely voluntary, and a number of boys preferred golf to cricket, and the course at Craigentinny was just east of Seafield. I knew one Academical from the generation previous to mine, who became a golf professional and spent all his working life in France as one of the professionals at Le Touquet, before returning to Leith in his old age, when I got to know him. In his nineties he was taken into care, but insisted on taking his clubs with him. He kept them by his armchair, threaping[1] that he might yet get the chance of a game.

Leith Town Council bought the Links from Edinburgh in the mid-nineteenth century and the general public was allowed to play golf

---

[1] to threap - to assert persistently

Everything Mixed with Mercy

on this common ground, but the rapidly growing population made golf on the Links a dangerous pastime, so in 1907 golf was forbidden on the Links. Schoolboys still knocked balls about until stopped by a 'parkie'. I possessed only a cleek and a putter, which were adequate for my standard of golf, but I gradually managed to increase my range of clubs, and at Baronscourt Terrace, I was living just about half a mile from the nine-hole course at Portobello.

My cousin Bertie Cummings now became keen on golf, and two or three times a week, one summer, he cycled up from Leith in time to cycle with me to Portobello, just after six o'clock when the course opened. It cost twopence for a round, and if we timed our arrival for around 6.15 the greenkeeper, who ought to have taken our money, would be on a green a good distance away, so we waved to each other, but no money changed hands. We finished the nine holes in time to go home for breakfast, and so to school for nine o'clock. Bertie worked at a cardboard box factory in Bonnington Road, where he also had a nine o'clock start. Bertie was a quiet, pleasant lad, two years my senior, keen on the B.B.s[1], and a fair performer on the piano. The Cummings, my mother's sister Elizabeth always known as Sis and her husband Jos, lived in Lorne Street, and there were four children. The eldest was Joseph (Josie or Joe) who worked with his father at Andrew White the paper maker in Bothwell Street. Ella was next. All I remember of her was her mass of long golden hair. She died of tuberculosis at the age of sixteen. Robert (Bertie) was next, and then Tommy, my own age, who lost a hand in the war and became a recluse. Morning golf with Bertie only lasted one summer. He became organist at Williston Church. He joined the army, and after the demob he didn't come back to Scotland, but to the family's shocked astonishment married a Roman Catholic girl and took over a sub-post office in Leicester. They had no children but adopted a boy, David.

Bert visited Leith annually to see his family, and I twice met his wife Margaret - a pleasant but colourless personality. The next we heard of Bert was from the news media. A man had come into Bert's post office with a gun, which he presented at Bert and demanded money. Bert leaped over the counter and went for him. The gunman took to his heels with Bert after him down the street. If the family were shocked at Bert's marriage, they were taken aback by this story of fearless bravado. The marriage was happy and long-lasting. Both are now dead.

Mother played the piano, and Dad the organ. Oddly, as I think now, I never once heard Dad play the piano, but he was fond of the organ, and I think it was in that winter of 1926-7 that Alfred Hollins, the blind organist at St George's West Church, gave a series of recitals on Thursday evenings. Dad took me along with him, and I marvelled to

---

[1] B.B.s - Boys' Brigade

see a man so triumph over his disability. That was a lesson I was to be glad I learned early.

Wireless was then coming into its own, but Dad would have none of it. He said, probably quite rightly, that is would interfere with our homework. As we had never had the wireless, and television was far in the future, we didn't miss them and entertained ourselves, like everyone else. Flora McLaughlan, the dux girl at school the year I was dux boy, belonged to a family very like ours. She went on to teach languages, and her brother Hugh, also a teacher, told me that in their youth they had lived in Assembly Street, in a spacious flat. The house was spacious, but there was a very wide landing outside, and when they had a party they moved all the heavy furniture out of the house and on to the landing, to make room for dancing in the house.

From the mid-nineteenth century Leith had been a chronically overcrowded town, and people had ways of coping with the situation. Another family in the Kirkgate Church - the Bairds - had had several children, all married and living in and around the town. John Turnbull, treasurer of the Kirkgate Church, and a war hero with two D.S.O.s and two D.F.Cs, had married Mary Baird. He told me that when they were courting he was invited to a party in Mary's parents' house on the top flat of a tenement in Great Junction Street. When they reached the stair foot they could get no further, as the staircase up four flights, was full of guests unable to get into the house. They spent the evening gradually making their way up to the old folks' house as those inside said their farewells and made way for the next batch of guests.

Another aspect of overcrowding I may as well mention now. Visiting a lady in Portland Street who lived with a much older lady, the younger one suddenly said to me, ' I think you are under a misapprehension, Mr. Marshall. You think this lady is my mother, don't you?'

'Why yes,' said I, 'You are listed on the Communion Roll as mother and daughter.'

'Yes, everyone calls us mother and daughter, but we aren't really related at all. The family at the other end of the landing had nine children, and this lady had none, so she took me and my sister to live with her, and we were in and out of both houses, so we were almost in our teens before we were able to sort out which lady was our real mother.'

Mother was a great enthusiast for 'company' and put out tremendous energy organizing parties. Her parties were well known and long remembered. She did the cooking with help from Sis, who was approaching her teens. Mother also directed the entertainment, and somehow or other she catered for up to twenty guests. The house was not big enough for such a crowd but we managed.

There was a hard core of guests who appeared regularly at these parties - family members and close friends, and as in a ceilidh, each was expected to contribute an item. Some guests were known for one particular song or recitation. So we regularly heard 'Apple Dumpling' sung by a jovial man who looked like an apple dumpling; 'Rocked in the Cradle of the Deep' by our favourite basso profundo; 'On the Road to Mandalay'; 'Doon the Burn, Davie Lad'. Dad sang 'Anchored'. Mother invited people a little out of the ordinary, so we had Bella Dagg, from the church choir, who was an astonishingly deep contralto, reminiscent of Clara Butt. Jimmy Grieve from next door was a born humourist, who made the funniest comments with a straight face and had me in stitches. Meg Robertson was a fervent clanswoman, a member of the Clan Donnachie. The Robertsons had been ardent Jacobites, and Meg in our day was an ardent royalist. Whenever the national anthem came over the air on some auspicious occasion, Meg jumped to her feet and stood to attention, alone in all the company. Andrew Dishington rattled out popular songs on the organ. There were parties at Christmas, Hogmanay, New Year, Hallowe'en, but no birthday parties. These only acquired importance after the Hitler war. In my mid-teens I was playing reels and country dances, Lancers, Quadrilles, Waltzes. I had the Students' Lancers, taken from the Students' Song Book from the start of the twentieth century. Mother was exhausted, and next day would inevitably have a bilious attack or "have the bile", a condition which struck after periods of excessive work or anxiety. My mother used to get it, and of course my granny. You couldn't get up, you had a terrible headache and did a lot of noisy vomiting of bile. Posh people didn't get "the bile" - they had bilious attacks or "sick headaches." Of course it was probably migraine but who knows? All I know is that it's one of the conditions which was very common and has disappeared. Like Consumption and Rheumatic Fever. The condition still exists but it must have a new name.

Sometimes Dad would have a gathering of business friends, discussing the state of business over a dram. Dad didn't like spirits but acknowledged his responsibility as a host. A couple at these gatherings were Alex Mackay and his wife. They came from a family up north, at Portskerra, near Melvich on the Pentland Firth. They were cousins of my father's in a Highland sense I never understood; but we once went on holiday at Portskerra, and everyone in the village was a Mackay. Mrs. Mackay, the grandmother, was very active. The family were all fishermen, and the old lady did her share in baiting the lines. She was over seventy and had never been on a train. Indeed she seldom got as far as Thurso but was healthy and happy. The Mackays we knew in Edinburgh lived in Elm Row, and Alex was in the same line of business as Dad. There was also a son, Alistair, a little older than me, and said to be a brilliant pupil at Heriot's.

On Tuesday 27th December 1927 Mother and I boarded a tramcar in Wolseley Terrace and mounted to the top deck, when I was suddenly felled by an epileptic fit. Of course I had no idea what had hit me. I came round in bed, and we called the family doctor - Robert Thin - a brother of James Thin the bookseller, and he didn't put any name to this mysterious visitation. He put me on luminal, a mild sedative, and strictly forbade me any kind of exercise except walking. The school Christmas holidays were due to end the following week, but school was not to be thought of for the time being. I was on my feet again the following day, and nothing further happened. Relying on the doctor, I didn't go back to school. From time to time the doctor called but was quite adamant about no exercise but walking. I felt perfectly healthy, but he insisted I was not well, and sure enough, after three months I had another fit, equally severe. Even then I had no idea that this was going to change my life completely, and it was years before I became reconciled to the fact that everyone seemed to know of my illness although I never knew how they got to know.

As school was apparently out of the question for a lengthy period my parents engaged a tutor to take me along in French and Maths. English they reckoned I could probably cope with on my own, and without a Science lab we just had to forget Science. My tutor was Mary MacLeod, a very personable student - a Leith Academical who was taking a degree in modern languages. She came in twice a week except for university vacations, and we got on well together.

Fits recurred at odd intervals, and of course always without warning, sometimes fairly mild, sometimes more exhausting. As a fit might occur in any circumstances I soon got the message about walking only, although eventually I did use the bike again. I liked walking, and soon took to exploring the environs of the city, setting off after breakfast with sandwiches in my pocket. The built-up area was then much less extensive than it has since become. In less than half an hour I could walk into open country. On these hikes I would cover anything from twelve to eighteen miles, and grew fond of my own company, and anyway there was no alternative.

I didn't get back to school until after the Easter holidays in 1929, and joined the class that had been a year behind me when I fell ill. This was the fourth year, where I was the same age as everyone else. In my old class, now the fifth year, I had been a year younger than my classmates; but I only spent the summer term in the fourth. In the autumn we had a sharp transition into the fifth, and only now were girls and boys taught together, and the fifth and sixth years were largely composed

Everything Mixed with Mercy

of those who were aiming at the university. We boys now came into contact with Miss Thomsen, a Swedish lady, a tall imposing figure with a mass of flaxen hair. She taught French, but was also the Lady Superintendent. She paid no attention to the boys apart from teaching French, but she criticised the girls' grammar and deportment, keeping them behind from time to time, presumably to offer sexual advice and education. But Miss Thomsen did more than teach. At intervals in winter and spring she produced cheap tickets for the International Celebrity Concerts in the Usher Hall. For sixpence school children could sit in the Upper Gallery. Not everyone took up the offer of these tickets, but I grabbed at every offer. It was at these concerts that I first heard Yehudi Menuhin - a boy of about my own age, Jelly D'Aranyi and other celebrities, and brilliant performances of the classics by the Scottish National Orchestra.

Science was taught by William Chalmers - 'Billy Cheese' as he was known throughout the school. He was a big corpulent man, and having qualified as a teacher before the war, he didn't have a degree. He had spent the war in a cavalry regiment, which afforded us much amusement. He closely resembled Captain Mainwaring in 'Dad's Army', better at giving instructions than in carrying them out himself. The Science lab had a very high roof, and on one unforgettable day he proposed rigging up apparatus to demonstrate the acceleration due to gravity. We spent a joyous afternoon over this experiment, managing to confuse 'Billy Cheese' even more than he was confused by nature. And the afternoon was not entirely wasted, for ever since that day I have remembered that the acceleration due to gravity is calculated with the formula $S=½gt^2$. It was about this time that Mother conceived the idea of a parent/teacher association, and set about raising a fund to endow prizes for the dux boy and girl. There were no endowments in the school, and a committee was formed and a series of events organised to produce the needed finance. The committee met weekly in each others' houses in rotation. Mrs. Heatly was on the committee, and her son, Sir Peter Heatly, the Olympic diver, told me that he and his brother always looked forward eagerly to the committee's turn in their house, as on that evening they were excused piano practice.

In Sport I played no cricket, but instead put in time at athletics practice. I was no sprinter, but went for the mile and the jumps. I liked rugby, and for my last two years at school I played hooker for the 1st fifteen. I must have done more than that for, to my surprise, in my final year I found myself in with a chance for the championship. Unfortunately (as I saw it), two new boys had turned up, the brothers Brownlie. They were the sons of the new Methodist minister in the town. The younger one didn't worry me, but the older one was my own age, and entered for the mile. I had never seen him on the track, but he beat me, and consequently I failed in the championship by 1½ points.

The family had now settled into a regular pattern for summer holidays. We never went to the same place twice. Dad took a house for a month, always within commuting distance from home. We all stayed at the holiday home for the month, while Dad came for a fortnight, and commuted for the next fortnight. So we holidayed in Mid- or East Lothian, and Fife. We were in Kirkcaldy where there was a sandy beach, and in Elie, and Saline. There was a wonderful, hot summer at Heriot, where we stayed in one of a row of cottages. The next-door cottage had a garden with blackcurrant bushes with a heavy crop ready for pulling and eating - which I did with great enjoyment. Later, the next-door neighbour accused me of stealing the currants, and while I stood in confusion wondering how to answer, I looked down and saw a vivid stain on the breast pocket of my grey shirt, where I had stuffed currants. She didn't lay hands on me, but I got a verbal drubbing which prevented me making a return visit to that garden.

While at Heriot we attended church, and I was astonished to see only four people in the congregation, and an old, old minister who mounted the pulpit and was quite inaudible. This sort of thing was apt to happen under the old regime, under which ministers were ordained *ad vitam aut culpam*. In fact a minister could remain in his charge until he died or was guilty of some crime or immoral behaviour. The situation in a parish could become quite scandalous and nothing could be done about it. This anomalous situation has now been changed, and ministers are retired at seventy. Even so, it is not easy to deal with an unsatisfactory minister. Over the years I have known four ministers who were alcoholics, and this can do immense damage in a parish, but in one case where the presbytery were aware of this trouble in a parish a committee was sent to investigate and report on the matter. They met with the kirk session , who unanimously maintained that their minister was a splendid preacher and an effective pastor - when he was sober. The case had to rest there, until it was solved when the minister died. There are other unexpected aspects to the relationship between a minister and his congregation. I once discussed church government with a Congregational minister in a small country town. He was highly regarded, and assured me he could do anything he liked, so long as the congregation was with him. It seemed to work all right.

Advancing through my teens I was still keen on scouting, and in the troop I was known as 'Paddy'. This came from my school cap, normally worn then by schoolboys. But in the 31st Waverley troop I was the one at school over the age of fourteen, and the younger members of the troop didn't go to schools which wore caps. Once acquired, a nickname is impossible to shake off. Later, in the Agricultural set at the university, no one knew me as 'Paddy'. Among that lot I was 'Bull', and again I was stuck with the name until moving to another kind of society.

About half a dozen of us scouts frequently went for weekend camps to Crichton Castle. Other Saturdays we walked the Pentlands. We also hiked over pre-arranged routes, carrying all the necessary gear on our backs. We'd take a bus to our starting point. Scotland's weather being, as always, unpredictable and forecasts being nothing like as detailed as they are now, we got many a soaking. Our most thorough drenching, I think, was one weekend when we arrived in Selkirk to find there would be no bus for a long time. The rain continued pouring and we were wet to the skin. Fortunately a local scoutmaster spotted us and invited us into the hall of his church, where we got warm and reasonably dry. We cooked ourselves mince, which was all the food we had, and spent the night on the floor.

Apart from these group outings I had become quite fond of my own company during that year off school, and I did some hiking on my own. I bought a small bivouac tent for two guineas from a Glasgow firm. It was supposed to sleep two, and I slept in it comfortably. I did try it with Terry, but while we slept eventually we were much too crowded. It only weighed two pounds so it was certainly portable and it withstood showers, but not heavy rain. Hiking in warm weather I sometimes just slept on the ground rather than bother pitching the tent, and I was always impressed by the way, even after a hot day, the temperature dropped after dark, so that I slept all right on lying down, but woke freezing at dawn. I also stretched out on the back lawn at home, and if I woke in the chilly dawn it was no trouble to finish the night in bed.

1931 was my last year at school. The question of what I meant to do afterwards had come up in conversation from time to time. I had proposed being an explorer. It was pointed out that a modern explorer would be as well to have a degree, and to have financial backing. I thought again that I might become a professional violinist, but Dad cut me down to size, saying that not only was I rather late in thinking of it, but that the ability to play for Scottish country dancing and traditional songs hardly put me in the same class as a would-be professional. I then announced that I'd like to go into Agriculture - which was what I'd really had at the back of my mind for long enough, but with no family connection in farming I was ignorant of how best to get into that world. I knew my father's folk had come from Fowlis Wester, but my grandfather had come south in the 1850s. Dad was very fond of Fowlis, where he had spent his school holidays, and where he was a great local favourite. We spent two or three summer holidays there, and I loved the place. We stayed with an old lady, a cousin of Dad's, who rather intimidated me as I could not understand a word she said. She had the Gaelic and no English, which I discovered later. We got milk daily at a local farm where milk was set out in a very large, wide basin on which the cream formed in a thick top layer. Mother was concerned about Sis, who remained slim and lightweight, no matter what she ate. Mother thought cream would put weight on her, and she was handed a tumblerful of cream to drink. I watched anxiously as she was told to drink up, but she only managed two or three mouthfuls, and with joy I finished it for her. Looking around the local fields and steadings on these holidays, I saw farming as a very desirable way of life.

I decided on a degree in Agriculture. As an afterthought, I told Dr. Thin of my intention, as he had always kept in touch with me. He was delighted and went on to say, 'As you are going to the university I think I ought to tell you that we know very little about your condition, and I'm afraid you will have to cure yourself. The best advice I can give you is to keep yourself physically fit and healthy.' With this general guideline I was fairly satisfied. It seemed to make sense.

In the meantime I had to finish my last term at school. Since I returned after my year and more off, the school had been functioning under grave difficulties, while Watt's Hospital was being demolished and a new school built on the same site - the same site, in fact, where the old golf house of the eighteenth century had stood. The new Secondary School was opened after the Easter holidays in 1931. The Junior School was now accommodated in the 1896 building. The opening of the new school took place with immense public acclaim, and of course it was an immense improvement on what we had been used to. £200 was spent on providing a series of Medici prints to adorn the walls of the corridors, and they were greatly admired. Great efforts were put into the annual concert which was mounted on the stage before the annual speech day and prizegiving, and I was persuaded, much against my will, to take the part of the village idiot. It was only later in the proceedings, when I was presented with the Dux medal to tremendous applause that I realised that this over-the-top applause was not really for the Dux, but for the village idiot, whose song began:

> *My father died, I can't tell how,*
> *And left me six horses to follow the plough,*
> *With a wim, wim, wobble O,*
> *Strim, strim, strobble O,*
> *Wobble O, pretty boy, Over the down.*

And the yellow smock I wore is in the fancy dress cupboard at Old Lathrisk where my daughter lives.

4
UNIVERSITY 1932 - 1938

It was at the May term 1931 that we moved from Baronscourt Terrace to 2 West Savile Road, Newington, so that I travelled daily to school for the summer term by the suburban railway, on the outer circular line, from Newington Station, round the city, to Leith Central. None of that line exists now, and the site of Leith Central has been redeveloped.

That summer the first school trip abroad was organised. We crossed to Holland, and from there, by train to Germany. We sailed up the Rhine to the Moselle, visited Trier and Cologne, and had an interesting time, marred for me by taking a fit in Cologne, and being kept in bed for three days in a youth hostel where we were staying. The Germans appeared to be just as cagey about epilepsy as people were in Scotland, and it was put about that I was suffering from sunstroke. In support of this theory I was induced to buy a beret. Youth hostels in Scotland had only been introduced in 1929, and I had visited one or two like Broadmeadows in the Borders, which consisted of two cottages joined together. The arrangements were basic, but we greatly enjoyed living there with the communal kitchen and simple sleeping bunks. The German hostel was five-star accommodation compared with the Scottish provision. This one in Cologne was a three-storey building with steel-framed, two-tiered beds, and everything spotlessly clean. The Germans were great on wanderlust, and the hit song was then 'I Love To Go A Wandering'. Hitler was not yet in power, but the Hitler Youth were everywhere, strutting and parading. We found these bumptious and avoided them, which was not difficult as we had our own programme to pursue. Apart from these unpleasant types, we got on well with the people we met, and I first tasted Moselle wine when we visited a vineyard in that area.

Back home I had a great sense of freedom with no more school, and I spent September exploring the city and browsing in some of the thirty-odd secondhand bookshops in Edinburgh. H.V.Morton, visiting the city, remarked that every other shop seemed to be a bookshop, and as a rather tatty book could be had for a penny I was soon acquiring quite a collection, and they were not all rubbish. Paperbacks were appearing, a novelty in Britain - with Penguins at 6d (2½p), and Ernest Benn were publishing a series of classics at 6d. Dowell's and Lyon & Turnbull in George Street had monthly book sales, and when I had any money I could pick up an odd prize at a reasonable price. But normally I was not bidding, but listening and learning which books were valuable and which stirred little or no interest. In this way I gradually acquired first editions of Scott, Dickens, Stevenson and others. Nowadays it is not that simple for the individual with little money to win such trophies. Books are auctioned in bundles in which there may be one that is of some interest. Secondhand booksellers have space which the individual lacks. The secondhand shops varied greatly from Grant's in George IVth Bridge, and Thin's, opposite the Old Quad, who operated secondhand departments within their main shop, down to antique shops with a few shelves of secondhand books.

One well-known man in this line of business was Mr. Hyslop who had a shop in College Street, next to the Old Quad. He never appeared in anything other than an old overcoat and beret, and his shop front was so narrow that it could easily be passed without being noticed. Over the years I was a fairly regular customer. The shop was cluttered, so with time to spare I could browse around. One day I asked whether he had a book I was keen to get, as it was out of print. Yes, he had it, and he disappeared into the back shop. After a while he reappeared to say he couldn't find it, but was sure he had it. He said he had several cellars around the district, and if I were to return in a week he might have laid hands on it by then. Looking around I asked why he gave shelf space to so many tatty books, which I couldn't imagine anyone buying. He admitted there was a great deal of rubbish on view, but said he could never bring himself to throw any book away, remembering all the trouble the author had in writing it. 'Well,' I said, 'you don't appear to have much passing trade.' He said most of his business was done by mail order. He also said that a regular customer came over every year from Belfast, and bought so many yards of books. I suggested he was pulling my leg. 'Not at all,' he asserted, 'people with large houses like to have a library with shelves of books, not necessarily for reading, but for decoration.'

Having matriculated, I found myself committed to lectures in Physics, Chemistry, Zoology and Botany. Physics was dealt with at High School Yards, Infirmary Street, and here I had an introductory shock when it was soon obvious that the Physics I had had at school came far short of the starting point for Physics at the university. Practically everyone else in the class felt the same, and at the end of term exams two men in the class achieved percentages in the nineties, another one or two were in the sixty per cent bracket, while the rest of us foundered in the twenties and thirties. To our relief, the pass-mark at the end of the year was declared to be 33%. Chemistry for Agriculture only required steady application. Zoology, in King's Buildings, opened the previous year, was a much larger class, with medicals added to our twenty or so agricultural students. Two incidents made the Zoology class memorable. One of the medicals was epileptic, and had a fit which set him screaming on a bloodcurdling note. This triggered a response in my own nerves. With a mounting sense of panic, I struggled to keep control, but when the screaming stopped my panic died, to my intense relief. Two epileptics performing at once would certainly have brought the class to an abrupt end that day. Certain types of sound, or certain types of stimulus to my imagination were very disturbing. I once read a book which started with a vivid description of an epileptic fit. I could not read it: I threw the book away.

On another day we were dissecting a frog when an aspiring surgeon from Falkirk with flaming red hair fainted at the sight of blood and fell face down into a tray of formalin beside the frog. Before drawing any hasty conclusions, I ought to say that that same man became a successful surgeon after all. Nelson was sea-sick at the start of every voyage.

Botany was a sizeable nuisance. Lectures were at the Royal Botanic Garden at Inverleith, the same day as Zoology at King's Buildings. There was an interval of just forty-five minutes to get from King's Buildings to Inverleith, with lunch to fit in on the way. I cycled to West Savile Road, where lunch was waiting, then on to the Botanics just in time. The other objection we all had to Botany was a compulsory excursion every Saturday morning, generally to somewhere along the east coast, where the flora was interesting, or to some other area exhibiting unusual species. We were always assured we'd be home again for lunch, but that never happened, unless lunch was set for mid-afternoon. The result of this was that none of us could take part in university rugby or soccer. Eventually I joined the Boxing Club which met on a Wednesday evening, which was small compensation.

I had one disadvantage. It soon appeared that everyone in the class had some farming experience. They were farmers' sons, or the sons of vets, or had other connections which gave them a knowledge of farming practice. I was only a spectator hoping to enter a strange world. It was conditional on my entering on the degree course that I would work on farms during vacations; so I applied for a job in answer to an advertisement in the Farmers' Weekly, and found myself at Newra, a farm near Muthill, in Perthshire, run by Mr. Arthur, his wife and father-in-law, and a dairymaid. I paid nothing to be taught farming practice, and I gave my services free, so there was no contract, nothing in writing between us.

The Arthurs were in their thirties, and Mrs. Arthur's father was approaching seventy, but spry, capable, and very experienced, with a lifetime of farming behind him. The girl was a local lassie, whose ambition seemed to be to get me to bed with her. She tried her best, but did not seem to understand that there must be some mutual attraction

University 1932 - 1938

for anything in that way to happen, and she did not attract me at all. Mr. Arthur had been to college, and had ideas on how to improve his farm. What he lacked was money. It was a mixed farm - arable, with about a dozen milking kye.

My day started at a quarter to five. Shortly after five the lassie and I began milking, and when that was done and the byre mucked out we went in for breakfast. The food was good and plentiful. This was in 1932, and there was little in the way of machinery about. I spent three weeks singling turnips, with help from others as and when they had time to join me. We cut hay and I managed to operate the tumbling tam. I was deft enough with the horses to be allowed to set up the tatties, although ploughing was reckoned to be a bit beyond me. Starting on a field of barley at harvest we scythed the head-rigs - Mr. Arthur, his father-in-law and me. This was back-breaking work, at which the old man was far and away the fastest worker. He worked with a smooth, regular, apparently easy movement. The one large piece of machinery was the threshing-mill, and it toured the district. It took about sixteen men to work as a team with the mill, so all available hands from neighbouring farms reported for duty. I built the stacks in the stackyard, although I wasn't trusted to finish them. Topping them off was a skilled job. There was a short break at midday for tea and a sandwich, and at the end of the day we worked on until the job was done, so that the mill was free to travel to the next farm the following day. The fairm wifie put on a huge meal for the evening, with broth and cloutie dumplings. The threshing-mill meant a week or ten days' work for the farm hands moving round the neighbouring farms in turn. The dairy lass and myself stayed where we were to attend to the myriad jobs to be done daily.

The social life of the district, apart from weddings and such-like, centred on the weekly dance in Muthill. This event, to which I was warmly invited, began at nine o'clock on Friday evening, and was kept up until two or three a.m. With so much necessary work with horses and cattle on the farms, nine o'clock was the earliest feasible time for the jollification. With my early start the Arthurs were not keen on my going to the jiggin, and Mrs. Arthur said that if I were not back by eleven o'clock I'd have to sleep in the hay loft, for the house door would be locked. I thought she probably didn't mean it, so I took a chance and stayed at the dance till midnight, and got back to Newra to find Mrs. Arthur had kept her promise after all, and I bedded down in the hay for four hours. I was undisturbed except for rats running over me. At first I didn't realise what they were when I felt them, but as they were obviously not going to eat me, who, after all, was an intruder on their territory, I didn't worry any more about them. And of course I was dead tired. I didn't get to the dance every week, but after that first night I stayed to the end of the dance, and didn't go to bed at all. Had I tried to sleep for an hour or so I'd probably have slept in. Instead I routed about in the hay loft, for I knew the hens sometimes laid away there, and sure enough I would find an egg, which by way of refreshment I broke into my mouth. To my acute discomfiture I found the egg was too big to be accommodated there, and I got egg all over my face. But it was a refreshment.

At these Friday dances there was no difficulty finding partners. Strangers on these nights were something of a rarity, but I soon met Isobel Honeyman - a very attractive lass, and intelligent, able to converse and contribute as much as she received. She was a farmer's daughter, with a sister Eleanor, and the Honeyman's farm, Drumdowie, was two or three miles south of Muthill. I walked her home. There weren't any cars available, and no one thought much of a walk of a few miles. By the time we had reached her home, and I made my way back gain to Newra, it was getting on for starting time again. When I had to leave for Edinburgh again Isobel and I were on a pretty warm footing, and we corresponded from time to time throughout the winter. Next year I was back at Newra but I was getting fed-up with unremitting work, early and late. Isobel suggested her father would be glad to have my help. That suited me, for her father and I got on well together, and I spent a week or two with the Honeymans. Then one evening Isobel and I were indulging in a bit of canoodling in the parlour, when I had a fit. This was a horrific shock to the Honeymans. Mr. Honeyman wanted to throw me out at once but Mrs. Honeyman pled for me to stay the night at least. And that was the abrupt end to a beautiful dream. I really couldn't complain. I realised by then that everyone was afraid of epilepsy, and the doctor had told me he didn't know much about the disease. True enough, I'd have to learn to fend for myself.

A fellow student offered to sell me his motorbike for two pounds. Even in those days two pounds was suspiciously cheap for a motorbike, but he insisted it was in working order. There was no driving test then, but I knew there were questions to be answered before a licence was handed out. I decided to find out, however, and proceeded to Waterloo Place, to the relevant office. I was handed a printed form with a long list of questions, to which the answer to each was 'yes' or 'no'. I went down the list, and in answer to the question as to whether I was subject to fits of any kind I answered 'yes', hoping the man behind the counter would not notice. But he noticed all right. He asked if I realised what I'd written. Again I answered 'Yes', and he must have thought I was deranged. He told me in a loud voice to get out, and came quickly round the counter to speed my going. So now I knew that if doctors didn't know much about epilepsy, the average citizen, even more ignorant of the disease, was very cautious, as the epileptic was quite unpredictable.

Isobel and I were still in touch. At first we were forbidden to see each other again, but Isobel persuaded her mother to let us correspond once a week so long as we did not meet. We were then able to meet 'by chance' at various cattle shows, and we even went to the Highland Show in Dundee. Isobel's grannie lived in Dundee, and I met her father there. He was very affable. Three weeks later I was back at Drumdowie, apparently on the old footing, and I met Isobel's sister Eleanor, who was in service somewhere and was on holiday.

Meanwhile at the university things were happening. I had had to resit a Zoology exam, but passed the resit; but I was increasingly dissatisfied with the prospect of a career in agriculture, in which I felt more and more the difficulty of advancing in an industry in which I had had so little experience. At the same time I felt drawn to the Faculty of Arts, where I felt more at home. Towards the end of May, then , I decided to study for the ministry. There and then I dropped most of my classes, and began working with Miss Lemon, a well-known tutor in Lauriston Place. I took Latin and Greek with her. She was a chain smoker, but a very good tutor. My idea was to sit part of the entrance exam for New College in September, but I learned that there was no need to do that before I had a degree, so I said goodbye to Miss Lemon.

My decision to turn to the ministry did not meet with universal acclaim. Dr. Thin was furious. Of all the stupid decisions to have made, this was the worst. Did I realise what a sedentary life I was heading for? Did I realise that I was throwing away all the benefits of an active, open-air life for day after day in the study? Most people who heard of my change in plans said nothing. The only man who congratulated me and wished me well was one of the lecturers in agriculture. He seemed to understand my dilemma. He pointed out the close relationship that has always existed between the ministry and the farming community, shook hands and wished me well. I was immensely heartened. My parents took it all quite calmly. 'If that's what you want to do, just go ahead.'

Towards the end of September I paid another visit to Drumdowie and found the atmosphere there had reverted to what it had been when I first had a fit there. Mr. Honeyman wouldn't speak to me. He refused my assurance that this was not a hereditary illness. I was forbidden to come to Drumdowie again, and Isobel was told that if she continued to see me the family would have no more to do with her. As I, of course, could not support her, that was the end.

Surprisingly, in little more than a fortnight I had forgotten about Isobel.

Look, no specs!
How young I was. Sartorial note from the thirties: the jacket served to keep the pullover clean. For many years that pullover was washed every spring.

Graduation, 1934
James Scott Marshall, MA.

Between classes and university social life I was very much engaged, and in any case in November I met Mary Tough, a very different type of girl from Isobel. We met at a Rover dance at the R.C. hall in Graham Street. I was late in arriving and saw Mary without a partner. We joined up then and started a conversation that seems to have been going on for seventy years now.

Transferring from the Science faculty to Arts, I was told that in view of the subjects I had been reading in Science I would be allowed to graduate in Arts in two years, provided Mathematics was included in my Arts course. I protested. I had done no Maths since leaving school, and my experience with university Physics had made me very reluctant to have another go at Maths. However, I was told that it was either Maths, or I'd have to take the normal three-year course for an ordinary M.A.. So I yielded, and in June 1934 I passed degree exams in English

University 1932 - 1938

and 1st Ordinary Philosophy, and in September failed 1st Ordinary Maths. In 1934-5 I took Inter-hons Philosophy, 1st Ord Maths and 1st Ord French.

In the Arts faculty there was far more opportunity for socializing. In agriculture there were no contacts with others outside the lecture rooms. The syllabus was so full we had no leisure. In second-year Agriculture, as well as animal and crop husbandry we had three short one-term courses in Geology, Genetics and Forestry, and it was in the Forestry course I first met Logan Patullo. It was but a tenuous acquaintanceship, and I only recognized him in Fife thirty-odd years later as he was one of those men remarkably unchanged in appearance over the years.

Now instead of farm work in the vacations I went off with Phil McNaughton hiking around the Border youth hostels; and in the summer I camped in Arran for a fortnight, and joined the family at Bridge of Earn for another fortnight.

Heading for the parish ministry it seemed appropriate that I join a Christian society, so I joined the Student Christian Movement (SCM); but having joined I was not much impressed. It seemed to me only too like the Church - a great organization failing to press on with the most important of its aims. It claimed to be an evangelical movement, but there was precious little evangelism done in Edinburgh. The SCM then combined with the Student Campaigners, but very few members took any active part in the campaign movement. After some months I saw the S.C.M as simply an association in which adherents of different Christian denominations could meet and exchange ideas; but even so, I never saw any R.C.s among the members. The Evangelical Association was streets ahead of the S.C.M. in active evangelical work, but I didn't join the E.A. My difficulty with them was that they withheld themselves from the world at large. They disapproved of films because of Hollywood's immorality. Theatres were bad because of the immorality of showgirls - and so on. Associating with activities of which we disapprove is doing evil that good may come - a bad principle. Their motto appeared to be 'No compromise', and it sounds fine, but they were a narrow-minded lot. I later decided to leave both the S.C.M and the E.A. alone.

I took this problem to Mr. Shedden. The Rev John Shedden had become colleague and successor to James Law at the Moray-Knox Church. I thought he was a splendid preacher, raising many points I wanted to discuss with him. I called at the manse on many a Monday morning to talk about things he had said the day before, not realising that Monday was supposed to be the minister's day off. His heart must have sunk on many a Monday forenoon when I called yet again; but I was certainly grateful for these talks. He had had a bad war, as the phrase went then, and he died a year or two later from war wounds.

I was teaching a Sunday School class of four boys, who provided me with entertainment in response to my teaching. One of them, known to me as John White, had been with me since October 1934, when I inherited a class from Miss Anderson. At the Christmas party I learned from Miss Anderson that my John White was really John Brown. When I asked him the reason for this, 'To escape detection' he answered. He had probably been reading too much Sexton Blake. These lads came from very poor homes around the Dumbiedykes, but they were a lively bunch. I invited them to come to our house for supper, and they were rather late in arriving. When they did turn up it appeared they had taken a tram to Newington Station, and as they got off the tram one of them lost the last remaining button on his trousers. His pals shepherded him into a telephone kiosk and tied his breeks up with a piece of string. Mother was hard put to it to keep a straight face, but she supplied buttons to solve his problem, and we had a pleasant evening thereafter.

The Christmas vacation in 1934 saw Mary and me recognized by the family as friends. After my experience with Isobel Honeyman, however, I was much more cautious. I had a slight fit early in December - the first since the end of August, so I was hoping I might be recovering. After having had a fit in Mary's presence, Mother spoke to her alone and asked what she felt about our relationship now. Mary said it made no difference to her. I think Mother was relieved, and from then on they were like mother and daughter. Isobel had had the same reaction to my trouble but her family effectively killed our relationship. The farmer's instinct was to avoid any contact with a disease that might be hereditary. I had no trouble with the Tough family. I did not realise it at the time, but my parents must have been extremely worried about my prospects as an epileptic in the ministry, and Dr. Thin's fury was understandable. Since so little was known about the disease, and my fits occurring so irregularly, no one was in a position to be categorical about it, so with the best will in the world, the best course must have seemed to be to leave me to it with all good wishes.

The Rovers' Annual Dance was held at Ritchie's in St Andrew Street. I was no longer in the Rovers, but Mary and I went as 'paying guests'. We had a great time, finishing at 2 a.m. We walked back to Maryfield. Mary is a difficult girl to say goodbye to, and after I left her door there was not a taxi to be seen, so I walked back to West Savile Road, by which time it was five o'clock. This was a walk I did frequently, for if I left Mary after midnight there was no transport of any kind available.

About this time Mary lost her job at the N.B. Rubber works in Leith

Walk. She was not all that distressed, for the seven o'clock start in the morning was inconvenient, to say the least. Mother and Dad were complaining about the late hours I'd been keeping - the result of Mary's home being so far from mine. We were keen on theatre, and spent many nights at the Palladium in Fountainbridge, which was cheaper than the King's or Lyceum, and we enjoyed repertory theatre. I took the Sunday School class to the first house at the Theatre Royal to see Rip Van Winkle, with Harry Gordon and Betty Jumel. Mary and I also went to hear Moonie's choir perform the Messiah before a small audience. I thought it a good performance, but it was fashionable then to go to the Choral Union's presentation of the Messiah at New Year in the Usher Hall, which was always packed. I sang with the Choral Union at New Year 1933, and again the following year, but was not thrilled by the prospect of singing it again and again every year, when I had no time to attend rehearsals for their other concerts.

With one thing and another it was always late when I got home after walking from Abbeyhill to Newington. On Christmas Day, however, I sought to make amends and rose at seven to make breakfast, and thereafter spent the day in the kitchen, lending a hand. We ran a buffet supper in the evening as we had invited far more than could be seated. It was a huge success, and left us exhausted.

Over the festive season I noticed various tobacconists, fruiterers, confectioners and the like - small shops - still open at eleven o'clock and much later on Hogmanay. Shop-girls in these places had a very long day on their feet, and it was obvious that the impending Shop Hours Act was urgently needed.

On 30th December Mary and I parted early enough. For some reason now forgotten we had gone for a walk on the Radical Road after dark, and were caught in a heavy downpour of rain - an 'onding', Aunt Mary would have called it. We were soaked to the skin and made for home at 9:30. It was on this New Year's Day of 1934 that sixteen of the family sat down to a five-course dinner at West Savile Road, which was an achievement for Sis and Mother, but I thought there was far too much preparation for a meal like that. Like the buffet at Christmas it was a memorable get-together. And after dinner we had a lively session of country dancing until we broke up at 11.30. Next morning we heard that Uncle Bob, true to form, had turned up at the Cummings' house at 2 a.m. minus his bottom set of dentures. (The previous year he'd arrived without his luggage!). Joe let him in, and as Uncle Jos refused to get up, Joe and his mother put him to bed. He was full of beans, as usual, and announced that Gordie was top in Latin and Maths at Aberdeen University. (I wondered!)

My sister Isobel was training at Atholl Crescent College of Domestic

Science for a certificate in Household Management, and these dinners and suppers at home were by way of practice for her.

Mother was normally the boss of the house, but with Isobel at home Mother became the home help, to their mutual satisfaction. At this time I got the notion of offering myself as a foreign missionary. I was advised to get my degree before finally deciding, and of course my epilepsy threw doubt on the possibility of being accepted, and in any case there is so much need for evangelism in this country that any decision would be difficult. Turning all this over in my mind I had four fits in one morning, followed by a blinding attack of bile. In fact I was asleep when this happened in the early hours, but I was left with a splitting headache as usual. I felt like a wet rag all day, and not much better the next day. However it was at this time I first heard George MacLeod expounding a plausible theory of 'Patriotic Pacifism', and was inclined to agree with practically all he said. He was a fine speaker with a good memory and a good delivery, but much of what he said was wasted through a toneless expression.

Thinking over the missionary idea, when I remembered the outburst from the doctor when I proposed training for the ministry, I guessed he would do his best to stop any idea of missionary work. Another idea of his from the onset of my trouble was that I must avoid constipation, so I had long had bran for supper. That was so tasteless that I soon changed to brose - that is a handful of oatmeal treated with boiling water. I found this quite palatable and sometimes varied it with pease meal. Dr. Robert Thin belonged to a family that had made its mark in the eighteenth century, as adherents of the sect of the Glasites or Sandemanians[1]. The sect had never grown much in numbers, but they had a meeting place in Barony Street, where they hung on well past the mid-twentieth century. Our Dr. Robert Thin had been chairman of the Dialectic Society about 1881 - half a century before my time, which was so long ago that to me he seemed to have belonged to another world. But he was no fool.

I was also a member of the Young Scots - a Liberal society which I joined at the instigation of my cousin Jimmy Denholm, a keen Liberal, who was living in Edinburgh, and working for my father. After Airdrie Academy he had gone to Glasgow University for a degree in Agriculture, but failed all his exams at the end of his first year, so his parents refused to support him any longer at the university. He was then unemployed, and Dad gave him a job, as he had no prospects at that time of high unemployment. Jimmy was an opinionated cantankerous man who managed to quarrel with almost everyone he had any dealings with. After 1939 Dad lost several men on war service, and he got Isobel to give up her job managing a nursing home at Peebles to come and

---

[1] The Glasite Meeting House closed in 1989

University 1932 - 1938

work for Nairn and Marshall. Jimmy Denholm twice proposed to her, but she couldn't stand him, so nothing came of it. He later married and went to live in Baronscourt Terrace, but his wife died, and he developed Parkinson's Disease, and after a long spell of suffering he suddenly died.

The Young Scots met monthly in a room at Surgeons' Hall, and they formed what might have been a supporters club for the Leith M.P., Ernest Brown, who hailed from Devon, and was a great favourite with the Newhaven fisherfolk. He was known as the man with the loudest voice in the House of Commons, and in the run-up to the General Election that year the Young Scots had promised to organise an open-air meeting at the Foot of the Walk. But when the members turned up no one was prepared to speak for an indefinite period, gathering a crowd in anticipation of the arrival of Mr. Brown. They all insisted on my taking on this thankless task, as they claimed a student was the best qualified for the job. A large wooden box was produced and I mounted it with my heart in my mouth and butterflies in my stomach. This was my first experience of open-air speaking, and there was no public address system in those days, apart from a megaphone, and the Young Scots didn't have one. Ernest Brown was due to join us after a meeting in Newhaven. I had no idea when he was likely to appear, and as no one else was prepared to relieve me on the soap box, I had to go on talking, without notes. There was no difficulty gathering a crowd, for the Foot of the Walk always had plenty of the unemployed hanging about. My difficulty was knowing what to say, and I was expecting heckling, but none came. They were all expecting the arrival of the M.P. and were writing me off as not worth their attention, but as I got into my stride I realised I was carrying on smoothly, while saying nothing original or important. At length Mr. Brown arrived and I stepped down, satisfied that while I had not impressed the audience I at least had done my bit. It was a kind of baptism.

The Dialectic Society was one of the five Associated Societies - long-established, traditional bodies. The Dialectic went in for debating, and a number of these debates carried on until we reached closing time, with plenty of steam left. I was secretary that year, and got the idea of having an extra meeting over lunch, when we could carry on talking if we had somewhere to enjoy these facilities. About a dozen men showed interest, and I managed to get a restaurant at Surgeons' Hall to give us a weekly lunch for 1s3d in a private room. This carried on through the spring term but faded in the summer and was never resumed.

Francis Dick and I were pretty close friends. We met in the Dialectic Society and talked together on every conceivable subject. His father taught English at Edinburgh Academy, but I never knew where his home was. We were both interested in chess and met once a week in my house and his digs on alternate weeks. These games would continue till the small hours, so each of us had a good walk home every other week. His digs were in Marchmont, and in those days, when there was very little student accommodation Marchmont was a popular area for digs, being just across the Meadows from the University. The landladies ('bunk-wives' in St Andrews) were a very mixed lot, and Francis' landlady was a close-fisted, no-nonsense character. When we were playing chess in Francis' digs his landlady always came into the room at nine o'clock precisely with a glass of milk and a biscuit. Francis was very embarrassed and would offer me a drink of his milk and half the biscuit. We did better playing at West Savile Road. As the practice never varied at his digs we just got used to it.

The death of my dog Ranger distressed me, for we had been daily companions during my year off school. Since then, however, with my work for the Highers, then farm work, and university life, I had had little time for any dog, but at home we always had a dog, a cat, and from time to time, a canary - all of which were just taken for granted as part of the family. I never thought of them as pets, but as real personalities, remembered now for their habits, preferences and escapades. When my parents married in 1910 they had a black and white collie, of whom I have only a vague memory, for he did not go with us to Fountainhall Road. In Leith Walk we had a black cat called Umbie. In the kitchen the crockery was stacked along shelves, and Umbie loved walking along those shelves, delicately picking his way between the dishes. He never broke a dish, and yet on one occasion he did make a *faux pas*. It was summer, the window was open, and Umbie lay sunning himself on the windowsill, two storeys above the ground. Suddenly there was a screech, and Umbie had disappeared. No one saw it happen, but I rushed down to the back green, expecting to pick up the body; but when I opened the back green door he shot past me up to the house again, as though nothing out of the usual had happened. I guess that was one of his nine lives.

Back in Baronscourt again we had a canary, a Border Roller. Hardly a cheep came from it until I started violin practice, when he simultaneously burst into song, and continued a steady tremolo apparently without pausing for breath until I stopped playing, when he also stopped. I could never decide which of us was the soloist and which the accompanist.

Our cat at that time was Smokey, and he was very fond of heat. He disappeared one day but we hardly noticed his absence as he habitually wandered around the house and garden. There was a range in the kitchen with the coal fire and oven adjacent. When Mother stoked the fire to begin cooking, the oven heated. We could hear mewing and the sound of scrabbling. It was some time before we identified the source of the noise and opened the oven door, whereupon Smokey shot out and careered round and round the room. I have already paid tribute to Ranger, and he was succeeded by Major, a Labrador, phlegmatic, with a quiet and steady disposition.

It was at this period that Terry, then aged ten or eleven, turned up one day, with guinea pigs in a box. He had got them from Collins, the pet shop in Fleshmarket Close. Mother was shocked. She couldn't stand the sight of those beasts, and the prospect of them proliferating was the last straw. She ordered Terry to take them back immediately, and after about an hour he was home again without the little beasts. 'Did the man take them back?' asked Mother. 'The shop was shut', said Terry. 'Then where are the guinea pigs?' 'I left them on his doorstep.'

In West Savile Road, Major was followed by Scottie - a Labrador crossed on a collie or some such. He had character and personality. He was Dad's closest companion and accompanied him to and from the office every day. Dad at that time was pretty deaf, and his eyes were not good either. Going home at lunch-time they passed the Mac Fisheries shop at Salisbury. On a long marble slab outside the shop window, there was always a display of poultry and game. Every day Scottie sidled past this slab with his head well down, and would snatch the carcass at the end of the slab - a rabbit, a chicken or whatever and make off round the corner into Salisbury Road. Dad never saw anything of all this, and Scottie continued home by a roundabout route, pausing long enough to devour his booty, and reaching 2 West Savile Road just as Dad got there. This went on for nobody knew how long, but one day Mother unusually had Scottie with her on the same road, when she saw him doing his daily snatch, and she called him. When she turned, the shopman was there. 'Is that your dog ma'am?' 'Yes, I'll pay for it.' 'You certainly will, and there are several others,' and he told her the story of how Scottie had been seen more than once, but he had always disappeared before anyone could get on his tail.

Wednesday afternoons were special. On that day the Salvation Army appeared in Hill Square, just round the corner from Nairn and Marshall. They took up position in a ring to give their weekly recital of hymn tunes. There was no service, but the weekly concert was much appreciated in the neighbourhood. However, when they took up position, Scottie would come out from the office, and when the first notes were sounded he would move into the centre of the ring, squat on his haunches, and join in with a descant of his best and most sustained howls. The Army couldn't get rid of him, and in time they grew to tolerate him, and someone from the office would come and

Everything Mixed with Mercy

remove him. I only witnessed this show once or twice. Wednesday afternoons were normally free of lectures, and I often used the time writing essays or catching up with required reading. But punctually every Wednesday afternoon an old chap with a barrel organ would arrive in Gilmour Road, round the corner from our house, and give us a recital of hymns tunes, like the 'Sally Army' in Hill Square, but the barrel organ produced the same recital every week, beginning with 'What a Friend we have in Jesus'. It effectively ended all concentration.

Anticipating my entrance to New College in the autumn of 1935, I thought it would be a good idea to read through the Bible. This was more for information that for inspiration. I remember going to Mr. Shedden to inform him that for the first time in my life I had discovered the book of Ecclesiastes and thought it was marvellous. He laughed and said he thought I had a peculiar view of it.

Our family had always been strong Liberals. In Dad's young days the hero had been Gladstone, and in my youth David Lloyd George filled that position, and Dada had me along to a meeting in the Usher Hall to hear the great man speak. The Party, however, had long been in the doldrums, so I went to lunch in the Union to meet Sir Robert Hamilton, late Secretary of State for the Colonies. The idea behind this meeting was to try to restart the Edinburgh University Liberal Club, which had been defunct for something over two years. About thirty men and girls attended the lunch, and Sir Robert had nothing in particular to say, and was thanked with a trickle of applause. Nevertheless three weeks later the Varsity Liberal Club was reconstituted., and I was excited over its prospects, but it came to nothing for Liberalism had little backing in the university.

The Dialectic Society still attracted those who enjoyed the cut and thrust of debate, but some of the motions proposed seemed rather silly, although a good speaker could dredge up some unusual aspects of an unpromising subject. I was invited to propose 'That Misogyny is the Inevitable Result of Bachelordom', and to my astonishment that was defeated by the narrowest of margins. Another subject was 'That the Soul of Man is Immortal'. I had meant to go to the Reid Orchestra concert that evening, but everyone else in the Society seemed to think this would be a red-letter evening, so I went along, although I thought the motion silly. Immortality is surely what characterises the soul. There is no such concept as a soul that is not immortal - and yet the motion was carried by an overwhelming majority.

About this time the Union debated the motion, 'That the S.R.C, Being Useless and Effete, should Dissolve Itself Forthwith.' This was an ironical situation. I attended only because I knew three of the four principal speakers and wanted to hear how they dealt with the motion.

59

University 1932 - 1938

Out of 4000 students just twenty-nine votes were cast. These twenty-nine voters appeared to be under a misconception. The Students Representative Council is a body elected by the students. If they are not satisfied with the S.R.C. they should dismiss them and appoint a more effective body.

Looking back over the years at the myriad of activities that took up my energies in the spring of 1935, one thing stands out. The Maths results were posted in mid-March, and, glory of glories, I got 52%, which put me in the first third of the class list. This was very important for me, as my graduating depended on the result of the Maths exam. I'd been doing quite well in Philosophy, and in fact I had just cashed a cheque for 15s for tutoring in Logic. French was no problem, and in all my time in Arts I had the fondest memory of Sir Herbert Grierson lecturing to the English class. He was to speak on Shakespeare, and he did mention him, but wandered off into a fascinating disquisition on 17th century literature. It was a large class, with quite a few girls who were all furious at Grierson's blethers which they could not get down in their notes. I was fascinated by his chatty style, and made no attempt to write notes on what was first-class entertainment. That evening I went to the King's Theatre to hear Edward German's 'Merrie England'. A great tonic. Next day at Murrayfield, I saw Scotland beat England 10-7. Then back to the King's with Mary. And it was in that same month of March, that the speed limit of 30 miles per hour was introduced.

Those final months before my graduation was a time of great social and political stress. Hunger marchers leaving Edinburgh for Glasgow, protesting against the Unemployment Act and the Means Test. The politicians worried over Germany's reintroduction of conscription, and the young generation here being compared unfavourably with their heroic fathers. This worried me a bit. I was also experimenting with fasting, to Mother's puzzlement. This was really a form of self-discipline. Over several months I found that in fasting, missing the first meal was the most difficult. Between meals hunger diminished, but getting over each regular mealtime was one more hard step. After two days I was definitely weak, and I usually gave up at that. Once I did reach a third day, which satisfied me that the prospect would be increasing weakness, in which I saw no profit.

The graduation took place without anything untoward taking place, and I pass without more comment to the 2nd September 1935, which marked a milestone in my life. We were with the family on holiday at Innerwick, East Lothian, and early on Sunday morning Mary and I went for a walk, and I took the opportunity to propose to her, and she consented. We had known each other two years, and I felt that graduation, with the intention of entering the ministry put me

Everything Mixed with Mercy

on a more secure footing than being an undergraduate. Mother was shocked. I think she may have felt that an epileptic in the ministry was not a very secure prospect. Dad just smiled and continued reading a map. But they liked Mary and quickly wished her joy.

Marriage, of course, could not be for at least another three years yet. In the meantime it was suggested that our engagement must not get beyond our parents' knowledge. Mary also insisted that I must ask her father's permission. I rather jibbed at this, but she assured me her father would be deeply offended if I didn't ask him. So I asked him, and he agreed. He knew well enough what my hopes were, and I'm sure his other children, who were all married, had not gone through this formality. I was naïve, and didn't realise that my epilepsy was a much more important issue to others than it was to me. I took each fit as it came and then continued with a normal life. It was not like having a limb amputated, or being blind or having multiple sclerosis, which would be with me all the time. But the public could see these disabilities and organise their reaction to them in their own time. A fit in public was a huge embarrassment to all witnesses. Both our families adopted the policy 'wait and see', keeping their doubts and fears to themselves.

New College was a very different place from the Arts Faculty. Here there was a close fellowship. Divinity was a three-year course, at the end of which we could take a B.D. degree or not, as we pleased, although everyone entering the college required to have an M.A. or its equivalent from one of the other faculties. But there was a warm camaraderie in the college - first, second and third years. We lunched together every day, played table tennis, and indulged in whatever pursuits we favoured, provided we attended the lectures and wrote the required essays. There was a bunch of brilliant students in the college at that time - men who became well known as preachers, professors, theologians. Tom Torrance was two years ahead of me and became a world-famous theologian. His sister was at Boroughmuir with Mary. David Read became a renowned preacher in New York. He also was two years older than me and we first met in the Dialectic Society. He early made a name for himself with a pretty stanza which was sung extensively for a term:

> *Baillie, Baillie, give me your answer, do;*
> *Why ain't Plato found in the canon too?*
> *On your own interpretation,*
> *He's as sound as Revelation.*
> *His style is neater than II Peter,*
> *And he wasn't a dirty Jew.*

University 1932 - 1938

David, as a chaplain, was captured as St Valery and spent the rest of the war in a prisoner-of-war camp. Later he spent many years at the principal Presbyterian Church in New York.

There were two brothers Baillie, both professors of Divinity. Donald was at St Andrews, and John, after years in the States, came to New College. They came of a Highland Family. John had a sharp, incisive mind, and at the same time was deeply devotional. Rumour in the College had it that he had a photographic mind, so one evening, when he invited a group of us to supper, we sat on afterwards talking in his study. Someone said we had been given to understand that he had a photographic mind: would he care to confirm or deny that? Oh yes, he could confirm it. He said he read a book every night before going to sleep. Someone mentioned a book. Yes, he had it and had read it. He rose and fetched it from a shelf. The man who mentioned it had also read it, and mentioned an incident in the book. Prof. Baillie thought for a minute, and then named a page. 'You will find it there or thereabouts.' True enough, the passage was on the page named. We were awestruck; how was it done? Prof. Baillie didn't know. It was neither a talent nor a feat of memory. No, as he turned the pages of a book the print seemed to register itself on his mind. It seemed miraculous, but John Baillie was an unassuming man who was greatly respected.

Professor Hugh Watt was much interested in my switching from agriculture to the ministry. He himself came from a farming family in Ayrshire, and occupied the chair of Church History. William Curtis was the only professor not to be in general favour for his extreme long-windedness. Once started there was no stopping him. We spent an evening with him, and after supper he began talking. What he was saying was quite interesting, but no one else could get a word in, and the evening ended with his thanking us for our conversation!

In my last year, Norman Porteous came as Professor of Hebrew. I wasn't taking Hebrew so I didn't see much of him. He was a small man in his thirties, and so just a few years our senior, and a clubbable spirit. I got to know him better in future years when he often joined us at our year's annual reunion. He was known to all of us as 'Mickey Mouse'. I last saw him when he was not far short of a hundred years old, and I can only assume he has died.[1]

A very different type was G.D.Thomson, who arrived in my last year. He was a tall man with a monocle, very definite views on everything, and prepared to argue and swear vociferously if he met the least opposition. I wrote an essay on Communism for him, in which I tried to imitate his own style, anticipating thereby a good mark. He gave me 5%, commenting that I seemed to have an irrational tendency to criticise and argue over everything!

---

[1] Norman Porteous - 9th September, 1898 to 3rd September, 2003

Everything Mixed with Mercy

In our last term a number of the men took supply. The fees were very acceptable as we were all very hard-up. I didn't look for supply, as I hadn't preached a sermon in my life, and felt it would be time enough to begin after I had been licensed to preach. However, Bob Fraser, a friend, got hold of me in mid-week, told me he had inadvertently accepted supply engagements for two different churches on the same Sunday - next Sunday in fact. Would I take one of these engagements? 'No!' said I, 'A thousand times no.' I had never preached a sermon, or conducted a whole service, and I'd need a lot more than three days to prepare. But Bob Fraser was insistent. Everyone who did supply was already engaged for next Sunday. I must take it. So I agreed, and on the following Sunday I arrived at Liberton Northfield. In the vestry before the service the beadle produced a gown. I told him I didn't want it; it was too big for me in any case. But he was insistent; a preacher must have a gown, and mounting the pulpit steps I tripped over the gown and measured my length in the pulpit. It was not the most auspicious start to my career but the service passed off without any more trouble.

The summer term of 1938 was my last term at New College. The final exam for the B.D. was looming, and I was specializing in Church History. About a week before the exam I was walking up Bank Street carrying a bag with my notes, for I had been working in the New College Library. I had a fit on the pavement and passed out completely. When I came to I was walking along George IV Bridge, and it was some time before I realised I did not have any notes. This was a devastating blow, as there was a great deal of work needed for the days leading to the exam. I could not get notes from anybody else as everyone was now swotting hard, and in any case I was the only one doing Church History. I had to withdraw from the exam and regretted it for a long time thereafter.

After New College we would all be probationers, looking for a paid assistantship, or a call to a charge. As a student I had been assisting Riddock Fisher at Lady Glenorchy's North - the church next to the Playhouse cinema. There was no pay attached to that, but I acquired much experience. Typical of city churches then, there was a mission attached to the congregation, and I had charge of a Sunday School in Greenside, behind the church. This was a very old part of the city. Tenements down in Greenside were fourteen stories high, and the youngsters were akin to those I had known in Dumbiedykes.

The senior minister at Lady Glenorchy's was Dr. Harvey, who had in fact retired, but paid the church a visit now and then for special occasions. One Sunday he appeared at the mission Sunday School with Dr. Robert Laws - Laws of Livingstonia, as he was universally known. He must have been in his eighties then, but was handsome, upright and interested to see the children.

University 1932 - 1938

Riddock Fisher and I got on well together. He was an enthusiastic supporter of the Oxford Group, which was very active in Edinburgh at that time. I had my doubts about their effectiveness. They claimed to be a missionary society, pursuing a different line from the usual missionary bodies. The Group concentrated on the middle classes, with Group meetings in good hotels. Here they confessed their sins to each other - rather than to God, I thought. They seemed to be ignored and forgotten with the outbreak of war.

Mary had gone to London to work at the Charities Commission, so we had to carry on writing letters. Since being thrown in at the deep end at Liberton Northfield, I had been doing quite a bit of preaching at Lady Glenorchy's, and taking whatever supply was offered me. Willie Graham was the Church's supply agent, and he was a member of Moray-Knox Church, so he knew me and my situation. He asked if, when I had finished at New College, I'd be interested in a vacancy at Watten in Caithness for the summer, and I gratefully accepted this.

It was only then that George MacLeod appeared at New College asking for volunteers to go with him to Iona to restore the Abbey and there practise a new type of evangelism. George was a charismatic character. He was a born orator and leader; he had a marvellous way with words, and was very much 'with it'. It was most unfortunate that we were all already settled with work for the immediate future. Not many would have gone with George, but a few would probably have gone to Iona. The difficulty many of us had with George MacLeod was that while we readily acknowledged his inspiring character and leadership, we could never find any coherent theology on which to base his ideas. He himself never made any claim to be a theologian, but maintained that theology was not all that important.

People, as it were, 'caught' Christianity from Christians. They were not to be saved by adopting any particular brand of theology. Older men might have been more relaxed over this, but students fresh from the Halls of Learning were not so comfortable with ideas which did not hitch onto what we had been absorbing in the past three years. This was exemplified year after year at the General Assembly, when George would electrify us with his Passionate Pacifism - a very topical subject at that time. He would sit down to thunderous applause, but only a handful of men voted for him. The Church had yet to discover what a genius George was in directing prayer and devotion, and what an original driving force he was in creating patterns of worship. The aftermath of the Second World War brought a change in opinion and a surge of support for George MacLeod by a new generation of ministers and elders.

5
ON PROBATION 1938 - 1939

The situation at Watten was that this small village had two churches - the Parish Kirk and the United Free Church. This latter had from the Disruption in 1843 been the Free Kirk, which since 1900 had been the United Free Church and since 1929 was the Church of Scotland, with as its parish part of the original parish. Since the Union of the Churches in 1929 this was the situation in villages all over Scotland. In these small communities there had never been any need for more than one church, but the Disruption had seen more than a third of parish ministers leaving the Auld Kirk. They called their new denomination the Free Kirk, and erected churches in all parishes where they could get ground. Before long there were more people belonging to the Free Kirk than were left in the parish kirk, and a popular jingle pointed up this fact:

The wee kirk, the Free Kirk,
The kirk without a steeple.
The Auld Kirk, the cauld kirk
The kirk without the people.

Indeed in many villages there were three kirks; for in 1847 branches of the Secession Kirk of the 18th century joined together to form the United Presbyterian Church (the U.P. Kirk). The Free and the U.P.Kirks joined together in 1900 to form the United Free Church (U.F. Kirk). In 1929 at the Union of the Churches the U.F. Church joined the Parish Church to form the Church of Scotland. In Watten the minister of the former U.F. Church had died, and the parish minister was due to retire in the autumn. As a consequence there was a drive by the Church authorities to have the two kirks united to form one parish church for the village. Local circumstances varied greatly over the country. In some places congregations would not hear of union; they were doing quite well on their own, thank you, and no power on earth would move them. Elsewhere, as in Watten, the people all got on well together, the congregations were intermarried, and the union would probably go ahead with no trouble. The former U.F. Kirk was just looking for a minister to tide them over the summer months until the union could take place. That is what brought me, a callow student, now a probationer, to fill this temporary post.

I lodged with a young farmer and his wife, members of the congregation, and I was blithe to be living on a farm again. I had a room to myself and no arduous duties. I took the service on Sundays, spent time reading and writing, and attended to any sick. One morning the farm wife said,

On Probation 1938 - 1939

'Would you like an egg to your breakfast?' I said, 'Thank you', and I was duly presented next morning with a boiled egg. It was a monster, a goose egg. I ought to have remembered they had a flock of geese. When I first arrived I found the farmhouse enclosed within a sizeable fenced lawn, and when I opened the gate the flock of geese flew at me, hissing like to burst. There is a surprising amount of food in a goose egg, but I managed it, just, for it followed a substantial plate of porridge. Next morning saw another goose egg on my plate - not in an egg cup, for egg cups are not made for that size of egg. Oddly enough, many years later, in Virginia, our hostess had never heard of an egg cup. Boiled eggs there were just shelled and then spooned from a bowl or saucer. I coped with the second egg, but on the third day I had to ask for a respite. The geese were laying, but there was no ready market for the eggs. The birds were bred for sale at the back-end, when the festival loomed.

I visited another farm - a much bigger place, and in the large, stone-floored kitchen a peat fire was burning. Under the fire there was a large cavity, into which the ash dropped. That fire, I was assured, was never allowed to go out. It had been burning since the seventeenth century. The ash-pit was cleared once a year, on Hogmanay, and the embers were carefully kept to start the New Year's fire. I found it an impressive sight, but while I believed the fire had never gone out I doubted that the present fireplace was three hundred years old. In the seventeenth century the house would be a much more modest building, and the fire was probably in the middle of the floor.

I had been told there were about sixty members in the congregation, but on Sunday mornings there were usually about 150 people present. I knew that in the Highlands, and particularly in the Free Kirk there was a strong reluctance to become a committed member of the Church because of the warning in the Book of Hebrews, that once having confessed the Christian Faith one could not deliberately sin again without accepting the dire consequences (Heb..x.26ff)

Now the beadle was a man in his seventies, fit, and surprisingly athletic for his age. And he was a committed member of the Church. I asked him when he had joined, and he put it at some years ago. 'And why was it only in your late sixties that you finally decided to become a communicant member of the Church?' I asked. He explained that all his working life he had been a roadman, and those were days before any tarmacadam was used on the side roads. The roadman sat by the roadside beside a large pile of road metal and a six-pound hammer. He broke the stones down into much smaller pieces, which could be scattered over the road surface, and passing traffic gradually embedded the stones. In the course of years of this kind of work roadmen often developed cataracts from the stone dust flying around in the wind. In time, therefore, the beadle gradually became blind, and his doctor said that nothing could be done about it unless he were prepared to journey to Edinburgh, where there was a very clever surgeon who might be able to help. So he made the journey, and had the operation, which was entirely successful, and returned to Watten with his sight restored.

Rather woodenly I commented, 'So that was why you joined the Kirk?' He looked at me pityingly. 'God gave me back my sight, didn't He? The least I could do in return was join the Kirk!'

There was no musical instrument in the church, which had been quite normal in the Free Church, so we had a precentor - a young fellow from Wick, nine miles away. He cycled out on Sunday morning, unless he didn't feel like it, or something else came in the way. There were no telephones to warn us what to expect, and he would usually arrive just a few minutes before the service was due to begin. When from time to time he failed to appear, I had to do everything - pray, read the lessons, preach and precent. This sounds a simple, straightforward programme to cope with, but as there was no let-up in the course of an hour, it could be quite tiring. On Sunday morning, then, the session clerk, the beadle and myself all stood outside the church peering along the road for the cyclist's appearance on the horizon. As the land was quite flat we had at least ten minutes' warning of his arrival or probable non-appearance.

After some weeks I noticed in a corner of the vestry a bulky object under a sheet. Curious, I lifted the sheet, and there was a harmonium! I asked the Session Clerk about it. 'Ay,' said he, ' but it's nae uise. It's perished.' And true enough, the leather bellows had succumbed to the damp. But that was not beyond repair. I pursued my enquiries, and at length the Session Clerk explained. The laird's wife, who of course belonged to the Parish Kirk, had heard that the U.F. Kirk had no musical instrument; so as a gesture of goodwill between the denominations, she presented the U.F Kirk with the harmonium. On their part, the office bearers of the U.F. Kirk, responding to the laird's wife's generosity, produced their own goodwill gesture by warmly accepting the gift and thanking the laird's lady. But they had never used instrumental music in their kirk, and had no intention of starting now. So the bellows of the harmonium ended the matter by becoming perished and useless.

A further lesson in proper behaviour came to me unexpectedly when a farmer at my digs said to me one day, 'Would you like to see a football match?' I said I'd very much appreciate the chance to see a match. He said there was to be a game between Watten and another village on the coming Saturday, and he showed me where to stand to get the best view. The game would be played on a level field, but there were no crowd facilities. Spectators just stood where they thought they'd get a good view. I assured him that would be all right with me. On the Friday however, the day before the match, he said 'Will you be a candidate for the vacancy?' I assured him that I was not in the running. 'That's all right then,' he said. 'I just thought that if you were a candidate I'd better tell you that if you go to the match nobody will vote for you.'

This pinpointed the striking difference in attitude to the ministry and sport between Watten and Edinburgh. In the capital city the Very Reverend Dr. James Black, minister of St George's West was a Hearts fan. He was a famous preacher, and a consummate actor, who filled his church to overflowing, morning and evening. Tynecastle lay within his parish, and on many a Saturday afternoon Dr. Black would appear at Tynecastle clad in frock coat, striped trousers and a silk hat, having come straight from a funeral, and his appearance would be greeted with applause from the crowd as he made his way to his seat in the stand. And in those days a band would appear at half time, playing popular tunes, including 'Abide with Me' if Dr. Black was present!

My time at Watten, however, was cut short by a bad fit. Alan Robson, then minister at Wick Central, and interim moderator in the vacancy at Watten, insisted on putting me up for a week, after which I returned home, deeply grateful for his kindness.

Looking back now, I am astonished that nobody ever queried to me the wisdom of trying to fill the role of a parish minister so long as I was so disabled with epilepsy. No doubt many people had their own thoughts on this, but no one felt it their place to try to stop me. Certainly the staff and students at New College must have known; and when I did have a fit in public there generally was alarm and a feeling of helplessness, for the public then was quite ignorant of how to treat this trouble.

Back home I was now taking supply when anything offered, and also looking for a parish. In the autumn and winter, the holiday season being past, there was a falling away in applications for supply, but I did get calls to fill in for men on sick leave. Over the months I spent some interesting weekends, and met a variety of interesting people and churches. Mary was working with the Charities Commission in London, and she applied for a transfer nearer home. She was transferred to the War Office at Irvine in Ayrshire. This rather grandiloquent title referred to a corrugated iron building where the work was quite congenial, and she had digs in the town. She was able to get to Edinburgh at the weekends by rising at five o'clock on Saturday mornings, dressing quickly and running about a mile to the railway station to catch the early train. Changing at Glasgow Queen Street she got to Edinburgh by mid-forenoon, and the rest of the weekend was ours, provided I was not taking supply.

Preaching at a newly-built church at Newtongrange, I was annoyed by someone persistently interrupting me from the body of the kirk, whom I could not place. It was quite some time before I realised the interruption was in fact an echo - the loudest and clearest echo I had ever heard. I complained about this after the service, and when I returned to that church years later I found a curtain had been drawn across the rear of the nave, which satisfactorily killed the echo.

Taking a service at Lauder Old Church, I discovered that the pulpit directly faced a pillar at the centre of the church, the interior of which took the form of a saltire. The beadle warned me not to look at the congregation, but to speak to the pillar. In this way the sound of my voice would be divided and would reach all the congregation. Otherwise, if I looked at the people I'd only see a quarter of them, and they would be the only ones to hear me. Architects, especially church architects, would appear to have some peculiar ideas.

I did what I was told, with fair success; but it was rather a weird exercise preaching and praying to the pillar. Added to the challenge of the architecture, the minister there was notorious as a miser, and a bad payer when it came to supply fees. Willie Graham, the supply agent, warned me beforehand that I might have difficulty getting paid. Normally the congregational treasurer would hand me a cheque in the minister's absence, but there was no cheque awaiting me, and as this was usual at Lauder it was difficult getting anyone to accept an engagement to supply there. But I needed the money and agreed to supply. I left without payment, but Willie Graham took the business in hand and I was eventually paid several weeks later.

In the spring of 1939 the Rev D.P. Thomson, the Church of Scotland's evangelist, was pursuing a scheme to involve young folk in the Church through working together, and to that extent adopting some of George MacLeod's ideas. He had taken over the ruined village of Lassodie in Fife, and I joined him there for a week, but didn't make much of it. When he heard that I had been an agricultural student I got a warm welcome and found myself labouring with barrowloads of material being shifted from one place to another, while I had no clear idea of what the overall scheme was. I gave up after that week. D. P. Thomson was an enthusiast, but his enthusiasms tended to move from one subject to another, unlike George MacLeod, whose enthusiasm was directed to the one end of restoring Iona Abbey, towards which everything was organised to the last detail, and all that held him up from time to time was lack of money.

As long as I continued living at home I had no financial worries. What

On Probation 1938 - 1939

I earned from supply was enough to cope with incidentals, and the intention was to marry as soon as I had a charge. With this in view I had in the years since we had become engaged been learning about household furniture. In those days household sales were much more common that they are now, and Mother had long been interested in attending these when she could. Many a time there would be nothing of interest to see, but often enough items of interest came under the hammer, and occasionally she would bring home what she thought a bargain. I didn't often attend these sales. I wanted to learn the good and the bad. I wanted to be able to recognise the classical furniture designs and hopefully after a while acquire some of these items for the future manse. Both Dowell and Lyon & Turnbull had regular monthly sales. The fine, genuine, classical pieces were usually to be found at Dowell's, and the more run-of-the-mill household articles were at Lyon & Turnbull, who also operated a 'lane sale' in a lane behind their George Street premises, where what was somebody's junk would sometimes throw up a real bargain for someone else's use.

I did acquire some knowledge in time, and I did acquire some furniture. We still have a Chippendale mahogany corner chair with claw-and-ball feet; a pediment barometer; a wag-at-the-wa' clock. There was nothing like the interest in antiques that there is now, and I picked up pieces, admittedly flawed, very cheaply. I attended the sale of Lord Balfour's furniture at Whittinghame House, and there got a large library table, which proved immensely useful over the years. This moved with us wherever we went until we came to St Andrews where there was no room for it. Fortunately Morag introduced me to Paul Harris, publisher and journalist, who had recently moved into a flat at Whittinghame after the huge house had been converted into flats, and I swapped the library table with him for a Victorian knee-hole desk which suited my new requirements. In those last days before marriage I also became possessed of two Hepplewhite semi-circular satinwood tables, and also a Hepplewhite Elmwood dining-room suite. I got this cheaply as an elbow chair was missing. The suite consisted of four hand-chairs and two carving or elbow chairs. Dad had done business with a firm at Gorgie which specialised in repairing and reproducing antique furniture, so I took the elbow chair to them and asked them to make a copy of it to complete the suite. They took on the job, but the war broke out, and after the war, when I called to collect my chairs the firm had disappeared and no one could help me.

The same kind of artistic interest kept me attending art exhibitions, but I couldn't think of buying pictures, which would hardly be essential when we'd have a house to furnish. But I did buy three Swarbrecks - coloured lithographs of Edinburgh in the 1830s. They cost me two

Everything Mixed with Mercy

guineas - 14s each. This was far more of a bargain than I realised. Many years later John Walter, a director of J.G. Thomson, the wine merchants at the Vaults in Leith, proudly showed me a dozen Swarbrecks he had bought in London for his boardroom. They had cost fifty pounds each. This kind of thing can really happen. A man I knew as a fellow member of the Bible Society Board, ran a laundry in Glasgow, and he had a notable collection of the Scottish Colourists. I once said to him that the laundry must have been paying well over the years. 'Not at all,' he replied. 'The laundry didn't pay for them. I bought them on their first appearance between the wars. They cost on average £20 each. I just bought them because I like them.' And of course he had no intention of selling them. When his family grew up he moved to a smaller house, and many of the pictures are distributed within the family, where presumably they will stay, barring accidents. Mary and I also visited an art exhibition in Dumfries, where she fell in love with a flower piece which lightens a wall in our parlour today - years of appreciation without any money involved.

Through the goodwill of Willie Graham I was getting fairly regular supply engagements, and at two guineas a time I had a modest income, and as the minimum stipend was then £300 a year, or six pounds a week, and with no wife or family to support, and living at home, I was not badly off; and supply could sometimes be interesting for reasons other than ecclesiastical. In Dumfriesshire on supply, I stayed overnight on the Saturday at a farm where they made cheese in a big way. This was farming as I had not seen it before. A large dairy had cheeses stacked along several shelves, maturing, and the two sons of the house, a year or two younger than me, ate cheese by the hunk - cheese on its own with neither bread nor oatcake.

For some reason that escapes me now I supplied a pulpit at Brodick in Arran. Saturday was a beautiful, cloudless summer day, but waiting for the ferry to start from Ardrossan I could see Arran shrouded in mist - and it was more than mist; we sailed into heavy rain, which persisted all day and continued on Sunday forenoon. The afternoon ferry on Sunday left wet, wet Arran and we sailed into unbroken sunshine. A man in Ardrossan with a twinkle in his eye asked what the weather had been like over there. My answer might have been unprintable, but he said it was not always like that. In further conversation I found him to be a Gaelic speaker, so I told him my grandmother had had the Gaelic. 'And where did she belong?' 'Easter Ross', said I. 'I'd probably not understand a word she said.' It was news to me that even within the Gaelic speaking community there are dialects.

In August I received an invitation to preach as sole nominee for the vacant parish of Twechar. I had never even heard of the place before,

On Probation 1938 - 1939

and I had not preached before any vacancy committee. How was it I was chosen as sole nominee? Me? New College knew I was epileptic. No one ever said anything out loud, and we did not know any other epileptics, so we could not benefit from their experiences, but in time I came to realise that Twechar was a difficult parish, especially for a beginner. I guess the interim moderator, a minister in Kirkintilloch whom I came to know rather well, told the Twechar office-bearers that they could either take me or resign themselves to a very long vacancy. Twechar was a mining village twelve miles north of Glasgow, between Kirkintilloch and Kilsyth. Locally it was known as "The Twechar", as it had come into existence in the mid-nineteenth century to provide homes for the miners of the Twechar pit. It stood at the western edge of the Scottish coalfield and to the passer-by it hardly looked like a mining village. In fact there were six pits in the area, but all winding gear and pit bings were scarcely visible as the whole district was heavily wooded.

Having been elected, Mary and I went to visit the place and see the church and manse. We travelled by train to Glasgow and thence from Buchanan Street Bus Station. In Queen Street station I had a fit on the platform, attracting a big crowd of course, and Mary had the greatest difficulty persuading a young zealous policeman to stop trying to undo my collar, whereby he was half choking me, and just keep the crowd back. We proceeded by bus, and I had another fit on the main street in Twechar. I thought my election would be rescinded, but it wasn't . Everyone knew what had happened, for nothing of any interest or importance could happen in Twechar without everyone knowing about it in next to no time. But nobody turned a hair, and in all our years in Twechar no one ever mentioned or hinted at my epilepsy, either to Mary or me.

The village today is completely changed from what it was in our time. It is now a Glasgow commuter village consisting almost entirely of council houses, and coal mining is a thing of the past. Before the war a beginning had been made with council houses, but four of the miners' rows were still occupied, a wash-house to every eight houses, and dry outside closets in the same proportion. All of the rows were the property of the mine owners, Baird's & Scottish Steel. There were no pithead baths and the men worked in appalling conditions, sometimes in water chest-high, sometimes working coal seams anything down to fourteen inches. And from time to time there were accidents causing injury and death. Living under these conditions the minister's epilepsy was nothing much to worry about. A third of the population were Roman Catholics, but there was no distinction down the pit or in the compulsory intimacy of life in the rows.

In the meantime the plans for our wedding went ahead, and the ceremony was fixed for Thursday 7th September. Riddock Fisher would conduct the service in Trinity College & Moray Knox Church in Jeffrey Street. This building had been erected when the railway reached the base of the Calton Hill in the mid-nineteenth century. Here the original Trinity College had stood, and the apse of that church was taken down stone by stone and re-erected in Jeffrey Street as part of a new church building.

After I was licensed Willie Morrell, the minister, invited me to take a service at Trinity College & Moray Knox, and in the pulpit I found the book board just a few inches above my knees - too far down for me to read any notes. As I had never before been in that pulpit this was rather disconcerting. I was told afterwards that James Law, senior minister at the time of the union, was a small man, and he had had the floor of the pulpit raised to suit him. Willie Morrell, his successor, was also small, and so did nothing to alter things, but I felt like I did in the 'gods' of the Usher Hall before the seating was altered: the steep rake of the top gallery made the audience feel like toppling. I later discovered this was not an unusual arrangement for small ministers.

I have but the dimmest recollection of the wedding service, but afterwards we all adjourned to Green's Hotel in Grosvenor Crescent. I say 'we all adjourned', as there were only about a dozen of us having afternoon tea there. This rather flat, low-key celebration had been forced on us by the war. War had been declared on the previous Sunday, 3rd September. I was conducting a service that day at Lauriston, near Falkirk, and when the service finished we were at war. At that point no one had any idea of what to expect, so we received apologies from all our intended wedding guests who lived outside Edinburgh.

Still we were married, which was all that really mattered. Again owing to the war I had made no detailed plans for a honeymoon. My ordination and induction at Twechar was to take place in a fortnight, so we had decided to travel on our wedding day to Perth, and then decide from day to day whether to stay where we were, or travel from place to place, as circumstance would allow. Our taxi took us to the Waverley Station, where we had about twenty minutes to wait for the train. The train was already at the platform, when suddenly I realised we were short of one of our luggage bags. I got Mary on to the train with the luggage we had, and sprinted for another taxi to take me back to Green's Hotel, where I picked up the missing bag and arrived back at the Waverley just as the train was pulling out. That was rather nerve-racking for Mary, but that was only the first of a series of jolting experiences.

We spent the night at the Salutation Hotel in Perth, and next morning

On Probation 1938 - 1939

I received a telegram from Twechar saying that the ordination had been postponed until the end of October. No explanation - there was no room on a telegram for an explanation. I never discovered who had made this decision, but I cannot imagine any miner panicking. I jalouse[1] the interim moderator was to blame. Some people became very jittery at that time, not knowing what to expect with a war on. Anyhow that telegram was a shocking blow to us. I only had enough money to last a fortnight and expected to live on my stipend thereafter. Now we had to live for six weeks without any income.

The first obvious move was to return to Edinburgh, and this we did with some hope, for Mary remembered that her sister Bessie, who was living at Granton, was being evacuated with her two children, Margaret and Francis - both toddlers. So we made for Granton and were warmly welcomed, for Bessie was very glad to have us occupy her house in her absence. Off they went then, but a few days later they reappeared. Bessie had found the conditions where they were evacuated quite intolerable. Benjy Miller, Bessie's husband, was in the regular Army, and the Granton house was very small. There was no room for us in addition to Bessie and the two kids. So once more we were on the street, with our luggage, and this time we had no idea where to go. But as we walked along with our bags I suddenly remembered Auntie Johan had recently been knocked down by a taxi, and was in bed with a broken leg. She lived in Wellington Street, a quarter of an hour's walk from Montrose Terrace - a flat I was familiar with. We rang Auntie Jean's bell, and were welcomed with open arms. She was delighted to have us live in her house while she went to live with Johan. That was our immediate problem solved. This kind of situation, this completely unexpected silver lining, which had kept recurring throughout my life, hammered home my mother's dictum that everything comes mixed with mercy.

Of course we were not yet out of the wood. We would need money for the next six weeks. Anyone knowing us, and our circumstance, would scarcely be worried. My people would see to it that we would not be reduced to sleeping in an entry with a newspaper to cover us. But we would only get help if we asked for it, and I could not face the humiliation of applying to the family for help. Yet the knowledge that the family was there made a world of difference between us and the homeless.

I went to see Willie Graham and told him our story. He promised me weekly supply as long as it was available. One particular weekend from that period I always remember - and bear in mind this was over sixty years ago. I had to take the morning service at Markinch, a place I had never visited before. I was booked to stay overnight on the Saturday at

---
[1] jalouse - guess/assume

the Station Hotel. The blackout was in force, and I got off the train in almost complete darkness. Making my way to the building pointed out to me as the hotel. I knocked at the door. It was opened, and dazzled by the light I found myself standing in the bar in full clerical garb. The bar was crowded and noisy, but on my appearance there was sudden, complete silence. It was then quite unheard of for a minister to be seen in a pub. The only contact between a public house and religion would be from a Salvation Army officer selling the 'War-Cry'. I went upstairs to my room and the rest of the weekend was uneventful, but my dramatic entry to that bar has remained vividly in my memory ever since.

6
TWECHAR 1939 - 1946

The minimum stipend was £300 per annum, and Twechar was offering £305. We moved in on 29th October for my ordination and induction, and on 11th November - the November term - I was paid for a fortnight's work. I would be paid again six months later, in May 1940. At the end of the year, however, I would receive five pounds. £300 of the stipend came from an endowment, and the congregation contributed the annual five pounds at the year's end. This was news to me - shocking news, as I had not been informed beforehand of this financial arrangement. Years later I met a minister from the West of Scotland who had experienced the same bizarre arrangement for paying stipend. I was angry. We were left to live for six months on a total of less than twenty pounds. Mary had to have a word with the butcher, explaining our situation, and asking if he could supply us until May, when we would pay what we owed him. He readily agreed, and it was only years later that we discovered that in Twechar no 'tick' was allowed, and the butcher simply provided for us from his own pocket.

The only shop in the village was a branch of Gartsherrie Co-operative Society, which belonged to the Coal Company. The public house, known to everyone as 'The Bully' (presumably 'bully' in the sense of 'first-rate'), also belonged to the Company, as did all the ground on which the village stood. Every miner had a 'store book', in which all that was spent in 'The Bully', or at the Gartsherrie Store was recorded. This arrangement looked very like the operation of the Truck system[1], which had been abolished towards the end of the 19th century under a series of 'Truck Acts'.

The original row had stood along the bank of the Forth and Clyde Canal, and six more rows had been added at the turn of the twentieth century as the need for more housing arose. Now in our time there were about 3000 people in the village, a third of whom were Roman Catholics. It was rather odd to find a parish church there at all, especially as the church had been built a little over thirty years ago - built within the bounds of Kirkintilloch Old Parish. There was no R.C. priest in the village, no R.C. chapel. Their interests were looked after by a visiting priest from Croy, a Roman Catholic village not so far away. There was also a branch of the Church of the Nazarene, small in number and without any pastor at the time of our arrival.

The laird was William Whitelaw (the late Lord Whitelaw) who lived at Gartshore House. Twechar lay within the grounds of Gartshore estate. At the beginning of the twentieth century William Whitelaw,

---

[1] The practice of paying workers in goods instead of money

grandfather of our William Whitelaw, was a major shareholder in William Baird & Co, the predecessor of Baird's & Scottish Steel. In 1903 Mr. Whitelaw fell out with the minister of the parish kirk in Kirkintilloch, and swore he would never enter that kirk again. He then built the church at Twechar and endowed it. So not only did Baird's & Scottish Steel own the pits, the miners' row, the local shop and the pub; the Coal Company, in the person of William Whitelaw owned the ground on which the village was built. The lives of the Twechar folk were completely bound up and dominated by the Coal Company.

The Whitelaw who built the church was fond of music, and especially the organ. He installed a large pipe organ in Gartshore House, and a replica of it was set up in the church. It was driven by waterpower, but in summer drought there was not enough pressure to work the organ and power had to be supplied by someone using a hand pump. The manse adjoined the church; indeed the two buildings shared the same roof, and these were surrounded by a large garden. The front garden was well stocked with roses and azaleas - all from the laird's garden at Gartshore, and these all flourished in the very heavy soil which suited them.

Coal was no problem. The miners got coal free, and we at the manse got it at 1s3d a bag; but this was delivered in bulk. A cart-load was emptied on the pavement for the use of church and manse. It was super quality, and the beadle and I shovelled it in to the cellar behind the church by the barrow-load. Dr Thin's horror of the ministry for me as a sedentary occupation did not envisage work in a large garden with very heavy soil.

Another unexpected bonus was that the manse was furnished. This was common in the Methodist Church, where the ministers moved in circuit every three years; but I had never heard of it in the Church of Scotland. Would that have been old William Whitelaw's idea too, so that even the manse furniture would also belong to the Coal Company? It suited us very well. We used what furniture we had, and moved what we didn't need into a spare room.

We saw little of the laird as he was in the Army, and only appeared from time to time on leave from the Middle East. If this break happened in autumn he dropped a brace of pheasants at our door. Annually, too, John Graham, the farmer at Easter Board, who was an elder, left us a sack of potatoes. Added to what we grew in the garden, this saw us through the year. The church and manse being so close together took some getting used to. From the vestry door a door led directly into the manse study. People living in the rows had no sense of privacy. Some council houses had been built, which enabled two of the rows to be cleared away, and the original Twechar row along the canal

Twechar 1939 - 1946

bank had gone some time ago. Families moving to the new houses did acquire some appreciation of the benefits of a kitchen, living-room and bedrooms. There were four rows still fully occupied - all but-and-bens where piped water had been introduced only recently. Outside sheds for coal storage and washing boynes[1] were shared.

After the ordination and induction we spent two exhausting days moving furniture and fixing things generally. We lay rather late, and at eight in the morning the church bell began to toll, and I sprang up as Albert Unwin the beadle walked into the bedroom and apologised for having forgotten to warn us that the early bell on Sunday morning was simply a warning to rise. The church service was at eleven o'clock. He was not in the least embarrassed, but just annoyed with himself for having forgotten to warn us of the early bell.

The senior elder was John Leishman, in his seventies, and still working. I had occasion to visit him in the rows, and knowing he was on the day shift I called on him in the afternoon when I judged he'd be free. In fact he had been late home from work, and when I knocked on the door he shouted to come in. When I did, there he was stark naked in a zinc bath, cleaning up. I was taken aback and embarrassed, but not he. He told me to sit down while he got himself dried and dressed. John had had twelve children who were all up and away, so he and his wife were on their own again. His mother, Grannie Leishman, was almost a hundred years old, and lived on her own in the rows a few doors away. She still rose every morning at five o'clock, as she had always done. She also had brought up twelve children, and by nine a.m. she had finished her housework and settled down to her correspondence, for she regularly kept in touch with her innumerable descendants and kept them in touch with each other in Scotland, England, Ireland, Canada, the States, South Africa, New Zealand and elsewhere. She held the family together, and after she died no one else had the time to maintain this service, and the family, especially those living abroad, drifted apart.

When we arrived in Twechar the men had for so long only been working three shifts a week at 8s6d per shift, so they had 25s6d a week. On the dole they would be paid 24s a week after the means test. So for their week's work, curtailed as it was, they were 1s6d better off than being unemployed and on the dole. And on strike they received no financial support until they had spent all their savings. Consequently they taught their children to save nothing. Another consequence of their poverty was that in practice they held everything in common, as the New Testament tells us the early Christians did. They lived in and out of each other's houses, and took it for granted that everything was shared. The onset of the war, of course, brought them all back to full

---

[1] boyne - a shallow wash-tub

employment, and in a protected occupation.

The irony of their situation was not lost on the miners - especially the young ones. One man told me bitterly that if he went to Glasgow to a dance hall, as soon as it was discovered that he was a miner he couldn't get a partner. The mining community was separate from the rest of the world, and was welcome to stay that way. But in wartime they were local heroes. We had a good choir in the church with half a dozen young men. One Sunday they all disappeared. Albert Unwin, the beadle, also sang in the choir. I asked him for the missing choir members. 'Oh', said he, 'they've aa jined up!' 'But mining is a protected job', said I in my innocence. 'Aye well, we'll wait and see.' The Coal Company did their best to get these very fit young recruits back, but the Army did not let them go.

I spoke to several of them on leave. Basically they all had the same thing to say. This was the first chance they had ever had of breaking away from mining, and they had no intention of ever returning. In the forces they were able to learn other trades, different skills, like driving lorries.

An odd coincidence occurred to me one Sunday, when I read the banns of marriage for a local lass. After the service a soldier on leave and in uniform came into the vestry and told me that the man mentioned in the banns was already married. He had a wife in Liverpool. I asked how he knew, and he said they were in the same unit, and it was sheer coincidence that he happened to be in church that Sunday at the end of his leave. I left this with the police.

The winter of 1939-40 was very severe. At New Year we went through to Eastwood to spend four days with my parents. When we got back to Twechar the first thing we did was light a fire in the kitchen, for all the cooking was done on the kitchen range. The coal was just beginning to throw out some heat when there was a thunderous explosion, and the kitchen was reduced to a shambles. When the plumber saw it, he congratulated us. A frozen pipe had burst at a joint; had it given way where it passed through the outer wall, the whole gable end of the house would probably have blown up. Even so, we had a major problem. The whole house was frozen. All the bottles in the dining-room sideboard had burst, and the mess was considerable. For the next six weeks the cooking had to be done on the small coal fire in the study, which became the living room, and we lived there and in the bedroom. But we survived in good health.

I think that my epilepsy, almost certainly quite well known, may in Twechar have been an advantage rather than otherwise. It was a disablement, and the villagers knew all about coping with disability.

Twechar 1939 - 1946

One day I had a fit while sitting in front of an electric fire in the study. When I came to, my right foot and ankle were badly burnt, and I was laid up for several weeks. Getting supply during the war was very difficult, but the Kirk Session was not unduly worried. Every Sunday Albert Unwin pushed me through to the church from the study in a wheel-chair just before the service, and left me behind the communion table, and I conducted the service from there. The congregation skailed as usual and Albert pushed me back to the study again. After a few weeks it all felt perfectly normal and nobody was bothered.

Another example of the imperturbability in the face of the unexpected happened one Communion Sunday. When the elements were being taken round the congregation, a lady sitting alone and rather apart was not noticed by the elder distributing the bread. The elder with the wine followed in turn and he saw the lady who had been missed. What did he do? He stopped, put his fingers between his teeth and emitted a piercing whistle, at the same time waving to the man with the bread. I cringed but no one else seemed to notice either then or afterwards. After all, the whistle was much quicker getting the required result than going the length of the aisle to recall the man with the bread.

Incidentally, at Twechar the common cup was used but instead of drinking from it each communicant had a silver ladle from which to take a sip - a present, I understood, from the laird, and much more seemly and dignified than individual cups - a practice that has always upset me.

We were unable to black out the church with its high windows, so we abandoned the evening service when the days shortened. Now there was another denomination functioning in Twechar - a branch of the Church of the Nazarene, originating in America and striving to get a foothold in Scotland. They came to Twechar at the invitation of Watty Neil. Watty was a fervent evangelist who had a large family of relatives and in-laws, over whom he was definitely the boss. He belonged to the Salvation Army, and he and his relatives formed the great majority of the Twechar branch of the 'Sally Army'. But Watty fell out with the Army over some matter, and left, along with all his following. The Salvation Army then faded from Twechar, but Watty seems to have owned the brick-built hall they used for meetings and services. They had no pastor, but before long they acquired one. This was Alex Pitt, who had been a Salvation Army officer in Wick, but he also had quit the Army, alleging that in Wick the books were 'cooked'. Somehow or other Watty Neil and Alex Pitt met, and the Church of the Nazarene became an established fact in Twechar.

In time I got to know Alex Pitt very well. He had married Miriam, a lassie from Durham, also in the 'Sally Army', and they had no children.

Alex was a very different character from Watty, who was a domineering man, determined to get his own way in everything. Alex was quiet and perhaps rather naïve; but he saw through the Neils and quietly pursued his own ideas for the Church of the Nazarene. In order to keep the evening service alive Alex and I agreed to hold joint evening services in winter in the Nazarene hall, which had no blackout problem. The pulpit there was roomy enough for us both, and we arranged that one of us would preach, and the other take the rest of the service, and switch these duties on alternate Sundays. This worked very well for some weeks, until one Sunday evening I rose to start the service when Alex tugged at my coat tail. 'You're preaching tonight', he breathed. 'I preached last week - it's your turn tonight.' We hadn't discussed this beforehand, as the arrangement was so simple. I realised I'd have to give way.

The congregation might have been diverted at the sight of us arguing in the pulpit, but we weren't there to entertain them. While Alex announced the first hymn, led us in prayer and read the lesson, I desperately thought of a text, clothed it with one or two ideas and in due course launched myself on the sermon. One more disturbing factor in the situation was that the front seats were occupied by all the Neil adherents, and as soon as I announced the text, they all, without exception, lay back in their seats and shut their eyes. Once started, the discourse, to my surprise, flowed along. Alex, of course, said it was good, but anything would have been good to him that evening. A truer assessment could be made from the fact that no one else made any remarks. Alex, for all his modesty, had ideas beyond the Salvation Army and the Church of the Nazarene. He applied to be accepted for training as a lay missionary in the Church of Scotland. I backed him, and he was accepted and was eventually sent to Shetland, to the Island of Yell, and we kept up a desultory correspondence.

Wartime conditions brought me some odd experiences. I had agreed to take a mid-week service at the Burns Church in Kilsyth almost three miles from Twechar. It was well on in the autumn and a bus was due to take me there just in time for the service. But the bus didn't appear. I waited a while, thinking it might be late; but if there was a breakdown no substitute would be supplied. This had happened more than once, and the next bus was not due for another three-quarters of an hour - too late for the service. There was no telephone available, and in any case there was no telephone at the church. I decided to run. If the bus did turn up late it would pick me up; if not, it would be better for me to arrive late than never. Jogging was not practised in those days. This was what might have been called a singular exercise. When I arrived at the Burns Church the door was closed but there was a chink of light to be

Twechar 1939 - 1946

seen. I knocked on the door, and it was opened by the beadle. 'I'm sorry to be so late,' I gasped, 'but the bus didn't turn up.' 'That's all right,' said he,' we just carried on, we've nearly finished.' 'How did you manage?' 'Oh there was a chap in the congregation with a sermon in his pocket.' I was left wondering whether this was an extraordinary coincidence, or whether it was quite usual for a man in the congregation to have a sermon in his pocket.

Twechar was sited on the bank of the Forth & Clyde Canal. A bridge over the canal was the only access from the village to the Glasgow road. The nearest railway station was at the chemical works in Queenzieburn a mile and a half away. A train ran to the city in the morning and back again in the evening. Shortly before we arrived a bus service was provided with a bus either way every forty-five minutes, but there was no transport over the parish to the villages of Drumgrew and Waterside and the various farms. There would have been no problem if we had had a car, but I could not even apply for a licence, so I bought a pony - a beautiful hackney, with a trap. Fortunately, as the manse dated from 1903, there was a stone-built stable, and adjacent to the garden was a stretch of permanent pasture, at the far end of which was an abandoned coal bing, bordering the canal.

Heather was a bay mare with a gleaming coat, and she was equally at home being ridden or driven. I rode her all over the parish, and with the trap we could get to Glasgow and back. She took us several times to Eastwood, the house at Fushiebridge, between Gorebridge and Middleton where my parents were now living, for summer holidays. Heather and my mother took to each other at once, and Heather tried to follow her into the house, but couldn't get further than the front porch. At Twechar I had to put her on a long tether to prevent her wandering, and some of the village lads took a fiendish delight in slipping her out of the tether. This happened sometimes on a Sunday afternoon while I was teaching the Bible Class in the study. From the study window we could look onto the field, and when Heather was untied we could see her wandering. That was the end of the Bible Class as the kids all set off to capture Heather. She could easily outrun them and would wait until they were just about an arm's length away, then she retreated as they advanced. We learned to approach her in a wide semi-circle and so get her retreating towards the coal bing, which she would gradually mount until I laid hands on her at the summit. This did not happen every week, but often enough to make the Bible Class popular.

We were grief stricken when Heather developed rheumatism and the vet said it was incurable. Now there was a family of tinkers who spent the winter on a piece of ground, about a mile along the canal towards Kirkintilloch, known as the Triangle. From spring to autumn they

Everything Mixed with Mercy

disappeared, travelling Scotland, but when they were at the Triangle I had a weekly visit from Davie Woods, the father of the family. It was said of them that when a baby was born the first thing they did with it was to dip it in the burn. I never witnessed that, but I knew that Davie Woods was driving his horse, pulling a float on the road from Twechar to Condorrat. His wife was seated on the end of the float, and the horse was trotting smartly when they had to turn a sharp right and his wife was shot off the float and into the ditch. A passer-by shouted to Davie, who turned round and saw his wife. 'Aye aa richt,' he shouted to the passer-by, 'a'll pick her up on ma wey hame.'

Davie visited me every week. He would press me to do a deal with him, and we exchanged all kinds of trumpery articles. He said it was bad luck not to make a bargain, especially with a minister. And a bargain was not complete until sealed by spitting on your palm and clapping hands together. He was a horse copar[1], and knew his business, and had me sized up. I showed him Heather and told him the vet said she was incurable. He denied this, and said he could cure her. I knew he was fly, but he said if I gave him Heather he would provide a replacement. This was what he liked - a bargain in which no money changed hands. He was as good as his word - whatever that might mean. I gave him Heather, and he produced Bobbie - a big, strong garron, full of beans, or oats. What Davie did not tell me was that Bobbie had never been broken in. He had come from a deer forest up north, where he had been used to transport deer carcasses. When I mounted him he threw me off at once. Gradually we came to an understanding, and I could ride him, but it took a long time, since he was unpredictable. Getting him into harness for the trap was another game we played, but once we understood each other he really was an asset. This idyllic period came to and end when, driving the trap on a secondary road skirting a forest, a motor lorry came along a forest ride from the pits, drove into us and smashed the trap. I got rid of Bobbie shortly afterwards as I couldn't afford another trap.

An interesting sidelight on this affair was that about six weeks after I had parted with Heather, with her swollen, painful joints I saw her in Bishopbriggs drawing a fish lorry, apparently in good health again. I reported this to Terry, my brother, a vet in Derby, and he assured me she was not cured. There were ways of ameliorating the rheumatism for a period, but a cure was unheard of.

Some time before that final smash, Mary's father was staying with us, and he was very interested in Bobbie. He had worked with horses a lot during his time with the Royal Artillery in 1914-18. He was saddling Bobbie one day when the horse suddenly shied, throwing him to the ground. He hurt his shoulder, and we called Dr Parker, who said he

---

[1] copar - dealer

thought Mr Tough had fractured his collar-bone, but he got him to the Glasgow infirmary to have an X-ray. When he got the result of the X-ray he was surprised to see no trace of a fracture. Looking more closely at the photograph he saw that the wrong shoulder had been X-rayed, and by that time it was too late to mend the fracture and Mr Tough had to live with it for the rest of his life.

Our animal interests extended over quite a range of livestock. We had a little cat called Dinah who spent every night outdoors, and every morning deposited a dead rat on our back doorstep. But Dinah could not cope with all the rats. The manse garden was adjacent to the school playground, and debris from school meals was thrown into a burn running nearby, so rats were everywhere. We had hens, and it was not unusual for a rat or two to join the poultry at the feeding trough. Mary came home one day to find a rat sitting on the kitchen mantelpiece. It didn't scurry away. It sat looking at her before strolling along the mantelpiece and disappearing into the wooden casing of a hot water pipe. The coal company decided to bring in a professional rat-catcher from Glasgow to deal with the plague of rats in and about the pits. We asked him to pay us a visit and deal with our rats. He came one afternoon and did some destruction among the rats in the school and church ground. He then said he was going home. 'You mean you've got rid of all the rats hereabout?' I asked. 'Nobody will ever do that,' he said, 'but I've had enough. I've killed over 700, and I'm sick of the job. I'm packing in.'

I also had a goat - a Toggenburg. She was a good milker, and as goat milk is free of the tubercle bacillus we were keen to use it for the children. But milking her was a high-risk activity, for she would not stand still. Time and again, with the pail half-full of frothing milk she would suddenly kick the pail over. I finally had to tie her hind legs to a couple of posts to get her properly milked. I tethered her on a brae on the opposite side of the road from our front garden, where I could keep an eye on her. One day Eddie Cairns, a small man, a miner, whose hobby was greyhounds, which he raced at the White City, Glasgow, came down the road with his greyhound on a lead. The dog caught sight of my goat, slipped the lead and made for the goat. I picked up a stone and threw it at the dog, and Eddie Cairns let out a yell. I managed to save the goat from injury, but Eddie was furious with me for attacking his valuable dog. In an equal fury I told him he ought to control his valuable dog, which was a danger to my valuable goat. We parted at that. His wife was a member of the congregation, but I had never seen him in church.

Not long after, I got word one morning before eight o'clock that there was a fire in the Twechar pit. I got down to the pithead at once and found half the village there, and a group of miners standing together.

Everything Mixed with Mercy

Twechar Parish Church, where we learned the priorities.
1939 - 47

It appeared that everyone working in the affected section had got out except one man. They had been waiting for some time but there was still no sign of him. Then Eddie Cairns, one of those who had escaped, announced that he was going to find the missing man, and made for the cage to go down. Everyone tried to stop him attempting the impossible. The real danger was not that of being burnt, but of suffocation. Smoke down there was much thicker than that of any fog above ground. But there was no stopping Eddie; the cage was away with him. Shortly after, the missing man turned up safe and well. He had found his way to another shaft and had reached safety with little trouble. The worry now was what had happened to Eddie Cairns, and a party went down to find him. They reached him not far from the foot of the shaft, (he was lying with his face jammed in the angle between a rail for coal trucks and the ground, where the last pocket of air would be). I saw him at the hospital in Kilsyth, where he was still coughing up soot. We got quite pally after that, but never again mentioned either goat or greyhound.

Twechar 1939 - 1946

In regard to food, what was on offer in Twechar was basic. Gartsherrie Co-operative Society was owned by the coal company, and the main shop was at Coatbridge. What Coatbridge could not sell was passed to Twechar, and we could take it or leave it. Twechar took quite a lot that was rejected by Coatbridge; but we did object to bread smelling of paraffin, the bread and oil presumably having been placed on the same shelf in Coatbridge. We could go to Glasgow, twelve miles away, and having no car we took the bus, and in Glasgow bought as much food as we could carry.

This state of things was eased unexpectedly when it was suddenly discovered that a small patch of ground near the canal was not owned by the Coal Company. There was an immediate rush to buy that ground, and Kilsyth Co-operative Society were the successful bidders, and before long they had erected a branch shop there. This led to an immediate improvement in what was for sale, and the two societies were soon competing over the dividend they were offering. By the time we left Twechar the dividend was 3s6d in the pound - more than could be had anywhere else.

The birth of our first child, Morag, caused quite a sensation in the village, to our great surprise, but it turned out that she was the first child ever to have been born in the manse, and everybody wanted to look in the pram. As well as praise and admiration Mary received all kinds of advice, since there was general sympathy for her, as her mother lived nowhere near. Nobody would have dreamed of going to hospital for such an ordinary event as a birth. There was a very good midwife in the village, who knew her job well, and the doctor turned up eventually to check that everything was all right.

We got to know Dr Parker pretty well. He was a G.P. in Kilsyth and included Twechar on his rounds. Everyone in the village knew him, and he had the reputation of being able to diagnose your trouble by just looking at you. The doctor said ninety per cent of the people had rheumatism, for which there was no cure apart from moving to a dry, warm climate. Twechar, under the lee of the Campsies, was a very wet place. Pneumoconiosis was widespread among the miners, and their bairns had all the usual children's troubles. The doctor's cavalier attitude towards his patients was matched by his patients' attitude towards the prescribed medicine. A man would take his medicine until he felt better and then put a stopper on the half-full bottle, which might come in handy for his neighbour one day. The doctor discovered we took porridge for breakfast, and he strongly approved of that. But he recommended the porridge he had every morning, which was made from four different meals: oatmeal, barley meal, pease meal and wheat meal. His wife was dead and his daughter was a dietician, and she kept house and cooked for them both. Mary asked her what she thought of her father's porridge. 'It's very good', she said, 'but of course he cooks it himself. I haven't got time in the morning to mess about with that complicated porridge.'

Dr Parker was forever at me to take a day off every week. I told him I didn't need a regular day off, as I always had the garden to do and I got plenty of exercise that way. He went fishing every Wednesday at a loch in the Campsies, but I never got around to joining him. I later learned that he didn't have a licence, and in fact, was poaching. This was known to the locals, and it probably endeared him to them, making him one of themselves as it were.

My medical record so far had not included what might be called run-of-the-mill illnesses, and now, to epilepsy and a badly burnt foot there was added an outbreak of eczema - common enough, it might be thought; but my eczema broke out on my face - over my right face and jaw. It was not a pretty sight and I applied to the doctor for a remedy. He produced a brilliant yellow ointment which, he said, must be plastered over the rash. I was nonplussed as I envisaged myself appearing in public with this revolting appearance, but I tried it. It was as bad as I had foreseen, so I didn't use any more of it. But I couldn't shave - at least I could only shave one side of my face, so I let my beard grow, and after a couple of weeks or so the eczema seemed to have disappeared. After waiting a while longer, and no eczema reappearing, I shaved, and the eczema returned almost at once. I grew four successive beards, with the eczema resurfacing every time I shaved the beard off, so I accepted the inevitable, but for years the barber had trouble with a patch of skin on and under my right jaw. Beards were not common then, and on my arrival in Leith in 1947 there was a persistent rumour in the town that I had been a submariner.

One difficulty in the village was that with almost everyone working in the pits, everyone was on an equality and no one could exercise authority. Finding a manager for 'The Bully' (the pub) was very difficult. The few who carried a natural authority - the pit manager, the manager of the chemical works at Queenzieburn, the headmaster, the pit surveyor - did not mix with the miners, and never even visited 'The Bully'. Various men tried the job but could not keep order and there was general turmoil and frequent fights. This problem was solved eventually when Willie Smith took the job. He was a son of the school janitor who had trained as a teacher and had married a teacher. He was tall, strong, and afraid of nobody. Born in the village, he knew practically every man's circumstances. When the miners were paid - and now in wartime they were working full out and had money to spend - they came straight to 'The Bully' and ordered drinks. When they asked for a second drink,

Willie asked to see their store book. When he judged they had spent enough he refused to supply any more drink. They accepted that, however reluctantly, and their wives were happy with this turn-up at 'The Bully', as they had to keep house on what was left in the storebook. This happy state of affairs came abruptly to and end when Willie, not being a miner, was called up, and went off to the R.A.F. 'The Bully' at once reverted to its former chaos until Willie Smith demobbed. He came home, walked into 'The Bully' and without asking anyone's leave, resumed his job as manager, to everyone's relief.

The trouble at 'The Bully' was an acute form of similar difficulty other organisations were having through no one being a cut above anyone else. I was roped in by no fewer than twenty-seven different organisations in the village to act as treasurer. I had to get a crash-course in bookkeeping from my father. But I felt things were reaching a state of absurdity when I was approached by the secretary of the local branch of the British Legion with a request for me to join. As I had never served in any of the armed forces, I refused, but the secretary repeated his appeal week after week. I suggested there must be some special reason for this urgency, and at length it transpired that what the Legion wanted was a treasurer. What was wrong with their present treasurer? After a good deal of probing it came out that the treasurer had not reported on the state of the funds for the past five years, and as there ought to be some hundreds of pounds in their bank account, the members were worried. Why could they not replace their treasurer? After a long time asking questions and evaluating the answers, it turned out that after each of their monthly meetings the treasurer invited them all to join him for a drink at 'The Bully'. This hospitality, of course, had come from the funds of the Legion, and as everyone had been sharing in this misappropriation of funds they were in a weak position when it came to dealing with the treasurer.

The two sisters Jean and Jessie Rollo became firm friends. Jean worked in a dentist's practice in Glasgow, and Jessie was a primary school teacher. She was the only school teacher in Twechar who lived in the village, and she taught Morag from her first day at school. She also had a flowing stream of commentary and anecdote from the classroom, which she retailed with a deadpan face. Both sisters were musical, Jean playing the 'cello and Jessie the violin, and they introduced me to the orchestra at the Athenaeum in Glasgow, ferrying me back and forward to rehearsals. I was very glad to have this stimulus, for I had had no lessons since my mid-teens and had been thrown back on my own resources, amusing myself with the violin in a desultory way. I particularly remember spending a whole war-time winter rehearsing Schubert's 'Unfinished Symphony'. Jean died while we were still in

Twechar, and Jessie moved to Waterside, taking charge of the school there until some years later she retired to Auchenloch, near Lenzie. There was no Church at Auchenloch, but Jessie organised a weekly service in the village hall, and for some years I paid an annual visit to provide supply there and enjoy a weekend.

Twechar came within the Presbytery of Glasgow. This was a completely different gathering from the Presbytery of Caithness, which I attended while in Watten. I was simply there as a visitor or observer, not then being either an elder or an ordained minister. There were just about a dozen scattered congregations in the Caithness gathering, and we all sat round a large table. We had lunch together and then re-convened to finish any business still to be dealt with. Glasgow was a complete contrast. Formal and routine business was covered in the forenoon; committee reports were heard and discussed in the afternoon, and as often as not there would still be some business in the evening. There was so much pressure to cope with all this that questions were discouraged by a convener announcing that 'This has already been discussed in committee'.

On one occasion however I did manage to get my oar in, when a Government Bill on education came before the presbytery. I took exception to a clause in the Bill, and got a majority when it came to a vote. I was then made a commissioner to the forthcoming General Assembly, where I would be given the chance to argue my case. I spent a long time preparing the ten-minute address to the Assembly which I thought would probably be cut to five minutes. When it came to the bit and I rose to address the Assembly from the bar of the House the convener of the Education Committee rose and said there would be no need for any speech from me, as the Committee had already agreed to accept the point I was making.

As well as the normal, ongoing work of the ministry I was usually involved in research, and setting out the results. I was especially interested in John Calvin, as one of the most influential reformers in the church. His preaching and teaching had greatly influenced John Knox, and it seemed to me that a selection of Calvin's sermons in English translation would be of considerable interest. I wrote to Butterworth the publishers and they said they'd be interested and would like to see my manuscript when it was available. I went ahead and found Calvin's mediaeval French straightforward, apart from the spelling. But I could only spend an hour or so a day on the work. Then one day I read a review of a newly-published book by an Oxford don - T.H.L. Parker. This was a selection of John Calvin's sermons! I realised I'd have to get used to that kind of thing, and just get on with other work. It was some consolation in later years to find T.H.L. Parker becoming a well-known scholar with several books to his credit.

Mr Filshill, the mining surveyor in Twechar had been captain of the Twechar B.B.s for some years. This was a strong company with a pipe band, unattached to any battalion, being too remote from other companies, so free in some matters to go its own way. Mr Filshill, however, became increasingly involved with civil defence, and dropped the captaincy of the B.B.s for the duration of the war. I agreed to take his place, although I had no experience of the B.B., having always been an enthusiastic Boy Scout. As Mary was running the Woman's Guild and the Girls' Guildry, we were now both immersed in this kind of social work.

The youngsters were a mixed lot, some from the families of church members, others wild and uncontrollable. I made it a rule that members of the Boys' Brigade must learn to live by the rules of respectable society or get out. Attendance at Church or Sunday School or Bible Class was made compulsory. Boys who tossed pennies or swore or prowled around private property were likewise banned. For the next year these three rules had an adverse effect on membership. Week by week the roll dwindled until I was left with four boys all told. The Girls' Guildry did not dwindle as the Brigade did. On the four remaining boys (little did they know it) the future of the Brigade in Twechar depended. They were twelve and thirteen years of age, and for the next year they were together as a Bible Class, and during the week they were employed on various odd jobs. We abolished their uniforms and held no Brigade meetings; but they were used as stewards at concerts, and as collectors for one or two of the numerous wartime funds. They also had one or two jaunts with the minister, and at Easter they all spent five days together in the country. For the five of them this was an unforgettable experience; and in the summer, with some of the Girls' Guildry in the Bible Class they had several Saturday afternoons together. By this time they thought of themselves as a gang - a squad of inseparables; and the Boys' Brigade restarted in the autumn with these boys as N.C.O.s and a roll of almost thirty - none older than themselves. At the same time the Life Boy team was revived amid the never failing enthusiasm of these youngsters, and by mid-winter all sections of the G.G. and B.B. totalled close to 200 members.

In the meantime a Horticultural Society had been started. This was an old idea, mooted repeatedly, and dropped as often for various reasons, but the war provided an excellent opportunity for reviving the subject with the wartime slogan 'Dig for Victory'. In the spring of 1941 it was proposed to hold a Show of Home & Garden Produce, and a committee met to elect itself, and then in true Twechar style nothing was done until the last minute. Then the minister, of course, was appointed treasurer, and he, with Jessie Rollo, the school teacher, was instructed to see the thing through, with power to adopt other helpers. Patriotism was then at an all-time high, and there was a good entry. The Show and Sale was a great success. The laird opened it, and before leaving he buttonholed the minister, expressed his keen interest in the proceedings and passed over a cheque for £100. 'Do what you like with it' he said. 'Thank you,' responded the minister, 'we'll start a Horticultural Society.' It was as easy as that. The hundred pounds did the trick. The most pessimistic committee could not deny it was a firm foundation on which to build. All we needed now was a group of keen members, and we had that - just a few, who hitherto had been contributing to other shows. In three years the Society grew from the original group of enthusiasts to a large and growing number who strove, by every gardening trick they knew to snatch the honour of having their name inscribed on one or other of the two trophies. The minister became president, and competed as in honour bound, and actually won prizes. The real success of the venture, however, lay in the sight of the growing number of cultivated gardens in the village, in place of the hideous stretches of couch grass, docks, thistles and groundsel. Plots began to appear that really produced food.

There were no Roman Catholics in Twechar until after the General Strike in 1926. After that long lay-off some pits did not reopen as the workings were flooded and many coal seams were no longer economic to bring into production again. One R.C. family was then allowed into Twechar. Before long a fair number followed them from Lanarkshire, and others arrived from Ireland. There was no sectarian enmity, but the R.C.s, and especially the Irish contingent were seen to be less law-abiding than the natives of Twechar; but they were good workers, and team-mates down the pit. The weekly paper, the Kilsyth Chronicle, always ran a column on cases before the Sheriff. The panel[1], as often as not, was from Twechar, and the panel more often than not was an R.C. The rest of the village just shrugged.

The Gibson family - Matthew, with his wife and two sons, John and Bertie, were Protestants ('Prodies') from Northern Ireland, and good members of the church. The older boy, John, seemed a born artist, squiggling, drawing, and painting everywhere and all the time. We got on well, and he was glad to use a room in our attic as a studio because of its North-facing skylight. He left Twechar, met Tyrone Guthrie and worked with him, scene-painting, learning the craft of the producer. Before he left Twechar he painted a copy of one of Van Gogh's pictures of the Bridge at Arles and gave it to me as a souvenir. In those early days of his career he was dissatisfied, for he had always wanted to be an artist, painting; but this stage-craft was a job, and a good job. We

---

[1] the panel - the accused

kept in touch by correspondence, and Mary and I met him in London, where he took us behind the stage at the Windmill Theatre, where a play was rehearsing, and we met a number of players as they came off stage, including young Richard Briers. John married a French girl, but died of T.B. in his early thirties. Bertie, his young brother, became a vet, returned to Northern Ireland and set up practice at Ballymena, where his parents retired, and we visited and corresponded with them until they died. Bertie's son also qualified as a vet, served as Terry's assistant for a year at Derby, and then returned to Ballymena to work with his father. The Irish troubles cut us off from them.

The lack of any church hall was a growing handicap. This had been felt long before we came to Twechar, and a hall fund had been started and abandoned. When the war was over I had the fund restarted, and a group of collectors went round the village every week, gathering contributions. As they moved from house to house in the rows the R.C.s became aware of what was afoot, and they pitched in with their contributions, which was gratifying. Hitherto there had not been any resident priest in the villages, but as the number of R.C.s had been steadily increasing, a priest from Croy had been visiting, from time to time, and I met him doing his rounds, and told him we were in need of a hall, and were raising money for the project. As his folk were helping us I thought it as well to be open with him on the subject. He said that his people also needed a chapel, and he added that he would have his chapel before we had our hall. I pointed out that we were a good way ahead of him. He didn't seem worried. In due course I heard from our people in the rows that the priest had visited each R.C. house, ascertained their income and told them what their contribution to the new chapel would be. They all said, "Yes Father", grumbled and swore a good deal after he had gone, but paid up.

After a week or two I became aware that several regular attendees among the men in the congregation were missing from morning worship. I mentioned this to Albert Unwin, who answered, 'D'ye no ken?', 'Ken what?' I countered. 'They're buildin' the Catholic chapel.' This was true. Work on the chapel was voluntary, and so could only be carried on at the weekends. The R.C.s were unskilled labourers, and the 'Prodies' were tradesmen - bricklayers, plumbers, electricians and joiners, all employed in the pit of course. The R.C. contributors to our hall fund were now getting value for their money. The chapel was indeed in working order in a surprisingly short time, and the priest showed me round. It was a little hall-church. Adequate.

There was a kind of all-round camaraderie between the denominations. The miners got a free issue of the best coal - more than they needed, so the surplus was delivered to the priest at Croy. On the other hand, if I travelled to Glasgow by bus, wearing my clerical collar, if the conductress was an R.C. she would ignore my hand outstretched with the fare. If the girl was Protestant she collected my money with no hesitation.

The Iona Community was carrying on with the restoration of Iona Abbey, and while I had never joined the Community, I had lined up as a Friend, and spent a week on Iona lending a hand. At the same time I took an interest in the Community's Glasgow base in Clyde Street, and in the autumn of 1946 I undertook to give a series of monthly talks on the Christian faith, and it was there that I met Oliver Wilkinson from Oxford, who had come to the Clyde Street rooms to learn more of the Community. He was interested in drama and playwriting, as I was, and he sold me the idea that a group could produce a script for a play, working together. But I could not do anything about it in Twechar, without any dramatic club.

As the war had progressed there had been increasingly urgent calls for chaplains to the forces, but those ministers fit and able had already joined up, and those who were left were too old, or suffered some kind of disability. As I saw it, if they were so hard-up for recruits they could surely make use of me in some capacity. Without reference to the presbytery clerk, who must know all about me and would do his best to stop me, I volunteered my services and was summoned to attend at Edinburgh Castle for my medical. As I expected I was passed A 1, returned to Twechar and waited, and waited, and waited, but heard no more. The presbytery would certainly have been informed, and the whole thing called off as stupid.

My predecessor as minister of Twechar had been a disaster. No other description would be adequate. He had married a wealthy lady and had no interest in the parish or its needs or its people. He was a keen bridge player and spent all his time in Glasgow at a bridge club. One of the astonishing facts I found shortly after my arrival in the village was that the average total offering at the Sunday services was 12s6d. In that situation any effort I made to improve matters would be successful, and in fact over the years my stipend had risen. As the congregation paid just five pounds per annum towards stipend, I put it to the congregational board that this might easily be increased, and I suggested that as the weekly freewill offerings increased and we paid all our presbytery and other dues, whatever surplus was available might be divided between the stipend and the hall fund. This was agreed without any difficulty and year by year brought small but significant increases to stipend.

I was becoming more relaxed over my situation in Twechar. After fully seven years in a very run-down parish things were now looking up. Attendance at church, membership of the Woman's Guild, the youth

Twechar 1939 - 1946

organisations, the horticultural society were all increasing and there was now a team of leaders contributing time and enthusiasm to the work of the parish. So why was it that one day, when I saw notice of a vacant parish in Leith, I was brought up short? From all accounts Leith was overcrowded, dirty, an unemployment black spot, a place presenting a considerable challenge to any minister. Twechar was a mining village, but it was set in a beautiful well-wooded area, with opportunities for enjoying country life that would not be present in Leith - and that counted for much with me.

But Leith had its peculiar attractions. I had happy memories of school there. I felt I belonged to the east of Scotland rather than the west. I liked the people of the west and responded to their warmth and openness; but I never felt one of them. I felt at home with the lifestyle of the east. This was the rather vague thinking that filled my mind as I waited to hear whether there would be any guidance in the reply to my application. When I received an invitation to conduct a service in a Leith church my mind was made up to respond, to go ahead positively and see what might come of it.

The service was to be in Junction Road Church, and as I indicated earlier I was somewhat disturbed at meeting my old English teacher James Paton, who was Session Clerk. The service itself went smoothly enough, and afterwards I met with the vacancy committee, when I was told there was no manse, and never had been, the minister always having been paid a sum of money in lieu of rent. This was a major problem, as in 1947, barely two years after the end of the war, housing, especially in Leith, was extremely difficult to come by and the Kirkgate Church's chances of attracting a minister then were slim indeed. The vacancy committee, however, promised that within a year they would procure a suitable house for a manse, but I did not build much hope on that. At the end of the meeting, the convener, Jim Alexander, said, 'Mr Marshall, in a sense we don't need a minister. We're getting along quite well without one, but the presbytery tells us that we must get a minister, and that's true. What we lack, and what we need, is someone to co-ordinate and direct our activities as a congregation, and to give us spiritual leadership.' We parted at that.

Back in Twechar, after a few days I received an invitation to preach at the Kirkgate Church as sole nominee. I mentioned this to several neighbouring ministers, who all warned me not to be so foolish as to go to a parish where I would be among men and women who had been at school with me. There would be all kinds of pitfalls in such a move. Far better to go where I was not known and would be able to start afresh, having learned from past experience. All this simply confirmed in me my intention to go to Leith if called. In my old age I realise, with some surprise that almost every big decision I have made in the course of my life has been made against the best advice.

Knowing that my parents were now settled at Eastwood was an added incentive. Dad was almost seventy years old, and Mother sixty-one. Dad was still attending to his business, going into Edinburgh two or three times a week, but with his increasing deafness was trying to retire. Mother was full of beans and much involved with the local church. She had always fancied herself as a countrywoman, although she had lived in Edinburgh all her life. Now she had two and a half acres, which included a well-stocked garden where she revelled working. They were delighted to have us come and live with them, even although temporarily, until a manse could be found for the Kirkgate Church. One last consideration for this move to Leith was that I'd be taking quite a drop in stipend, The Kirkgate Church was paying the city minimum which was £350 per annum. I had been doing better than that in Twechar, but again there was what is nowadays called job satisfaction, and schooling for the children. I already had Morag's name down for a place at Esdaile, but Donald would soon be presenting a problem if we still lived in Twechar.

That winter was very severe, and spring was very late. Our removal from Twechar was arranged for April, and we set off in snowy conditions. The removal man was Joe Crispin, an elder in Kirkgate Church, and the first real contact I was making with Leith. The packing was done in a day, and Joe stayed overnight with us. He was an interesting man, ready and able to turn his hand to almost anything. Originally a joiner, he became chauffeur to Sir Robert Sleigh before the First World War. Sleigh had a motoring business in Edinburgh (later Rossleigh) and later became Lord Provost of Edinburgh. Joe had some very entertaining stories of his pre-war adventures with his motor-car, travelling to London and back several times. The wheels were solid rubber, the roads were not all macadamised, and there were no filling stations, no roadside cafes or Little Chefs. Everything had to be carried on board - petrol, food, tools and repair equipment. After the war he joined the furniture removal firm, and it was as well he was prepared for anything, for when we reached Fushiebridge the snow had drifted to four feet from the roadway up the drive to the house, so instead of getting home that evening he had to spend the night with my folk, and next day we cleared a path to the house in two or three hours of shovelling. And that was my introduction to my new charge.

7
THE KIRKGATE CHURCH - PHASE 1

The first essential was to establish a routine on which to base my daily work in Leith. The vestry became my office, and I commuted there every morning getting the bus at the Birkenside terminus, and the tram to Leith from the Edinburgh Bus Station at Clyde Street, where formerly the St Andrew Square picture house had been - a very respectable howff. It was awkward having my books at Eastwood, but it was convenient to have the vestry as a base from which to visit homes and hospitals and attend meetings, afternoons or evenings.

The children's schooling was also a problem. Morag was six and Donald four. Not knowing where I might be living in future years I had entered Morag as a pupil at Esdaile, in Edinburgh, where she could board, if necessary. As Donald was still below school age I had not yet made any arrangement for his schooling. The trouble with Esdaile was that pupils there were not accepted until they were ten years old. In the meantime both children were sent to St Brendan's, near Eskbank - about four miles from Eastwood, so we were dependent on buses. It wasn't a good school, and has long since closed, but it served our need at that time. Morag soon transferred to Cranley in Edinburgh, travelling by bus. Donald, just beginning school, remained at St Brendan's until, after a year, the church bought a manse at 8 Dudley Avenue, and we said goodbye to Eastwood. A month or so later, my parents unwillingly left Eastwood and moved to Park Road, Newhaven. This was to lessen the strain on Dad, who was still unable to retire, since no one seemed able to buy the business.

The house at Dudley Avenue had belonged to a lecturer at the Leith Nautical College, who had died, and seems to have been a bachelor, for the contents of the house were sold off by auction. Mother and I attended the sale, and I got possession of what I took to be a Regency drawing-room suite in rosewood. It became mine without much opposition. This was before the modern passion to acquire antiques, and we had no furniture for the sitting room, as that had been supplied to the manse at Twechar.

Before long Mary became a close friend of Mrs. Gilmour in the congregation, wife of a chief engineer in the Ben Line. She had been an upholstress, and as soon as she saw our new suite she asked us to let her re-cover it. She seemed quite fascinated by it, and chose the present pattern, which she said was typical of the Regency period. When she finished the job she said she had removed no fewer than six previous coverings, which offered striking circumstantial evidence as to the age of the suite. Mrs. Gilmour refused to accept any payment, saying that the opportunity of doing the work was a great privilege.

I now had the job of finding a school for Donald. Morag continued at Cranley, but in those early post-war years there was a great shortage of school places. I tried Leith Academy first. Having been dux there I imagined that might count in my favour. I was wrong. The headmaster of the junior school turned me down flat. When I mentioned my connection with the school as a former pupil he was still unimpressed. I then approached all the Edinburgh schools, and all had the same answer. The summer term was just beginning, and the rolls were full. No more entrants would be accepted until the annual entrance exams in the autumn. That was no use to me. If Donald missed the summer term he would lose a year. In the meantime he was attending Gillsland Park, which was only a prep school. Finally Edinburgh Academy came up trumps. They said they had two vacancies they would be prepared to fill now. There would be an entrance exam next week. Mary took Donald along to Denham Green, the junior school for the Academy, and found a great crowd of forty mothers with their offspring. When Donald's turn came he showed no interest in the teacher examining him, but found the room full of interest. The teacher showed him a picture of a motor car, and asked what it was. At this obvious question Donald wondered what the trick was, so he took his time before informing the teacher that it was a vehicle. He was accepted! That reminded me of the old Border joke about the inspector visiting a school and showing a class of young boys a picture of a sheep and asking the class what it was. Dead silence! Growing impatient the inspector pointed to one boy and asked him for an answer. Still silence, then the boy said, 'A canna richt see whether it's a tup or a gimmer.'

The congregation was formerly United Presbyterian, since 1900 United Free, and Church of Scotland since 1929. In that tradition there were no endowments. Everything had to be paid for as it was acquired; so the managers, who were responsible for church finances, were an important element in the congregation. On the other hand the Kirk Session was the ruling body in the church, responsible for worship and church discipline. The two bodies were not quite at daggers drawn, but they were keen rivals to exercise authority.

I was soon made aware of this when, after a service at which I had appealed for funds to help foreign missions the preses of the managers said to me, "I hope we're not going to hear any more of that. We need all our money to pay our bills. Charity begins at home. " I said nothing, but realised that there was a problem here. The Kirk Session also had its intransigent members. The minister of the Kirkgate Church when war broke out went off as a chaplain, and in Egypt he had blotted his copybook by heavy drinking. The elders at home were shocked, but one or two were furious and wrote to him repeatedly until he resigned his charge, and after the war became a teacher. A missionary back from China took over the charge until the end of the war, when the congregation could look out for a new minister. The older men in both management and Kirk Session were the most difficult to deal with, entrenched in the attitudes of the twenties and thirties. The younger men, and especially ex-servicemen were much more relaxed and tolerant. One or two elders and managers I recognized from my schooldays. I got the two bodies to attend a joint meeting - a hitherto unheard of event - reminded them of what we all had in common, and got them to agree to joint quarterly meetings, when we could discuss matters of joint interest and hear of each others' plans and aspirations.

At the annual meeting of the congregation in March 1948, I took the chair, opened the meeting with a hymn, a Bible reading and a prayer, and then invited the preses of the managers to carry on. After the formal business we broke up for tea and biscuits, then reconvened for general discussion. During the interval I was told that never before had the meeting taken this form. I was mystified until I learned that the minister never attended this annual business meeting, which was run by the managers. No one had thought to tell me this, and once I had started no one liked to stop me. I was surprised at the large attendance, but discovered that this was the one chance in the year for the congregation to examine the managers. The managers were reminded of the promises made at the last AGM. Why had these not been fulfilled? Comment was made on the state of the building, what repairs were needed, and what was going to be done in the coming year. A very stimulating and entertaining meeting. And as for the form of the meeting, everyone seemed quite pleased, and the new style of the meeting remained like that in the following years.

Responding to repeated invitations to visit them, we went in August 1947 to the Island of Yell, in Shetland, where we had a great welcome from Alex and Miriam Pitt. I'd been wondering how we'd fill in the time living on a small island, but it was soon evident that without the facilities of life in the town, the necessary household chores were much more labour intensive, and took up a great deal of time. Alex asked if I'd like to give him a hand digging peat, and I agreed. The peat bank was barely half a mile from the house, and here we set to work. The weather had been dry so the top two or three inches of the ground were fairly dry, but further down the peat was like a wet sponge, and the peat that was cut was very heavy to lift and set on end to dry. A couple of hours of this was the most backbreaking labour I had ever known, even on the farms. Later, when dry, the peat was shifted to the house and stacked for winter use.

The weather was fine; indeed we had no rain at all while we were on Yell, which local people said had never happened before in living memory. I said to Alex that I'd like to do a bit of sea-fishing, but he was doubtful. I was a minister, and that was a guarantee of ill-luck. We asked around, and while no one was rude enough to say "No", everyone had a reason for not fishing when I wanted to go. A few days later I met a boy of fifteen who lived in the house nearest us - about a quarter of a mile away. He said that if I wanted to go fishing he would take me in his boat. I told him I was a minister, and would likely bring him bad luck. Said he, "A dinna believe in aa that." so we set out one evening. "Mind you," said my young friend, "we micht get naethin. Naebody has caught mackerel this year, and aa the men are worried."

However, a little later we found ourselves in a shoal of fish, and began hauling them in. For me this was an eye-opener, and when we had a great heap of fish lying in the bottom of the boat I suggested we call a halt. What were we going to do with ninety-four mackerel? (We had counted them). The boy indicated that would be no problem. We toured round the nearest neighbours, distributing from our haul. Next day I had four invitations to go fishing, but I must have had other things to do, for I didn't go out again. But we had mackerel to every meal for several days. The local people hung up their fish to dry and ate them during the winter.

The next memorable episode was my attempt at sea bathing. We were enjoying such fine weather that I was surprised that no one ever appeared to be bathing in the sea. I went in and swam around, while the rest of the family and the Pitts watched from the shore. When I tried to emerge from the sea I found my legs entangled in seaweed. The more I struggled the more entangled I became, and I found myself being dragged under water, while the spectators laughed at what they thought was a game I was playing. I panicked and thought I was drowning, when suddenly I got my head above water and managed to free myself. Now I knew why sea-bathing was not popular locally. The seaweed was known (perhaps sarcastically) as "Lucky Lines", and that was my first and last experience of bathing in Shetland.

Morag, aged seven, was the next to suffer. She was kicked by a pony - a small Shetland pony - kicked on her forehead, which was laid open. We summoned the district nurse, who was quickly with us, bound the wound, and took her to Mid-Yell, where the doctor stitched the wound, and sent her by ferry to Lerwick, where the surgeon said he could not do any better a job on the wound than had already been done, and sure enough the scar healed cleanly and in the course of years faded

The Kirkgate Church - Phase I

almost completely. It was a coincidence that the doctor at Mid-Yell was in fact originally a surgeon at Edinburgh Royal Infirmary, whose hobby and passion was sailing. He gave up his job in Edinburgh to take up a vacancy at Yell, where he acted as a GP and attended people there and in various neighbouring islands, using his boat to do his rounds. For my part, I could only murmur to myself, "Everything is mixed with mercy."

Another coincidence of a different sort was that the minister at Mid-Yell was Fred Houston. News travels fast on an island, and Fred had heard of our staying with the Pitts, and he urged us to pay him a visit. I knew Fred. He was one of a family of four brothers who were brought up in Henderson Street, Leith. That was a notable family. One brother became the Leith Registrar, another was headmaster of Portobello Secondary School, the third brother I did not know, and Fred, the youngest, was a "character". When he was ordained to the ministry and called to Yell, he married a nineteen-year-old girl from London, and we reckoned this would probably be a failed marriage, but on the contrary she loved the life in Shetland, and no greater contrast to London life could have been found in the British Isles.

We arrived at Fred's manse for lunch, and he showed us round. There was no gas or electricity, and no piped water. There was a well at the foot of the garden, and water had to be pumped from there to the kitchen sink. This enabled cooking to start. From the kitchen, water could be pumped upstairs to the bathroom. Considering these necessary arrangements we sat down to a surprisingly good lunch. Almost inevitably they kept hens, and also, in an adjoining field they had a few sheep. From the backend, and all through the winter and early spring, Fred explained, all the daylight hours were occupied doing the necessary daily chores - pumping water, attending to poultry and sheep, cleaning and replenishing the oil lamps all over the house - only then could the minister attend to his proper job.

There was no television, of course, and no wireless that I could see. "Oh," said Fred, "we make our own entertainment, and in fact there is to be a concert tonight in the village. You'll stay for that of course." This was interesting, and I asked who'd be performing. "I'm relying on you for one." I could hardly believe my ears, and after some incredulous comment I discovered that he had sold two hundred tickets for the concert. That was the capacity of the village hall. The money would go to some local fund, but no programme had been organised. Fred had persuaded two other men to join us, and in the late afternoon we four met to devise an evening's entertainment. I and one of the others had to sing; the other stranger could play the piano, but the main offering of the evening was to be a play. It didn't exist yet, but Fred said, while the pianist provided an interlude, which followed an opening solo from the singer, we would get together backstage. We had in mind the general subject for the play, and when the pianist finished two of us would enter on the stage and start talking. The two still backstage would listen to the stage talk, and when the time seemed ripe one would join them. With three on stage there was scope for one or two to go off for a breather while the remaining one backstage could take up the running. It was the most nerve wracking experience I had ever had, and all through the show I expected many to walk out. Instead we finished the show to thunderous applause, and Fred said he heard many appreciative comments as the audience dispersed. I could only accept that since they were not all simpletons, they realised what we were up to, and were applauding the efforts of two ministers, with two friends to provide an entertainment well worth the two shillings they had paid for their tickets.

I took a service at Fetlar, which was then vacant, and Mary and I lunched with Sir Arthur and Lady Bruce. Fetlar is known as the Garden of Shetland, and he showed us his own garden, which was laid out in small plots, each one surrounded by its own box hedge about a foot high. This was a device to assist the growth of vegetable seedlings, which would never stand the chance of developing in the gale-force winds so common there.

On our return home we had occasional letters from Shetland, but after a year or two we had a letter from Miriam with shocking news. Alex had got himself a motor-bike which was a great help in getting about the island. One day, however, he had an accident, and when he recovered consciousness found himself in a ditch, with the motor-bike, and to his astonishment saw his right foot lying beside him. Another unbelievable coincidence was that just then the district nurse came cycling by. She jumped off her bike, grabbed the severed foot and ankle, somehow managed to bind them on to Alex's leg, and got him transported to Mid-Yell to that notable doctor/surgeon, who did what he could and had the patient ferried to Lerwick. Unbelievably Alex recovered, with two ankles functioning, but with a pronounced limp. He went on and trained on a modified course for the ministry, and was ordained and inducted into a parish in Ayrshire.

That was the end of our contact with Shetland. When we were living in Leith in the 1920s there was a fish shop a few yards away on Leith Walk from our flat, and the window of that shop always mystified me, for there never was anything in that window but a great stack of rolls of what I thought was cardboard. Mother said that Shetlanders ate those rolls, and there were many Shetlanders in Leith. I still found it hard to believe this information, but now, having caught all that mackerel it

The Kirkgate Church - Phase I

was interesting to see what dried fish looked like - no more appetizing than in that Leith shop.

Shortly after entering the ministry at Kirkgate, in the autumn of 1948, John Curran, the recently appointed beadle, came into the vestry one day with a book in his hand. There were urgent appeals at that time for waste paper to be salvaged and recycled to meet the paper shortage following the war. John said "We're emptying a cupboard and getting rid of paper. I see this book is not printed but just written. Are you interested in it?" When I glanced at it I got a shock. This was the minute book of the Kirk Session from 1788. I told the beadle to stop throwing anything out, and to look through all they had already gathered, and to let me have anything else they found in manuscript like this. I joined the men doing the salvage and found two more books of session minutes. The result was a run of these minutes from 1788 to 1838, but disappointingly nothing before or after that half century.

This was the beginning of my interest in the congregation's history, and as one thing led to another, my interest extended to the town of Leith and the city of Edinburgh. The congregation had originated in a breakaway from South Leith Parish Church in 1740, protesting against a minister being appointed to the vacant charge without the congregation being consulted. The rebels joined the newly formed Secession Church, and without going into details, they became Antiburghers, then Burghers. In 1820 they became members of the United Secession Church, then briefly they were the Calvinistic Secession Church, and then joined the United Presbyterians, and in 1900 United Free, and in 1929 they became Church of Scotland. Few Congregations can have had such a mixture of sects in their history, but the congregation I was ministering to had no knowledge of all this, and I devoted a number of evening services to sketching their history.

A good deal of interest was expressed in that history, and I decided to do something to make a permanent record of it. I had no money to employ a printer; all I had was an old flat duplicator, acquired I know not where. I set to work with it, aiming to produce a part of the history every month, for which I could charge 1s 6d. I made a hopeful guess that 150 copies might be sold to make the venture pay for itself. This took a great deal of time during 1949, and the duplicator was very messy, but the job was completed, and I arranged with a bookbinding firm to bind copies for those who wished it. It was a story appealing to a very small market - which was confirmed a year or two later when a man told me he had bought a copy at a jumble sale in Broxburn for twopence!

There were many ex-servicemen and women in the congregation, and they provided a stimulus and a clubbable atmosphere which I did not realise would be temporary. The Youth Fellowship numbered about eighty ranging in age from sixteen to about thirty-five. They were delighted to be meeting up again with friends they had not seen for seven or eight years. But as the months passed they got jobs away from Leith, they married and no longer thought of themselves as "youth".

The minister of Junction Road Church, the parish adjacent to the Kirkgate, was Jack Prendergast. When war broke out he was in Paris studying to become a professional pianist, but the war had brought all that to an abrupt end, and he had entered the ministry. He was delighted to discover my interest in the violin and we got into the habit of meeting every Monday morning to practise together. He invited me to join a Ministers Concert Party. Jack was the accompanist, Tom Morton from Hawick an elocutionist and light baritone, Bob McIntyre, North Merchiston, a strong baritone and Leonard Small, compère. The addition of myself as violinist and tenor was apparently highly desirable.

As our services were free, we got no end of invitations from churches looking to raise money for various good causes, but shortly after I joined the party, Leonard Small resigned, pleading the lack of time with his large congregation at Cramond. We performed all over the city, and occasionally in the Borders. Lawson Memorial Church in Selkirk invited us on two successive years, and shortly after our second visit there I had a visit one Sunday from a vacancy committee inviting me there to come and be their minister! I was astonished. On the strength of two visits to Selkirk to play the violin and act as compère they were prepared to call me as their minister! I pointed this out to them, but they assured me I would be acceptable as sole nominee. I turned them down, not having been long in my present charge. Vacancy committees can be desperate. Many years later I took the service at Craiglockhart Church, when there was a vacancy there. After the service the Session Clerk and two or three others said, "Had you been twenty years younger we'd have voted for you." But I was not a candidate then.

The Ministers Concert Party was fine while it lasted, but like all amateur groups it was not likely to last. Bob McIntyre became the first industrial chaplain in Scotland, travelling all over the country. Tom Morton had a spell of ill-health, Jack Prendergast moved to Springburn in Glasgow, and there were no new additions to the company.

Feeling the loss of this musical fellowship I cast about for a group to get together to play at congregational concerts, and at Scottish country dances. I soon had a six-piece band. They were from varied backgrounds, had varied personalities, and music brought them together. Cathy Dunlop, the pianist/accompanist, worked with a Portobello undertaker, and became a partner in the firm. John Anderson, a bachelor, played the drums and could stand in as a pianist. Jimmy Hepburn had a ship repairer's business and played the violin. John Watt was in the Navy and came home to find his house had been completely destroyed by the only land-mine to hit Leith. His wife had got another house, but they had lost everything and were starting up again. Playing the violin was effective therapy for him. John Williamson, also in the Navy, was torpedoed in the Adriatic, and pulled out of the sea full of oil. He had been a long time in hospital, had a weak chest, was studying to be a C.A. but was back in hospital from time to time. Of all things his instrument was a double-bass. We enjoyed playing together for several years but it gradually became depleted and had to disperse.

A more long-lasting enterprise was the Dramatic Club. This had been founded by Jim Alexander in 1946, and they had mounted their first three-act play in that autumn, and when I arrived they were still wondering what to do next. Jim Alexander had real talent as a director and producer, and I sat in on the rehearsals for the next play. I brought up Oliver Wilkinson's idea of a play written by a group, pooling their ideas, and we discussed it. Both Jim and I were rather doubtful about it, but we thought it worth an experiment. We summoned those interested to discuss the idea. Could we agree on a subject? Interestingly that did not take long. Those were the early days of football pools, and the Church was against them. We discussed possible plots, but in the end it was left to me to write a script. As fifty-odd years earlier Scottish literature was bedevilled by the Kailyard School, so in these early post-war years amateur drama was immersed in kitchen comedy. On the wireless the McFlannels had been immensely popular during the war years. We had James Bridie and Dorothy Sayers to aspire to, but we recognized ourselves as being in a different league. Anyhow 'Money for Nothing' our one-act play on the pools was frankly kitchen comedy, and we decided to put it on in the church hall instead of the evening service. The response certainly impressed us. We had a write-up in the 'Evening News', and there was a long queue outside the hall before the doors were opened.

There was now pressure to do it again - with another play. We did this. At monthly intervals we produced about half a dozen one-act plays. They were all well received, but we couldn't keep it up. I was working on scripts into the small hours as no one else would take on that work. Added to all my normal work, there was neither time nor energy to keep it going. Also the dramatic club were spending more time on these plays than they felt was justified.

Membership of the club brought with it a deal of hard, concentrated work. For years now there had been two three-act plays in spring and autumn, a one-act play entered for the SCDA (Scottish Community Drama Association) competition, which ran throughout the spring months, and another one-act play for the Kirk Drama Festival in May. These one-act plays were staged in the Gateway Theatre, the building that had once been Pringle's Palace, and which became a television studio for STV. From the forties to the seventies there were kirk dramatic clubs all over the city, and indeed all over Scotland. The Kirkgate club also had backstage helpers, and could not have functioned without them - joiners, scene-painters, electricians, a wardrobe mistress and seamstresses. But the heart of all the activities was in the rehearsal room, where players were rehearsing all the year round once or twice a week, except for two months off in summer. Here, Jim Alexander bullied everyone into learning their parts as a first essential before working on stage setting, moves and drilling the cast on details. Drawing near to opening night the rehearsals became highly charged, and more than once Jim had the girls weeping, but once the first night was over everyone enjoyed the tension of actually playing on stage, and on the last night the party after the show was a hilarious climax to the whole enterprise.

It was not always like that. Inevitably players would leave for various reasons, and replacements were slow to appear. Membership was time-consuming, and needed dedication. Over the years there was a long, slow decline until in 1955 Jim Alexander and I were wondering whether we could continue for another session. Then by one more of the string of coincidences that have laced through my life, the two St John's churches (East & West) failed to agree to unite. The presbytery ordered the two churches to close and their moveable assets were moved to a church extension charge at St John's, Oxgangs. The St John's East members mostly joined South Leith Parish. The St John's West members mostly joined Kirkgate Church, and with them came members of a dramatic club they had had. That proved a shot in the arm for our dramatic club, for among the St John's contingent there was one born actor, Andrew Spiers, six feet four inches tall, with a natural stage presence, a beautiful sense of timing and an ability to learn words quickly. His joining the club attracted others and our fortunes took an upward turn. Jim Alexander now had some talented players to work with and he became chairman of the SCDA. Other clubs in the city were also wilting, and we gained new players from some of these. We pursued a steady course thereafter until the 1970s, when with our joining with South Leith we could no longer provide space for rehearsing, and Kirkgate Dramatic Club had to find themselves facilities elsewhere for rehearsals. By then, attracting members from all over the city they changed their name to 'Leitheatre', presenting plays in the Churchill Theatre and at St Serf's Hall during the Edinburgh Festival.

Mention of 1955, the year the Dramatic Club was saved from imminent

The Kirkgate Church - Phase I

death, reminds me that that was the year when a massive X-ray campaign was carried out in Leith to identify cases of TB. Every house in the town had to be visited, and this was achieved by a committee brought together for that one purpose. Never before had this group met and worked together. Representatives from the trade unions, churches and all kinds of societies were gathered under the chairmanship of Dr. Vaughan, the registrar at Leith Hospital. The whole town was divided into areas, and a committee member assigned to each area to do the visiting and arranging for X-ray photographs. Everyone but the priest managed their allotted task, and afterwards the committee met for the last time. Dr. Vaughan congratulated us all and asked if we thought we must just part. We had learned to work together; could we not continue on some worthwhile project? Two nurses who were present said that they were worried at the number of people living alone who were found dead after many days, and even weeks. Could anything be done to prevent this? It was agreed that this was something to be looked at, and those who were interested should meet together to devise a plan. We met and decided to start a lunch club - not free, but at a subsidised rate. This was not so much to feed the elderly, but to provide a *milieu* where lonely people could meet and get to know each other and keep an eye on each other's health. It was a great idea, but we had no money, and nowhere to set up the club, but Leith had always been a closely-knit community, and especially since the amalgamation with Edinburgh, fiercely independent.

We asked the directors of Leith Provident Co-operative Society for a room in which to hold committee meetings. This was granted free. When the Provident directors learned what we were aiming at, they said we could start our lunch club in their boardroom for as long as that was possible, with no long-term guarantee. Our most immediate and clamant need was for money. One day, when the committee was hammering out ideas, Willie Merrilees, Chief Constable of Lothians and Peebles Constabulary, walked in. He was a Leither, always with his finger on anything significant happening in the town. "A' hear ye're lookin' for money," he said, and when we agreed he went on, "Will ye still be here in an hour's time?" We said we'd wait for him, and off he went. An hour later he returned with a cap full of coins. We counted out almost £100. "Where did you get all this?" we asked. "At the dock gates; the men were leavin' for their mid-day break."

This was immensely heartening - evidence that Leith still would look after its own. The next hurdle was to find a place on which to erect premises to house the lunch club, as we could not be beholden to the 'Store' for ever. Again the response was unexpected. The flour mills in Leith were moving to new automatic mills on the waterfront, and the Swanfield Mill was now closed. The owners, the brothers Barry, said we could have the mill yard for a peppercorn rent - a shilling a year. From the start, when the lunch club opened in the Co-operative boardroom, about fifty women and two men attended, and lunch was delivered cooked, and only requiring to be reheated. After a few weeks more men began to trickle in, and eventually we were catering for fifty women and fifty men. John Crichton, an active town councillor, and I, attended the club weekly to sample the food and keep an eye on the enterprise.

With the Swanfield Mill yard now available we made a start on building premises, and the same strong determination to achieve this amenity for Leith prevailed wherever we made an appeal. Tradesmen contributed their time and even materials, either free or at a very low rate, and in 1957 I invited Compton Mackenzie, then living in Drummond Place, to come and perform the official opening, which he did readily. Unfortunately, but inevitably, the onset of inflation made it impossible to continue in these premises, as the continuing overheads increased beyond what the club could afford. Numbers attending also reduced over the years, as the massive poverty and overcrowding gradually improved. Numbers were reduced to some twenty-odd regulars, who were taken in hand by South Leith Parish Church.

Now here is a little story that couldn't have happened now. It belongs very much to the Leith of the early post-war years. We settled at 8 Dudley Avenue in 1948 - a house too small for the traditional manse. The garden was very small, which bothered me as I had always been accustomed to a large kailyard. All the same, the ground needed feeding, and there were no garden centres in Leith. As horse traffic was still quite common I decided to collect horse dung from the street. I rose one Sunday morning at five o'clock, collected a canvas bag I had, about three feet long and twelve inches wide, which could conveniently be slung from the handle-bar of my bike. I set off for the docks, where most horse traffic converged, and sure enough I was able to fill the bag with enough dung for my miniscule garden. I came home from the Shore, up Coburg Street, and as I drew near to Ferry Road a policeman stepped into the road and stopped me. He pointed to the bag. "What's in that?" he asked. "Oh, just some horse dung." I said. It didn't sound very like the truth. How many men would be likely to be carrying a bag of dung on a bike? "Open up", said the dedicated young cop. He plunged his hand in, but found nothing. He took it well. "There's been a lot of salmon poached and landed here. Your bag looked an ideal hidey-hole." "You're lucky it's dry." He nodded and we parted amicably and I was home in time for breakfast, but I didn't mention anything of all this in that morning's sermon.

The Kirkgate Church - Phase I

On holiday in 1948.
Mary and I with Terry's wife Edith and Morag,
Donald and Edith's daughter Sheena

Before I forget, I ought to say that after coming to Leith I had no more fits during the day. I did have what might be called minor fits, but these all took place in bed, and it was a long time before I was sure I had left all that behind me, and the law still forbade epilepsy sufferers from having a driving licence for life. In the late fifties, the law was relaxed to the extent that, had I been free of fits for the last thirty years I might sit the driving test, but by then I had no interest in motoring and did nothing about it. I used my bike a lot for going up town, as the bike could be left anywhere for any length of time. I did pastoral visiting on foot, for I enjoyed walking. I did eventually get myself a motor-bike - a BSA Bantam, and moved around on it while I twice failed the driving test, but I was not put out. Suitable clothing for the bike was not suitable for meetings or funerals. In any case, on his sixteenth birthday Donald took over the motor-bike, and at once took it to bits "to see how it works". When I came home and saw all the bits and pieces scattered over the floor I thought he had had an accident, but he put it all together again with nothing left over, and not long after he got a heavier bike, which made me uneasy.

Mary told me I'd have to learn to drive, for if I didn't I'd never be able to visit the family. I was more immediately concerned to be able to drive

Everything Mixed with Mercy

my father around. My parents had come to live with us at 4 Claremont Park, and Dad was becoming frail. I sat the test twice and failed, the second time in the summer of 1960. I thought I knew the man testing me, but he showed no sign of recognizing me. This disturbed me. Once he had failed me he smiled and said, "Don't you know me?" He was the son of Sam Law, the Session Clerk at Twechar, whom I had not seen since leaving the village. He was now living in Corstorphine. This was all irregular. I ought to have objected and got someone else to test me, but as he had shown no sign of knowing me I was less than confident. Anyhow Dad died two months later, so I felt relieved of responsibility, but Mary was now determined to get a licence for herself. She passed at the fourth attempt, after being assured by her instructor before each attempt that she should easily pass. But after it all she turned out to be a very good driver.

To go back ten years or so, in the summer of 1951 Terry suggested that Mary and I should join himself and Edith in a trip round Europe in his car. We agreed with alacrity. The children, theirs and ours, stayed at Derby with Granny in charge. In the course of that tour - our first trip abroad since the war, an odd assortment of incidents lodged in my mind. The first was the sight of the car being lifted on board the Channel Ferry grappled in mid-air by a crane. Next was in Paris, where one-way streets had just been introduced, and not being familiar with the signs, Terry was half way along a one-way street driving in the wrong direction, when we were stopped by a police whistle. Instantly about half a dozen gendarmes converged on us at the double. Terry put his head out of the window and said to the nearest copper, "No speak French", and in an instant they were all smiles and conducted us out of the street.

We slept that night in a comfortable inn where they served no meals. In the morning I rose early and sat in the lounge reading. After a while an English couple came down, looking for breakfast. They asked the porter for breakfast - asked in English, that is, and the porter explained that they could have *petit-déjeuner* in a restaurant over the street. They did not understand, and I was reluctant to interfere. Eventually the porter agreed to bring them breakfast, but they would have to pay extra for this service. We came across a similar situation at the Italian border, where a long queue was forming at the customs barrier. Terry had some talk with an English couple leaving Italy, who had spent their holiday in Italy without knowing that there were petrol coupons available for tourists, of which Terry had taken full advantage.

But the most hair-raising part of our journey had been on the Simplon Pass (I think it was the Simplon) where, on a narrow mountain road there had been a landslide. The narrow, twisting road was covered with

The Kirkgate Church - Phase I

loose rubble, and a gang of roadmen were eating their pieces, seated on the edge of the road with their legs dangling over a drop of several hundred feet, and on the other side, where the landslide had taken place there was a threatening overhang. We managed to inch our way round that fearsome bend, but at the time I little realised the strain on the driver. All Terry said was he hoped never to have to do the like of that again.

In Venice our hotel was adjacent to the bell tower of a church which stood eight or nine feet across an alley from our window, and that bell sounded regularly every quarter of an hour. A long-term resident might hardly be aware of this, but we only had a one-night stand.

Over the Alps again and into Switzerland, we stayed at a hotel where we had not booked in advance. It was a cold and foggy night and we were accommodated in an annexe as the hotel main building was full. Here, for the first time, I found on the bed a huge cover like an overblown duvet, feather-filled. The sleeper had to lie perfectly still, for with any movement the cover rolled off the bed. It took some getting used to, and one night was hardly enough. Finally, crossing into Belgium we joined the usual queue at the customs barrier. When our turn came we handed over our passports and the customs officer remarked, "Ah, English!" "Scots." answered Terry. The customs officer looked at us, and with a broad smile he stood up and performed the first step of the Highland Fling before waving us through - surely a fitting climax to our European tour.

In Dudley Avenue we were getting into financial straits, mainly due to the way school fees were rising, while the stipend remained static. Drawing near to Christmas, Mary had worried herself into taking to bed, but one morning when I opened the front door, there stood a large wicker hamper stuffed with all kinds of high-class groceries. No note, so I racked my brains but could get no clue, but that hamper was a life-saver. Years later I learned the truth. The mother of one of my elders had married a second time to a man who became an alcoholic, and was notorious in Leith for being thrown out of many pubs. Eventually he died, and his widow was very embarrassed, as she did not think any minister would agree to take the funeral. I heard about this and assured the widow I would gladly conduct the funeral. If it was a sin to drink too much, then she was sinned against. Everything went smoothly, and with many funerals to conduct I soon forgot all about this one, but the widow had a good job as a senior shop assistant to a top-class Edinburgh grocer.

In those days the word 'alcoholic' was not in general use. People just "drank themselves to death"; but the problem of alcohol abuse was growing, and two or three of us ministers hired a room in Bank Street

Kirkgate Church
The only example of an Italian Romanesque Church in Edinburgh.

for five evenings a week, and let it be known that anyone with a drink problem and wishful to get rid of the habit would be welcome to spend an evening with us. We soon had one or two regulars, and others turned up irregularly. It was less than a drop in the ocean, but there was no Alcoholics Anonymous, *faux de mieux* presumably we got one or two sent to us from the Infirmary. I spent an evening at Bank Street when I had the time, but the Church took over the work as part of the general social work that was being developed at Queen Street.

Casting around for gainful employment, my eye caught a newspaper advert seeking volunteers for the Cold Research Unit on Salisbury Plain. There would be no payment, but free transport, board and lodging was offered. I decided to volunteer. If nothing else was gained, at least it would be one less mouth to feed in Leith. They would try to give me the cold, but that was an acceptable risk. When I got there I found the Cold Research Unit consisted of a group of wooden huts left by American troops after the war. As usual with research work, the Government refused any help until they could prove they could cure the cold - which of course was what they were trying to do. The huts they got for nothing but there was no gas or electricity in the huts, and no central heating. By the time I arrived electricity had been installed but no heating. Each volunteer was supposed to be isolated. Meals

The Kirkgate Church - Phase I

were left at the door of the room, to be picked up by the "inmate". In the afternoon there were two hours free, during which the volunteer could take a walk or amuse himself in any other way he chose, provided he made no contact with any other volunteer. Walking sounded more attractive than it was, for the lanes on Salisbury Plain were sunk twenty to thirty feet below the surface of the plain so that no wide view was obtainable. In practice, three of us were housed together. One was a man demobbed from the Navy, who was studying for entrance to a teacher training college. I myself was working on books for another project, and the third man was a doctor on the staff who had dropped far behind with his paperwork and welcomed the chance to catch up. We got on very well together, each of us interested in what the other two were doing. The doctor said the search for money was a never-ending worry, and that the cold was caused not by a virus but by an army of viruses, so that a cure for the cold was not only the victory over one virus. The work would therefore continue for years - provided the needful money was forthcoming. I was injected without any success - that is, I did not catch cold. I began apologizing, but they brushed that aside, as a negative result was as informative as a positive one. I was then given a purple liquid to sniff, as they wanted to know how long it would take to work its way round to my mouth, and how much actually made the trip.

Home again, having completed the history of the congregation I turned my attention to local history on a wider scale. The 'Evening News' published articles from T.W. Jack and others, and I thought that I could contribute something at least as interesting and original as these articles. In the course of research for the congregation's history I had amassed a great deal of notes on related matters. I sent in an article, and it was accepted, but I had a lot to learn. A thousand words was acceptable; a little less was all right, but more than a thousand might still be accepted, but the sub-editor would simply cut off a bit from the end of what I'd written, even if that bit contained some fact that made sense of the rest of the article. Also the material must be original; failing that, rejection was inevitable. Again, however, if I hit on a subject never before explored, I could write two or three articles, to appear on successive weeks.

It usually took about twelve hours work to complete a thousand-word article, for pursuing the original was slow work. I was very fortunate in that the Edinburgh Room at the Central Library in George IV Bridge was then confined to a single attic room where the collection on local history was in its early days. My frequent visits there built up a confidential relationship with Miss Marie Balfour, the librarian in charge of the room, and I had the run of the place, which later became impossible with the extension of the collection and its removal to a larger room. One of the most valuable tools for a researcher was the eighteen folio manuscript volumes compiled by Charles B Boog Watson. He had a paper mill which provided him with enough to retire on in his mid forties, and he spent the rest of his life examining the Edinburgh Town Council minutes and extracting an amazing amount of information that he wrote down and indeed in beautifully clear handwriting. Over the years, hundreds of researchers in Edinburgh have relied heavily on these eighteen volumes.

Eventually I was sending in an article almost every month for two guineas a time. It was hard but fascinating work, and the fees were paying our electricity bills - until it came to an abrupt end when the Canadian, Roy Thomson, bought the 'Scotsman' and the 'Edinburgh Evening News'. In a ruthless drive to increase profits he cut the staff of the News and those left had increased workloads. He also refused to take any work from non-union contributors, which brought my journalistic career to a sudden end.

It was now that Mary decided to get a job. Nowadays, with a young married couple, that decision would be par for the course, but that decision would be made when the children were much younger. In 1953 Morag was thirteen and Donald eleven, and their mother was a minister's wife. Inevitably the congregation was divided between the traditionalists who were shocked, and the younger people who rather admired her courage. She had discovered that it was possible to return to the Civil Service after passing an exam. Before marriage she had been a shorthand typist, but that had been sixteen years ago. Now, failing the Civil Service, any job with a salary would do. She was soon working with the press office at 121 George Street, delivering reports and news items to various newspaper offices all over central Edinburgh. In less than a year she had passed the exam and was installed with the Telephone Exchange, and through the next twenty years she progressed from Great Stuart Street to the GPO and finally to West Port House, lamenting from time to time that had she returned earlier to work she could have progressed much higher up the scale than was possible at her age now. Her salary, however, made an immense difference at home.

By that time I must have acquired some reputation as a spokesman for Leith, for I had a phone call from the 'Evening News' asking if I'd be agreeable to meet Moray McLaren who was preparing a series of articles on Leith and would like me to correct any mistakes he might be making. We met in the North British Hotel for tea, and I found nothing amiss with his articles. Also about then I was approached by John Walter, a director of J.G. Thomson, wine merchants at 'The Vaults' in my parish, asking if I'd consider writing the history of the firm. This was not for publication, but was intended for an advertising brochure. I was thrilled. 'The Vaults' was the oldest building in Scotland still in commercial use after some six centuries of commercial occupation. Here in the old days, wine imported at the wine quay was transferred from the ship's hold about 100 yards to 'The Vaults', where it was auctioned. The canons of St Anthony came from the Preceptory by an underground passage to 'The Vaults', for their main income came from a tax on imported wine. At the turn of the seventeenth and eighteenth centuries the Thomson family had begun business at 'The Vaults', importing wine from Bordeaux, Cadiz and other ports on the Atlantic seaboard.

Mr. Walter had a number of family papers to put at my disposal, and I was soon deeply involved in this work, and was invited to lunch with the directors of the firm at their monthly lunch in the boardroom, when I reported progress to Mr. Walter. Sometimes, instead of the boardroom lunch Mr. Walter would invite Mary and me to join him at one or another of the top-class restaurants in the city - customers of the firm- where we always had a sumptuous meal, and conversation on the progress of the history. John Walter was a keen antiquarian, and in the Sherry Room at 'The Vaults' he had collected a small museum of mementoes of the wine trade. The other directors did not share his antiquarian enthusiasm, but were simply interested to hear what I could tell them about the firm's history.

The wine trade of Leith had been a going concern for centuries, and to glean what we could from Bordeaux, which had been trading with 'The Vaults' for generations, John Walter arranged for Mary and me to visit Bordeaux and inspect their records for the past two centuries or so. We arrived in Bordeaux and visited the wine firm there, only to discover that a fortnight previously they had had a disastrous fire, in which all their records had been lost. We did have other letters of introduction, however, to vineyards near the city, and also to another vineyard at Rheims, in champagne country, where we were well received and shown around, with a good dinner.

Back home I finished the history and received £100, which, added to the meals and hospitality both in Scotland and France, was a sizeable sum in those days. The word must have got around, for William Muir of Bond 9 asked me to write their history, but they had nothing but ledgers and accounts to offer me, so I had to turn them down. Another firm of Thomson, who made gin, also had to be refused for the same reason. You can't make bricks without straw.

The year after our trip abroad with Terry and Edith we hired a house in Ullapool for the summer holidays, and enjoyed ourselves each in our own way. For Donald, that meant fishing from beneath the pier, which he seemed to do all day and every day, although I never saw him catch anything. Every morning Mother went down to see the boats come in. Before transferring to Kinlochleven for sale, the fishermen went rapidly over the crans, pulling out mackerel and throwing them on the pier, where Mother picked up as many as she wanted. Mackerel then had the reputation of being the scavengers of the sea and could not be sold.

One dark night, sometime near midnight there was a knock at our door, and Edith and Terry appeared. They had been camping in Skye, but Edith had been badly savaged by swarms of midges. Terry had escaped but Edith was badly swollen and had to spend a day in bed. This ended their camping holidays. Then Mary, walking with Donald along a headrig of a field, stepped on a wasps' byke and was pursued by a swarm of wasps which lodged in her hair and took a deal of dislodging.

Being in a Gaelic-speaking area we decided to avoid the Church of Scotland. There were two services available - the Free Kirk and the Free Presbyterian. We tried both on successive Sundays. In the Free Church the service proceeded as we had anticipated, although we understood none of the language. When the sermon had continued for a little over twenty minutes a psalm was announced, for which we remained seated. After this we rose to our feet for what I thought was the benediction. But no, it was a prayer, after which the sermon continued for another twenty minutes. The only other place I came across this sermon in two halves, with a hymn at half-time, was in the Groote Kerke in Amsterdam. There were other unusual features in that Dutch church. As we approached the entrance we found a group of elders in the vestibule smoking cigars in preparation. Then when the offering was taken, an elder, dressed in black, approached me, sitting next to the aisle, with an offering bag, to which I contributed, upon which he switched another similar bag from behind his back, to which I contributed. He presented two other bags but I had to deny support for the fourth bag as I had run out of loose money.

There must have been some special appeal that day, but we have no room to criticise, for the Free Church in Ullapool had its own peculiarities, among which I found the oddest was the fact that while we sang four psalms, all of them were sung to the tune 'Coleshill'. The Free Presbyterian Kirk had its own odd features. The minister wore no gown, but a black jacket and a white stock (the predecessor of the clerical collar) so that he looked like his predecessor of the 1840s. This service enjoyed the leadership of two precentors. The first one took us through two psalms. Then just before the sermon, a second precentor

The Kirkgate Church - Phase I

came in from the door and gave us 'St Andrew', which also did for the concluding psalm. Apparently each precentor had his own tune.

It was, I think, the following year, 1955, that we took a house in the Isle of Whithorn, where we joined the Derby branch of the family - my brother Terry, his wife Edith and their children, Sheena and the twins Duncan and Gordon, eleven of us all told, and this holiday has left two imprints on my mind. The first is that Donald, who had thus far had no success in learning to swim, met a school friend of Morag's, whose people had a farm here. She dived into the sea and swam across the harbour with apparently no special effort. Mortified by this display from a mere girl, Donald must have thought "Anything she can do I can do better", and jumped in, and actually started to swim!

Then Eric Wilson, my cousin Annie's son, turned up with a car, and offered to drive us to Dumfries for the afternoon. He was an apprentice with John Brown the Clyde shipbuilders, and knew a good deal about cars and driving. On the way to Dumfries the engine emitted a faint whine, which gradually became more pronounced. On the way back to Whithorn the engine finally stopped, and Eric jumped out, looked under the bonnet and announced, "There's nae ile!" Not having a car of his own, Eric had hired a car from a garage in Stirling. We waited a long weary time while the garage sent us another car, apologising and explaining that an apprentice had been left to attend to the car that had been hired, and had forgotten to put in the oil.

Quite a different kind of work was wished on me when James Rennie, minister at Wardie, asked me to take his place on the board of the National Bible Society of Scotland. When I rather reluctantly agreed I little thought that this was the start of over thirty years on that Board, in the course of which I would fill every unpaid position in the Society. The Board I joined consisted of 120 members from branches all over Scotland, meeting monthly in Glasgow and Edinburgh alternately. We met in a building at 5 St Andrew Square, Edinburgh which had been given to the Society halfway through the nineteenth century, but that huge board was unwieldy, and as every matter had to be discussed and voted on it worked very slowly. After some years the Board was reduced to nineteen members. This made for much greater efficiency, and the entire outlook and method of working rapidly changed after the formation of the United Bible Societies in 1947. From that date the National Bible Society of Scotland became one of a large number of national bible societies all over the world, who pooled their financial resources to meet any emergencies, like earthquake, war, flood, persecution, etc., where bible societies could be of help. Poorer societies drew from the pool and richer societies contributed to the general need.

Everything Mixed with Mercy

Mary and I attended an international conference of bible societies at Woodschoten in Holland. That was the first of several such get-togethers through which we learned much about the work worldwide. The Scottish society over the years became stronger and more influential *vis-à-vis* the other societies. But the onset of inflation forced us to think hard about our future. We were reluctant to quit our traditional headquarters, but eventually we bought the former Wester Coates Church and employed an architect to convert it into premises suitable for modern office and shop requirements. The architect found this a thrilling assignment, and to pay for it we sold the St Andrew Square premises, for which we received not far short of £1,000,000. I was in charge as chairman at this time, and we invited the Queen to open the new premises. This she agreed to do, but on the day before the event she went down with 'flu', and delegated Princess Anne to stand in for her. I was surprised to find the Princess much smaller than I had anticipated, but we were all greatly impressed by her knowledge of the Society's work. She asked many questions and made some shrewd comments. As she had had only twenty-four hours' notice she must have put in some considerable work over the assignment.

In 1951 Sis (my sister Isobel, who hated my calling her Sis, but a lifetime habit is apt to cling) married Nigel Johnstone. After the war she had trained at St Colm's to be a Church Sister (in modern language a Deaconess). She wore a grey uniform which she heartily disliked, and was not paid any salary. All they received was a sum of money in lieu of rent, and they found their own lodgings. She worked in Dundee and Aberdeen slums, and it was quite a Spartan life. Her meeting with Nigel came about at a gathering in the old Little Theatre in the Pleasance, and Sis was taking a collection for a good cause. Nigel contributed half a crown, which lay in the collection plate shining amidst all the pennies and threepenny bits. Sis supposed this must have been a mistake, and said so to Nigel, who assured her that he meant it. Anything less romantic would be hard to imagine, but their friendship took off from that night, and after their marriage Nigel was ordained and inducted to Canisbay, on the north coast. It was a large and sparsely populated area, stretching ten miles in all directions, so as well as the parish church Nigel had four preaching stations which he visited in turn, week by week. The manse was a large house with no modern conveniences and stood as part of a steading with a glebe of six acres, which Nigel rented to a local farmer. When we visited there, the beadle told me that until the mid-twenties the minister had a household staff of five - housekeeper, cook, scullerymaid, gardener and coachman; but there was no staff now.

The church was a pre-Reformation building, the walls were eight

The Kirkgate Church - Phase 1

feet thick, and the pulpit stood in the middle of one of the long walls opposite a small transept. At the east end, a narrow staircase was built into the thickness of the wall, and this led to the vestry which, once the door was shut, was completely sound-proof. In that vestry Nigel on a Sunday morning could not hear the bell toll, and depended on the beadle telling him when to come and start the service.

Now the Queen Mother came north every summer to the Castle of Mey, and attended Canisbay Church quite regularly during her stay. When we were on holiday at Canisbay we went to the morning service. We arrived in good time, and a while after we were seated, the royal party arrived and took their seats in the pew in front of us, which had traditionally been the laird's pew directly facing the pulpit. Then nothing happened, and we were a little uneasy. We were accustomed to see royal occasions when everything took place punctually. But the Queen Mother had become accustomed to the way things happened here, and she liked to feel part of the congregation in a part of the country where time was not all that important.

Each Sunday morning a bus toured the parish, picking up those who lived miles away but preferred attending the parish church to the local preaching in a little hut. And when it was known that the Queen Mother would likely be attending, a great many wanted the bus, who did not use it every week. When the bus reached the church the service went ahead. It was twenty minutes beyond the normal starting time, but no one was worried. On another occasion, I was coming north by train. We left Georgemas junction and started on the final lap into Thurso, but the train suddenly stopped and went into reverse to pick up a regular who was late. The engine driver had spotted him crossing a field and kindly waited for him. On this occasion when the Offering was announced and the plate came round I noticed from the seat behind her, that the Queen Mother had no money, so she jogged her purse bearer, who produced the needful. During her annual stay she always invited my sister to tea, and Sis always enjoyed the garden at the Castle, even more than the tea.

When we thought of sending postcards home to the family, I went to the village shop, which also acted as a post office. I asked for the postcards, and the wifie behind the counter said, oh yes, she had postcards, and produced a bundle, each and all of which were pre-1914 cards, which today, in any of the big cities would sell for sizeable sums.

Nigel promised to take us over to Stroma, if possible. Crossing the narrow strait from the mainland to the island depended very much on the weather. Even at the best times the tide race on the Pentland Firth was surprisingly strong, and we had to wait a fortnight before the venture by a small boat was possible. Stroma was almost deserted,

Laying a flagstone path at Canisbay, where my sister Isobel's husband Nigel Johnstone was the minister, 1953

and we saw only one family still living there. There was little to do on the island, but some satisfaction in having been across there, as a few years later it became a desert island. We also visited John o'Groats House which had the reputation of being the northernmost point on the Scottish mainland. It is the northernmost house, indeed, but the northmost land is at Dunnet Head, a few miles west of John o'Groats House.

For some years I had been going for violin lessons to the Synod Hall, where little Miss Gavine was a well-known teacher. I was working on the Mozart Violin Sonatas, with an occasional foray into the Beethoven sonatas, when one day she said, "Mr. Marshall, you're wasting your time and your money. You now have the bulk of the main violin classical repertoire, and you can play it after a fashion. But you're never going to get any better, because you're not able to practise more than you're doing. You're a minister; you have a job which takes up most of your time. Your hobby is violin-playing, but there is an immense gap between the amateur and the professional. You can never practise for eight hours a day. Take my advice and don't come back here. And I wish you all success and happiness in your ministry."

Well, that was that. For some time I had felt it would come to this sooner or later. From then I realised my limitations, and just enjoyed playing in my own time in my own way. Not long after, however, I got a frozen shoulder which cleared up after some weeks, but two years later it returned - my right shoulder; and while the pain eventually

The Kirkgate Church - Phase 1

subsided I found I could not lift my bowing arm for more than about a minute and a half. Still, I realised I was lucky, for at about the same time the news came that Lionel Tertis, acknowledged as the greatest viola-player in the world, had got a frozen shoulder, which deprived him of his career, and all that that must have meant to him.

I haven't played the violin since then, but I still have the violin, and piles of music. Maybe I ought to pass all that to someone who could make use of it, but I can't bring myself to do that. I get such a thrill from hearing the violin that I could never get, were it not for the feeling that I'm playing it myself. All the years of practice have left me with something I could never have acquired in any other way.[1]

---

[1] At Christmas time 2002 James gave his violin to his 13-year-old great-granddaughter Katie who was able to play some Scottish fiddle music to the delight of the family gathering on Easter Day 2003.

8
The Kirkgate Church - Phase 2.

The closing of the two St John's churches not only did our dramatic club a very good turn but also presented the Kirkgate Church with a quite unexpected opportunity. Here, I must introduce John Turnbull to this narrative. John had been a navigator with the R.A.F. and was a war hero, having collected two D.S.Os and two D.F.Cs. After his return from the war he had been treasurer for the congregation. He was a chartered accountant, was a keen gardener, and was treasurer to the Royal Caledonian Horticultural Society. We got on pretty well together. My only gripe with him was that he never paid any tradesmen's accounts until just before the annual congregational meeting. This he did, so that the congregational accounts might benefit from more bank interest, the more money that was kept in the church's accounts. The result of this practice was that tradesmen dunned for payment, and somehow or other I paid, and John squared with me in early March. At the same time he could always quote me the exact amount we owed any tradesman to the last halfpenny.

The closure of the St John's churches was unexpected because, while their representatives in meetings with various Presbytery committees and Assembly committees had firmly refused any kind of union, so that they were finally closed by order of the Presbytery, I knew for a fact that they got on very well with each other, and after the closure, office-bearers in both congregations said to me they would have been quite happy to unite, but not at the diktat of a committee from outside of Leith, who knew little or nothing of the local circumstances.

Well, having overplayed their hand and lost, they could do nothing about the moveable assets of the two churches, which were moved to Oxgangs where a new Church Extension charge was created. St John's West Church now had a manse to dispose of. The St John's East minister had owned his own house, being a wealthy man, but St John's West were open to receive offers for their manse. This property was at 4 Claremont Park, and I eyed it and thought about it. Dudley Avenue was certainly too small for use as a manse, but in 1955 a bigger house would be beyond the means of the Kirkgate congregation. I spoke to John Turnbull about it, and he was interested, and asked if I was really prepared to move into it, if that became possible. I assured him I was. Of course I had not been inside the house, but the garden was in a fearful state of rank grass and matted weeds. For the past thirty years it had been neglected. The minister, Mr Murchison, was a Gaelic-speaking Canadian, who conducted Gaelic services in Edinburgh as

The Kirkgate Church - Phase 2

well as his services in Leith. But he had a bad heart and had neglected the garden. We asked the St John's West people what they had in mind as a purchase price for their manse, and they said they'd be satisfied to receive whatever we got for the sale of 8 Dudley Avenue. John and I thought that was a wonderful bargain, but when the congregation heard of our plan they couldn't believe it. Why should I want to move from the relative neatness and tidiness of Dudley Avenue to the rampant half-acre of Claremont Park? I said we were cramped where we were, and I'd always been accustomed to a larger garden. So they, as it were, shrugged their shoulders, knowing that the presbytery would have to agree. As expected, the presbytery sent a committee to interview me, asking if I realised what I was taking on. I said yes, I knew what I was taking on, so the committee withdrew reluctantly.

Dudley Avenue sold for £2000, which sum we passed to the St John's people, and Claremont Park was ours. No one could deny it was a bargain, and the value of the property would increase as it was improved. The presbytery was still not satisfied, and another committee under Charlie Smith the presbytery clerk interviewed me, apparently wondering whether I was in my right mind. I assured them they need have no worry, and so they left. It turned out a far greater bargain than anyone at that time would have thought possible, as it sold in 1991 for £175,000. But that was after many years of hard graft - which I greatly enjoyed.

Before entering the manse I got the corporation to cut the grass, as it was obviously too massive a growth for any hand mower. The mower they sent could not cope, so a bigger one was brought in. It also was not up to the job, so a third, much heavier machine finally managed to pare down the surface so that I could go to work with a motor mower. There was some good stuff in the garden - apple trees dating from the 1914 war, a magnificent lime tree on the lawn, which I think was there from the time the house was built, as it featured in the O.S. map in the mid-nineteenth century and quite a small forest of raspberry canes. Originally the group of Georgian houses at that part of Claremont Park each stood in half an acre of ground, and had a summer-house as well as a lime tree. In the late nineteenth century however, these gardens were each reduced to one third of an acre to make room for Blackie Road, which was not made until many years later, Blackie being the owner of a market garden in this area.

4 Claremont Park had one more distinguishing feature, for it appears to have been the first manse built by the Free Church after that denomination came into existence at the Disruption in 1843. A great deal has been written about the fortunes of the Free Church, especially in its early years. Ground for building churches was hard to get in

parishes where lairds and heritors were opposed to the new church, and where sites were acquired, churches were built as soon as possible - plain, barn-like buildings, as everything had to be paid for from voluntary contributions. In these circumstances, no manses were built. Ministers found lodgings for themselves and were given a sum to pay rent. The minister of St John's Free Church had lodgings in Charlotte Street, but a manse was proposed for him. Building began in 1850 and the manse was occupied in 1851.

Again in the circumstances of the Free Church at that time, we in the twenty-first century might well ask, 'Why build a twelve-roomed house?' The answer is simply that nothing less was then regarded as fit and proper for a minister. Even in the 1920s when North Leith Parish was looking for a new manse the presbytery was consulted as to the minimum standard to be sought for a suitable house, and the answer was that among other things there must be six bedrooms, as a minister had to extend hospitality to visiting ministers on the occasion of a sacramental sabbath. So 4 Claremont Park was built, but only the essential features were included. A wine cellar with stone shelves was built under the staircase, but no painter was employed to paint and paper the walls and ceilings. Inessentials could wait until money was available, but it was almost another thirty years before tiles were laid on the hall floor. As with many old houses there were mysterious features. The original coach-house was there but no recognisable stable. Four very substantial iron rings, two on each gable-end at about five and fifteen feet above ground have baffled everyone asked for an explanation.

The road that became Claremont Park was the old stage-coach route from Edinburgh to London. It continued from Seafield to Portobello - a dangerous stretch, for that area was all marsh, and a line of white posts marked the only viable route for the stage-coach. When we arrived at No 4, the road had been laid with granite setts at the start of the century, and trams ran to Seafield and Portobello as the marsh had been drained with the coming of the first railway in Scotland, running from Niddrie to the docks carrying coal for export. Shortly after we arrived, trams were superseded by buses, and the granite setts were removed by the lorryload. Seeing this good material apparently going to waste I asked the lorrymen where they were taking the setts, and they said they were dumping them, so I asked them to dump a load in my garden. This they did. I wanted the setts to edge the paths, and I put them down at once and found that one load was not enough; so next day I asked for another load, but the men said I'd have to pay this time, as the free issue yesterday had been an oversight.

When we moved to St Andrews in 1990, I took the opportunity to

The Kirkgate Church - Phase 2

move these setts to Morag's garden in Fife, where I used them to edge vegetable plots.

Tom Cochrane, our Session Clerk, worked for MacLaggan and Cumming the printers, and they wanted to clear out a large number of lithographic stones. These looked like convenient paving for the garden paths, and I took a good number of them, only to discover that in wet weather they made very treacherous walkways as they became very slippery.

A wide area between the back of the house and the lawn was gravelled and proved a hotbed for weeds. Again I found men lifting Caithness flagstones from the Claremont Park pavement. I knew these are used as fences in Caithness, and that they were ideal for walking surfaces. I bought enough of them to cover the gravel, which proved one of the best things I ever did in the garden, but I could never have afforded this improvement at today's sky-high prices for Caithness flags.

I pointed out to the office-bearers that this new manse they had reluctantly allowed me to occupy could be a reliable source of income if we held a garden party there. This they agreed and gave their help to organise a garden party annually on the first Saturday in June, and over the years this brought in from seven to eight hundred pounds a year. And the weather, while mixed, was never bad enough to cancel the event.

The year 1950 was significant for the family, for it was then that Morag acquired a pen-friend in Francine Goldstein, and both girls kept the correspondence going, bringing the two families together for the next two generations. The Goldsteins lived in Hesdin , the second city of the Pas-de-Calais, where Arras is the county town.

Seventeen years after the end of the war Morag married David Wood, and it had taken Edinburgh that length of time to build Leith Town Hall. The wedding was the first such reception to be held there, and it was highly successful, and of happy memory, as the rent then was surprisingly low, *pour encourager les autres*. Two weeks later the rent for such an occasion was trebled. They went to live in Freuchie, and two years later Mary and I went on holiday to Hesdin, marking our silver wedding, and learning a great deal about the French.

Henri Goldstein was an important man in Hesdin - recognized as a city, although the population was merely 3600. It was an agricultural market town, and as many of the inhabitants also had gardens and smallholdings in the surrounding country there was no recognized division between country and town, as in Scotland. M. Goldstein was deputy mayor, and also the chief clarinetist in the town band, and was a member of almost every committee in the town. He owned a shop

Everything Mixed with Mercy

Mary sporting the 'New Look'. Papa just a little older than his raincoat, meeting Uncle Bob and Aunt Mary at the Waverley Station, with Mother in 1950

where he made and sold furniture, and here we had a warm welcome and enjoyed the French style of living. Workmen started at seven in the morning, and there was a break at 8.30 for *petit déjeuner* - coffee and bread. Croissants were luxury items for visitors like us. The baker's shop showed one tray of croissants and dozens of varieties of bread. The popular flutes were delicious, eaten fresh in the morning, but tough and tasteless by evening. At one o'clock the shop was closed for *déjeuner* and a two-hour siesta., after which business was resumed until six o'clock, following which dinner was served at any time, until as late as nine p.m. in some households.

When the shop closed at one o'clock we sat down to *déjeuner* in the same house, so customers hardly paid attention to the closure, but simply knocked at the shop door till M. Goldstein rose to attend to them. As there were usually two or three such interruptions, the meal became much extended, occupying much of the siesta time. But the meals here were really excellent, as they were wherever we visited in France. The art of housekeeping is taken seriously in France. Cooking has a high priority, and elegance in its presentation is as important as the food itself. Dining with a young married couple, the wife placed on the table an immense ashet with a salad, in which, around a central mound of grated carrot, a great variety of vegetables was set out separately. Mary was invited to help herself, but was very reluctant to destroy the picture the salad made. Two glasses were usually set out -

The Kirkgate Church - Phase 2

one for wine, the other for water. Tap water was undrinkable, so all the table water was bottled.

The great annual, autumn fair took place on our first weekend. Lasting four days, it is centuries old, and began with a torchlight procession on the Friday evening about ten o'clock. The town band came first, followed by the fire brigade, and then all and sundry, waving torches, setting off fireworks, and making a terrific din. The presence of the fire brigade, which we thought was a precaution against fire amid so many torches, in fact was there because it was the only body in town possessing a uniform. The town band wore peaked caps, but that was the extent of their uniform, unless the instruments were thought to dress the band with some distinction. But the fire brigade all had beautiful, highly polished brass helmets and blue tunics. The fire brigade were well to the fore during the next four days, as they paraded on every possible occasion, and sometimes on a quite inappropriate occasion, as on Sunday morning, when they turned up as usual in their brass helmets at church. We then discovered that the helmet and tunic completed the uniform. Apart from these two necessaries every man pleased himself. One man in the front row had on the helmet and tunic, an old pair of breeks, no socks, and his feet in a huge pair of sandals, through which his corny feet were plainly visible. And he was typical of the others.

The *Ducasse*, normally a sort of harvest festival, was this year devoted to celebrating the twentieth anniversary of the Liberation from German occupation. When you have lived in an occupied country, the liberation is certainly something to celebrate. Deputations from many surrounding towns gathered at the church for the celebratory service, and the town band, which all through the torchlight procession had played one tune with many variations, struck up again as they led the parade away from the church -the same tune, with yet another variation. No one could deny that the clarinetist, M. Goldstein, doubling as bandmaster, was ingenious and adaptable with such music as he had.

Celebrating our silver wedding, we invited several friends to dinner. Eighteen or twenty of us sat down at tables normally used for ten. You might wonder how we could entertain a set of French people, when only some of us could speak French and only two of them knew any English. Not to worry! The French are splendid company, and without the aid of any record-player, piano, or any kind of musical instrument, without any attempt to pair off stable companions, the din was so great that we half expected to be summoned for disturbing the peace. There are strong similarities between the French and the Scots. We admire the same virtues and abhor the same vices; we have the same sense of humour, so can follow one another's thoughts with ease. So language difficulties melt away as we enjoy each other's company.

We became closely acquainted with another type of Frenchman in Michel Garcin, who came to Scotland to improve his English, as he was hoping to enter the diplomatic service. His parents were quite wealthy, and he came to stay with us at Claremont Park for some weeks. He was thrilled to be allowed to enter the kitchen, where he struck up a warm friendship with Granny. (My parents had come to live with us as Dad had become completely deaf, and almost totally blind. Mother, with unfailing energy, took over the housekeeping as Mary was at work.) Michel had never been allowed into the kitchen at home and was fascinated to watch Mother at work. She offered him stewed rhubarb, which he had never tasted before, and he became very fond of it. His English seemed excellent to us, but he was despondent. He was due to sit the vital entrance exam for the diplomatic service, but only a few entrants would be passed - just as many as were needed to fill existing vacancies.

He invited us to visit his parents in Paris, and we agreed to this as part of our summer holiday. We arrived in Paris in the middle of the day, and spent the afternoon looking up some other acquaintances, and having a look at the new United Nations building. When we decided to move on to our destination it was after six o'clock, and we reached the *Gare St Lazare* about a quarter to seven. Now we had forgotten that with the Paris offices closing later than in Britain, this was the peak of the evening rush hour - about an hour later than in Britain. The Paris rush hour is notorious all over the world. It compares with the Japanese railways, where passengers are packed in until the doors can hardly be shut. The train journey to *Bois Colombes* was very fast, taking barely ten minutes for the four miles. The station was a sea of moving people, streaming towards the trains. I got tickets, and soon we were in the proper stream - not at all like a Scottish queue. We reached the platform before the train had arrived. The crowd increased by the minute until the platform itself could hold no more, when the train moved in, and we all sprang aboard. More and more and more people came on board until I suddenly found I was as securely wedged in as though I had been tied hand and foot. I was standing but could neither move nor breathe. Suddenly I had an attack of claustrophobia, always associated in my mind with an epileptic fit. I just had to get off and draw at least one breath of fresh air. I had the very deuce of a job getting off that train, and after I got out at least six more people forced their way on board. Then the train started, with the doors still open, and I was left on the platform with no luggage and no tickets. A man who had seen me get off said to me that that often happened. '*Vous devez monter un fourgon*' he said - ('You should get on a lorry'). I didn't

The Kirkgate Church - Phase 2

stop to ask where I could get a lorry. All I knew was that I was going to walk to the Garcin's house. I had already looked it up on a map and set out confidently. After about two hours smart walking through Paris I arrived at the address, and found it to be an apartment block, but the concierge assured me there was no one there of the name Garcin, although, he said, letters often came here addressed to people of that name. He advised me to go to the police. I went to police headquarters, which were not far away. I didn't see *Maigret*, but got a very efficient gendarme to listen to my story. I worried now, because I didn't know what Donald and his mother were now doing. I was looking for *Avenue Jean Jaures*. (It should have been *Rue Jean Jaures*, but we'll let that pass for the moment.) As soon as the gendarme heard me ask for *Bois Colombes*, he started laughing. 'This is Paris.' he cried. 'I know.' I shouted. 'Where's *Bois Colombes?*' 'It's not here', he answered, 'This is Paris.' After going round in circles like this for some time he finally explained that *Bois Colombes* was several miles away. Apparently there were at least six *Avenues* and *Rues Jean Jaures* in Paris, and I had got the wrong one, having moved steadily away from the one I wanted. Eventually I did arrive, after going back to *Gare St Lazare* and taking a train, I arrived about half past ten, when they were thinking of fitting out an expedition to look for me.

We had V.I.P. treatment for those three days in Paris. Mme Garcin, who taught maths in a local school, told me she had first met her husband when they were both refugees on the main road south from Paris when the Germans occupied the country. Since then they had risen as it were from nothing, and M. Garcin was now the Paris manager of Olivetti. Next day we had a chauffeur-driven car to take us to Versailles, and in the evening we took a fabulous trip with the Garcins on the Seine on one of the famous *Bateaux-Mouches*. These are huge barge-like boats which cruise up and down the river after dark, providing a marvellous view of the lights of the city, while a splendid dinner is served. We ended that night in *Montmartre*, surrounded by artists painting and presumably hoping to look like Modigliani, Picasso or Toulouse-Lautrec.

In the morning Michel and I did a tour of the Sorbonne University of Paris; and then I spent some hours at the *bouquinistes* - the bookstalls on the bank of the Seine. There are hundreds of these stalls, which are to be found both open and closed at any hour of the day. None of the stallholders earns a living there. It is a spare time occupation, or a sideline. They are either booklovers, or students, or retired from their proper job, or they are disabled. Many reasons bring men into this line.

In Leith I was becoming involved in a new line of country. In the course of hunting up material for various articles I had asked Tom Brown, the minister of South Leith, for permission to read some Kirk Session minutes of South Leith Parish. These ought to have been lodged with the Scottish Record Office in obedience to an order from the General Assembly, but Tom Brown kept all his church records - about 500 items - locked in a huge cupboard in the church halls in Duke Street. He said he intended writing a history of the congregation whenever he had time, which I knew would never come about, as he was on many committees, attended many meetings, and was an assiduous pastoral visitor in his congregation. For all this devoted work he was granted a D.D. degree, but he died two days before it could be conferred by Glasgow University. Latterly he had given way and allowed me complete freedom with the records.

Reading these records I saw towards the end of the seventeenth century a notice of an irregular marriage. In Scotland it was never necessary for a minister to be present at a marriage. If a man and a woman declared before witnesses that they took each other as husband and wife, that constituted a marriage, and it was perfectly legal and binding, if it could be proved. And there was the rub, and the Kirk was strongly against these irregular marriages. Usually there was no record made of an irregular marriage, so nothing could be proved. The religious feuds of the seventeenth century resulted in a large number of irregular or clandestine marriages. As the Church swung from Presbyterian to Episcopal government, and back to presbyterianism again in the late years of the century, many ministers refused to swing with the change in Church government, and so were 'outed', and any marriages they conducted were irregular. A regular marriage was one conducted by the parish minister. All other forms were clandestine. An act of the Scottish Parliament in 1661 tried to end irregular marriages, but it was ignored. In 1698 a second act was passed, with severer penalties, and it was at this point that these irregular marriages began to be noted in the South Leith minutes. If a girl married a man in a clandestine way, without any written record of it, the man might later deny the marriage, and the girl could not prove it. If the man was a soldier or sailor, and was killed in action or drowned, the widow was not informed, and she could not claim any widow's benefit from the kirk session. More usually, when a child was born, the couple would confess their marriage and ask for baptism for the child, and this is how the facts appeared in the kirk session minutes. They would then have to pay a fine, and then the usual fees for marriage and baptism, the fine going into the poor box.

With the change from Episcopal to Presbyterian government in the Church in 1689, ministers who refused to change were deprived of their stipends and manses, and were then unemployed. Also, most of these

The Kirkgate Church - Phase 2

'outed' ministers were Jacobites, and as often as not their congregations still supported them and got them to officiate at marriages, for which service, in their desperate financial state, they were glad to receive the fees. But these marriages were irregular; and when patronage was reintroduced in 1712 the number of irregular marriages doubled. Under patronage the laird could fill a vacancy in the parish where he was patron without consulting the congregation, so many people sought marriage by someone other than the parish minister.

If no other minister was available, there were other ways to be married. In the parish of Falkland in Fife a local girl told the kirk session of her marriage to a soldier. He had assured her he would find a minister to marry them, but when she arrived for the wedding she found that not only was there no church, but the 'minister' was a drummer in the regiment. She demurred and hung back, but the man said this was quite all right, and usual in the Army.

Soldiers and sailors seeking irregular marriages were not men of evil intention. The marriage of men in the armed forces was strongly discouraged by the authorities. Men could not be forbidden to marry, but officers did everything in their power to put obstacles in the way. The country never had the resources to pay soldiers and pay was usually far in arrears, and no pensions were paid either for disability or long service. No government could do anything to provide for the widows and children of men killed on active service. So the men were encouraged to visit brothels, but never to marry.

In Dysart, as late as 1780, a local girl was reputedly married to a soldier, who, as it turned out, was not her husband at all, although they had been living together for over a year. The man's commanding officer had refused to give him a certificate of bachelorhood, without which no minister would agree to marry them, either regularly or irregularly.

All this, and much more emerged as I continued through the South Leith records, and news of what I was doing gradually leaked out, and Rudolf Ehrlich, the successor to Jack Prendergast in Junction Road Church, urged me to get in touch with the Scottish Record Society to see if they would be interested in publishing the results of my efforts. I did so, they indicated their strong interest, so in 1968 a 'Calendar of Irregular Marriages in the South Leith Records, 1697-1818' was published as Vol 95 of their records.

Our children at school were expected just to get on with it, with both their parents fully occupied in a variety of ways, we gave no assistance to them with homework. According to reports Donald did well at English, but always there appeared as an appendix 'Could do better', which prevented boasting. But on one occasion the teacher added

Everything Mixed with Mercy

'but I must admit he's very good company.' On reading this I had to point out to him that I wasn't paying out all the money on fees for him to learn how to be good company. There were some other things to be learned. Morag just seems to have enjoyed school, with exams a minor consideration. With a quick, receptive mind she did most of her swotting on the eve of exams, but she was brought up with a jerk when she failed Lower Latin, and realised she wouldn't get to university without a Higher pass. But she was not to be easily defeated. She asked her Latin teacher if she would be allowed to sit Higher Latin next year, and was firmly told that would be impossible without having a pass at Lower level. Thinking over any remaining options, she remembered the Headmistress had taught classics before becoming headmistress. She sought an interview, and put her case to the Headmistress, who was gratified at this enthusiasm for Latin, and granted permission to try for Higher Latin. This time Morag worked, and passed! Donald was rather disgruntled. He also passed his exams, but only after long, grinding preparation.

Mary had a friend from Applecross, whose sister was married to a Norwegian pastor. We had been asked several times to pay a visit to Norway, as the Scottish girl was yearning for some Scottish company. Morag had also had an *au pair* girl from Norway, Eldbjorg Vik, who strongly urged us to visit her people, so we finally took the plunge.

With Isabella, Mary and Morag, and Francione and Nicole Goldstein, each sporting a winning ticket from the recent flower show!

The Kirkgate Church - Phase 2

We had no knowledge of Norway and knew no word of the language. When I tried to get a Norwegian dictionary I found there were two languages over there. One was official, but the other was universally used colloquially.

We sailed from Hull to Bergen. Waiting for the ferry at Hull, I got into conversation with a local man whose passion was growing leeks. I had met people with various odd hobbies, but this was new to me. He insisted that that's what gardening was all about in his part of the world, but I had to cut the conversation short, to go for the ferry. The crossing was uneventful, but as we sat in the car waiting to drive on to Norwegian soil I reminded Mary this was her first time driving on the wrong side of the road. She said that would be all right, as she would just follow the car in front of us, which would serve as our introduction to this strange system. It seemed a foolproof plan, and we set off tailing the man in front, but whether he had spotted us and decided to shake us off, we couldn't know, but he drove all round the docks, stopping nowhere, then suddenly he shot through the dock gates up a brae into the town and disappeared. We were now thrown back on feminine ingenuity. In a move worthy of her daughter, Mary spotted a filling station and drove on to the forecourt. To our relief the man understood a little English - enough to follow Mary's explanation that we had newly arrived and would like to park here while we had lunch. With some reluctance he agreed, and we walked along the street about a hundred yards and found a restaurant. We sat down and a waitress approached us. 'You are English?' she asked. 'Scots,' we answered, 'but we understand English.' We had booked to stay in a university flat, and the waitress directed us.

Next morning we were confronted with the Norwegian breakfast. Innumerable cold meats, cereals, eggs, coffee. Serve yourself. It being Sunday we attended church, where, of course, we expected to understand nothing. To our surprise, a lady seated behind us leaned forward and asked if we were from Scotland - which was even better than the waitress on the day before. She explained all the service as it proceeded, and after the Benediction we talked. When she found that we were not only Scottish, but lived in Leith she became quite excited. Her husband had for years been the pastor at the Lutheran Church in North Junction Street. That little church had been erected in the mid-nineteenth century to serve the numerous Scandinavian sailors then passing through Leith. These seamen formed a significant element in the population of the port, and Leith Technical College offered classes in Norwegian - the only place in Scotland where this facility was on offer. Between the wars the Scandinavian trade with Leith gradually diminished, and merchant shipping generally was in slow decline. The

Everything Mixed with Mercy

Lutheran Church had finally been closed just about a year before our visit to Bergen.

We visited a most impressive maritime museum, where a great deal of money must have been spent. Numerous ship models were on display, and we looked in on classes being run on seamanship and maritime fishing. One more oddity we noticed in Bergen. The weather was brilliant and the sky cloudless, but everyone appeared to be carrying an umbrella. In the next few days we discovered why. When it rains it pours. The rain may not last long, but ten minutes in that sort of downpour will soak anything exposed to it.

We had clear directions to Eldbjorg Vik's village, and the run there was pleasant and easy, except for our confronting a company of soldiers on a very narrow road cut into a cliff face. This was a test for Mary's nerve, but the soldiers obligingly broke up and sidled along the cliff wall while we passed them at a respectable walking pace. As we approached the village we were aiming for, I realised that while we had been directed to the village, we had still to find the farm. No problem, I thought: in the village everyone will know the Viks. We stopped at a filling station on the outskirts, and asked for the Viks. The man stared blankly, then broke into a smile as he realised we were strangers. 'Everyone here is Vik.' Shades of old Scotland!

We explained that Mr. Vik was a fruit farmer, and also an inspector of crops. This was enough, and we had no more trouble. It was the middle of the apple harvest and every available person was picking fruit. We were welcomed and shown to a wooden house a few yards from the main house. The Viks had been farming here since the seventeenth century, and we would be occupying what might be called the Dower House, where the older generation of the family lived when retired from work. This house was built entirely of timber. It was roomy, comfortable, and in the meantime unoccupied. A most interesting dwelling, as not only the walls and roof, but all the furnishings were also timber.

We had a cup of tea, and it was made plain to us that we would not eat until the day's work was done. We understood this from farming practice in Scotland, so I offered to lend a hand and was provided with a ladder and a pail. The fruit was carefully hand-picked, and any that fell to the ground had to be ignored. The ground was grass, and I could not see any harm come to an apple falling. There was a fair number of windfalls and others on the ground, but they were not sold along with the perfect, top-class, hand-picked fruit.

There was a gallery in the village devoted to the work of the local sculptor - Vik, of course, of national repute, and very much the local hero.

The Kirkgate Church - Phase 2

After two or three days with the Viks we set off for the Fagerheims' place at Tonstad. It was a long drive, and we aimed to spend the night at Stavanger. Unfortunately we missed a turning and passed through a tunnel for which we had to pay a toll. It was several miles further on before we realised we were not on the right road, but it was impossible to make a U-turn on this fast road for about another twenty miles, and when we did manage the reverse run we had to pay toll again to get through the tunnel. All this added not only mileage but also time to our journey. Mary announced she had had enough for one day, and when we reached Stavanger she was stopping at the first hotel we saw, whether it looked like bed -and- breakfast, or five-star. We stopped at a modest hotel entrance on the waterfront. We registered, took in our bags, and found the place quite crowded with naval officers. We then discovered that the entrance we had used was in fact the back door, and the main entrance - impressive and five-starish, was on a street parallel with the one we had parked in. I also discovered, on discreet enquiry that, as I had jaloused, these naval types were here at the Government's expense.

Next morning we set out for Tonstad. We reached there in the afternoon, and, directed to the Fagerheims' house, we found a large man in the front garden, swinging his arms around, and in each hand he held a large polished brass ball of considerable weight, as I tested for myself. This was the Rev Fagerheim (His first name escapes me now.) and we were soon on warm friendly terms with him. His wife, Daisy, taught English at the village school, which served a large catchment area, and she was not yet home, but she appeared after about half an hour. I asked Mr Fagerheim what the garden exercises were all about, and he said that at this time of year (late September) he had to get fit for winter skiing. When I suggested he didn't ski with his arms, he assured me that the skier must be fit in every limb and every muscle. Again, when I suggested the minister would not of necessity have to ski very much, he pointed out that this house was at one end of a large parish. The far end was twenty-five miles away, and a large gang of forestry workers lived there.

I was intrigued by Fagerheim's excellent command of English, and learned that during the last war, and before he had become a minister, he had been sent with a party to Scotland to teach the Scots how to ski. Skiing in Norway has nothing to do with ski slopes and funicular railways. Skiing was all cross-country, and a fit man could cover seventy miles a day on skis. It was during this Scottish interlude that he met Daisy, his future wife. After Scotland, the Norwegian skiers were sent north to the country around Murmansk, and from there they made their way south through Russia and Eastern Europe. When the snow came he was still able to visit the forestry workers at the far end of the parish and get home again in a day - fifty miles.

The Church here was the Lutheran Evangelical Church, which operated under a form of Episcopacy. Fagerheim's bishop had only been appointed to the bishopric a few years ago, and before that he had been parish minister in an adjacent parish to Tonstad, so our Mr Fagerheim was not prepared to take any nonsense from the bishop. And thereby, as the phrase goes, hangs a tale.

The forestry workers at the far end of the parish asked the minister for permission to build themselves a church. They were too far from the parish church to attend there more than occasionally. The work would not cost the parish anything, as the building would be entirely of timber, and timber was all around them in abundance, and the necessary skills were represented among them. So the Rev Fagerheim gave permission, and reported this development to the bishop. Fagerheim visited the building site regularly while the work was in progress, and when all was completed he directed that in the vestry there ought to be a toilet, with washing facilities, and a bed, which would be needed if a visiting minister required to stay overnight. These features, not mentioned in the original plans, would have to be paid for by the parish. When this was reported to the bishop he refused to sanction these additions, which, he said, were quite unnecessary. 'All right,' said Fagerheim, but nonetheless he asked the bishop to come and dedicate the new church. His Grace agreed, and, as Fagerheim suggested, by divine Providence, on the day the new church was dedicated, there was a sudden heavy fall of snow, making it impossible for the bishop to leave until the next day. Permission for the toilet and sleeping facilities was then granted. Having heard all this, I was only too pleased to accept Fagerheim's invitation to visit the forestry workers' church, and found it a very handsome building in a forest clearing. Inside I found a large painting on the east wall behind the communion table. The workers had no idea of a subject for the painting. They employed an artist, and left it to him. What he produced was a picture of Judas kissing Jesus. Everyone was taken aback, and some were angry, but they came round to see the point, for it was a stark reminder of the treachery that ended with the crucifixion, and the worshipper might well reflect on John Wesley's thought, 'There, but for the grace of God, go I.'

Fagerheim had other interests. He was a good linguist, and it was his hobby to try and rescue Ancient Finnish from complete oblivion. Like Gaelic and other minority languages Ancient Finnish over the years had been spoken by ever fewer people, and was no longer in daily use. Fagerheim could read, write and speak the language, but latterly he could find only one other man with whom he could correspond, and he

The Kirkgate Church - Phase 2

had died recently. Fagerheim then claimed to be the last to know and use Ancient Finnish. There is a fascination about this kind of thing - about being the last to exercise some skill now being forgotten or about a way of life now generally abandoned. Master tradesmen value their skills, acquired as apprentices, which are now no longer taught. I have known or heard of several men claiming to be the last surviving riveter in the shipyards since welding became universal. The last islanders from St Kilda must feel a certain pride at being among the last to share the way of life on that island.

Daisy Fagerheim was very insistent that I should come to the school with her and speak to her class. I was most reluctant. It was a good idea - for someone else to take up. The prospect of addressing a class of foreign youngsters in a language they were just learning, filled me with dread. What was I afraid of? For some obscure reason I thought I would appear a fool. I did not realise English was a very important subject for them, and just as my grandparents did not teach their children Gaelic, as they thought that being known as Gaelic speakers they would never get on in the world, so in Norway it was commonly accepted that unless they knew English they would never get on in the world. As Daisy said, 'It is one thing for them to hear me speak English, for that is my job. It is quite another thing for them to hear you speaking English - actually using English as a means of communication.' So I spoke to the class. I can't remember what I spoke about, but Daisy said it was wonderful, and the class were enthralled! Nuff said.

The Queen and the Duke of Edinburgh came to Scotland each year in July to spend a week with Holyrood Palace as their base, and on one of these occasions about this time it was said that the Duke told the Lord Provost that he thought it was a damn disgrace that the city's slums should be within a stone's throw of the Palace. People were prone to say that the Duke put his foot in it every time he opened his mouth. Not so. This caustic remark began Edinburgh's clean-up of the Royal Mile. Expensive repairs and modernising was carried out while preserving the antique facade of the buildings facing the street. For years and years in Leith we had been crying out for something to be done about the existing heart of the port, but for years and years we had been told there was no money for such work. Money appeared as if by magic to spend on the Royal Mile. What about the Kirkgate in Leith? Suddenly the city acted. The whole of the Kirkgate area was demolished in 1964. Everything was destroyed except the Church and Trinity House. There was impotent fury in Leith. The frontage of the Kirkgate was as historical and interesting as much of the Royal Mile, but Edinburgh was ignorant of all that, and made no attempt to become informed. To Leithers the Kirkgate was known as 'The Channel', but all that was now replaced by a council housing scheme. Some of the inhabitants of the old Kirkgate were now housed in the new scheme. I said to one old chap, 'You really are in a far healthier house than before. You get far more sunshine and fresh air.' 'What dae ah want wi sunshine an fresh air?' he replied. 'Aa that juist gies ye pneumonia.'

The Rev Dr Rudolf Ehrlich now enters on the scene. He had arrived in this country shortly before the war. He belonged to Hamburg, was a considerable scholar, and was now minister in Junction Road Church. He was interested in my activities outside my congregational duties. As my investigations into Leith's history gradually became known I was called on to speak at clubs, societies and churches all over the city. It was an odd week in which, as well as preaching, teaching, visiting and taking funerals and weddings, I was not also delivering an address somewhere or other.

I had for long been a supporter of the Scottish National Party, and now I became a paid-up member, and was urged by the local branch to stand for the Town Council at the next election. In the course of canvassing I was shocked to discover that about a third of the people I visited had no intention of voting at all, and another sizeable percentage were voting for Labour or Tory because that was the party the family had always supported and had no reference to what that party's record may have been. As one man said, 'The Labour Party got me a job in 1931, so I'll always vote for them. That's me saying thank you.'

I addressed a fair number of meetings before the election, was warmly received at quite well attended meetings - largely S.N.P. members or sympathisers, of course. There was just one telling criticism that followed me around wherever I went. 'How do you propose, as a minister, to fulfil your duties as a town councillor?' This was also worrying me. John Hamilton, minister of St John's East, had been a Labour councillor for many years, but he was well-off and was able to afford to pay an assistant to do his parish work for him. My case was different. When I agreed to stand for election I didn't think the S.N.P. had an earthly chance of being returned as member for Leith. I was standing to fly the flag for the S.N.P., to make our ideals and proposals known to as wide a public as possible; but as the election drew nearer I was getting a lot of support. I couldn't afford to pay an assistant to do my church work, so if I won it would be a tremendous boost for the party, but a disaster for the congregation. In the event I didn't succeed. I was defeated by exactly 100 votes. This was much better than the local S.N.P. branch had expected, and they were all the more urgent on me to stand at the next election three years later. I finally agreed as I jaloused my support would have diminished in the interval. I was right. To my relief I was not elected.

The Kirkgate Church - Phase 2

To come back to Rudolf Ehrlich; he had read articles of mine and heard some talks. He said I ought to apply to study for a Ph.D. As he said truly, I was getting no financial benefit for all the research I was doing; surely I might see whether I might not at least have some academic recognition. The man to see was Gordon Donaldson, Professor of Scottish History at the University. I knew him. He was a Shetlander, but from his early youth he had been in Leith, living about a hundred yards from my manse. He shared my concern for the port, and years ago, when I first wrote to the 'Evening News' about the city's neglect, he at once wrote a supporting letter. I now asked him if he would accept me as a Ph.D. student in his department. 'Convince me' he said, 'Convince me that you have access to enough original material to justify working for a degree.' This I did, and we agreed I should matriculate in the following autumn.

The next hurdle was that I would require to have two foreign languages. I only knew French, but Rudolf ran a class in theological German for students at New College. If I attended that class for a year and passed the exam at the end of the course, that would satisfy the requirements for the PhD. degree. I duly took that class, but it hardly made a German linguist of me. I leaned very heavily on Karl Barth and his like, which hardly equipped me for ordinary conversation; but was enough for my purpose, and I passed the exam with little trouble.

Prof. Donaldson had about eight or ten PhD. students, and he arranged for a weekly seminar, where we heard what each of us was doing. We could discuss difficulties and ask for ideas on research and criticise each other's work. I found it all interesting and helpful. As the weeks passed, one or two in the group dropped out as they found the time needed for research was more than they could afford. One of these was Donald Gorrie, who had intended writing the history of his regiment. He soon emerged as a Liberal councillor and is now an M.S.P. Prof. Donaldson kept asking me how things were going, and I said I was happy enough, but he wanted to see something in writing, and when I kept putting him off, he finally said, "Write down what you know. You'll never know everything about any subject. If you insist on knowing everything before writing it down, you'll be an old man still ferreting around, and with nothing to show for it. When you've made your contribution, and if the subject is important enough, someone else will contribute what you missed, or didn't think important. That's a good thing. If no one pays any attention to your work that may mean it was of no importance anyway. So let's have your first chapter.'

That came as a great relief to me, and I went ahead fairly steadily. As a part-time student I was allowed five years for the work, and it was completed inside that time limit. I still had to meet two external

Everything Mixed with Mercy

examiners, and I waited and waited for several weeks before receiving a summons to appear. In fact only one examiner was present, who was, I believe, Deputy Head of the Scottish Record Office. His only criticism was that I paid much more attention to people than to statistics and the details of commerce. Why was that? The simple answer was that that was the way the available evidence pointed. After that it was handshakes all round. William Ferguson, Prof. Donaldson's assistant, and a man with a distinguished career ahead of him, apologised for having kept me so long for the viva voce exam, and explained that it had been difficult finding an examiner, as from my manuscript it appeared that I knew more than anyone else on my subject.

I had for many years been a member of the Old Edinburgh Club and had served as Chairman for a spell. I was impressed by the number of members who were experts and authorities on a great variety of subjects, who found common ground in their love of the city and its history, and who, as often as not, were researching in odd historical corners of the city's history - like the man who was gradually covering the older parts of the city taking note of windows which had been bricked up in the mid-nineteenth century to avoid paying the Window Tax. This was of no apparent importance to anyone, but simply satisfied one man's curiosity.

The Scottish Church History Society also claimed my interest, and I had been a member there for many years, serving as Treasurer, Secretary, Vice-Chairman and Chairman. Originating in the early twenties, it was in low water after the Second World War, when I attended meetings with no more than four present. Like other learned societies, most of the membership came from far afield, and they were indeed learned, but were seldom able to attend lectures, which were published annually, and circulated all over the world. Over the years the reputation of the Society for original historical work has grown steadily, as has the membership.

With the children safely married and out of the way, as one might put it, I thought it might be possible to acquire a few works of art. For some time I had been admiring a painting of Temple village by Willie Gillies. I knew Gillies by reputation, as he lived in Temple where Nigel was now minister, and he and Isobel got on well with him. Every time I passed Aitken Dott's window in Castle Street, the more that painting grew on me, till finally I went in and asked Bill Jackson, the manager, how much it was. 'Fifty-five pounds' I was told, and I wrote a cheque, knowing that I must enter a period of austerity to recoup myself. A few months later I added another Gillies to my shopping list - a still life. I knew Gillies as a student had lived in Willowbrae Road, and was sure he must have painted Restalrig Village. Bill Jackson said he knew of no

The Kirkgate Church - Phase 2

such painting. I asked him to ask Gillies, but the answer was the same. I asked him to ask Gillies to look under the bed, which I knew was the depository an artist usually needed for abandoned works, and lo! I became the proud possessor of an unframed canvas of Restalrig Village in the low-toned style of his early years. No one likes it but myself, which has never worried me.

At an exhibition I saw a coloured woodcut by Jennifer Hex, which I found very attractive. In conversation with her I found she lived in Ayrshire, but had a brother in Leith - a known member of S.N.P. I got her to bring a selection of her work when next she visited her brother, and I chose the Amphitheatre, which she had done in Rome. She claimed to be the only artist in woodcuts to be responsible for all the work from the original piece of timber, which she got from her uncle, a timber merchant, to the finished work.

Elizabeth Wardlaw and I had got a Leith Festival going annually in June, and an art show was one feature. I knew that James Cumming, who was an abstract painter, lived in Ferry Road, and I had bought one of his pictures at Aitken Dott. I invited him to put on a show in Leith, which he did, and I met him. I told him I had one of his paintings, and he was astonished. 'I must congratulate you.' he said, 'You are the first person ever to have bought anything of mine. My customers have all been galleries and the like.'

Emilio Coia did a charcoal drawing of me in fifteen minutes to illustrate a lecture he was giving. At the end of the meeting I said to him, 'I don't look as old as that.' 'You will', he said, 'You will.' 'Still, I'll buy it: it's a neat piece of work.' But when we turned round the picture had gone. A woman had bought it and was making off with it. Coia sent after her and retrieved it, for which I was grateful beyond words.

Christian Salvesen, the ship owners were moving from their premises in Bernard Street to East Fettes Avenue, and the day after the removal I had a phone call from the janitor in Bernard Street, telling me that a great collection of what they reckoned to be junk had been left for him to dispose of. He thought I might be interested to look over it for anything I might be interested in. I went along and confirmed that it was indeed junk, except for one very dirty picture of a sailing vessel. I took it home and cleaned it with detergent and turpentine, and found it to be a painting of a Leith smack, 'The Comet' 1809. Artistically this was no great picture, but historically it was an important find. The Leith smacks had existed for barely fifty years. These ships were built specifically for the run between Leith and London. By coach, that journey took several days. With favourable wind and weather the smacks could cover the distance in thirty-six hours.

Everything Mixed with Mercy

Admittedly the smacks were poor performers in a contrary wind. After a good run from the Thames they could be held for days off the May Island waiting for a favourable wind to let them dock at Leith, but the public were prepared to take their chance of a fast sail, when they knew the coach journey was inevitably long and uncomfortable. By the 1840s the smacks had been superseded with the advent of steam. But there was no known picture of a Leith smack -until now.

The picture was too big to get into the house. It comfortably filled a wall in the vestibule, and I thought it was safe enough there. Its sheer size and weight would make it difficult to move. But I was wrong; it did disappear one day. I phoned the police, and a few hours later they phoned to say they had found it in an antique dealer's shop in the Grassmarket, with a price tag of £250! They pursued their enquiries and learned that a man with a trolley had removed it, pushed it up Leith Walk and sold it to a friend for one pound! This friend, with more sense, had got £100 for it in the Grassmarket. The picture was duly returned, and the antique dealer phoned and acknowledged he had lost £100, but said he would willingly pay me £250 for the picture. I said I wasn't selling, but he asked me to think it over, and the following day, while I was out, he offered my mother £300 for it, to which Grannie answered, 'The Master is not at home, so I can't answer you.' Next day, when the Master was at home, the dealer phoned again with the £300 offer. When I pointed out he had already lost £100 on this deal, and was now offering £300, he would have to make a sizeable profit over £400. Who would pay that money? He said that was no problem. Americans interested in ships and sailing would readily pay whatever was asked for that painting. We left it at that. When at last I retired to St Andrews there was nowhere to hang it and I gave it to Edinburgh Town Council on condition they had it cleaned and restored. I have heard no more.

When I asked Tom Whalen to do a sculptured head of Gayle, my granddaughter, then aged two, he was reluctant. He said children were very difficult, their attitudes and moods unpredictable. Artist and model would have to hit it off together. So we arranged a meeting, and they were quite happy together, so that Tom was able to do preliminary sketches, and the head that finally emerged was quite a triumph.

Eduardo Paolozzi is now a world-famous artist, and he was a Leith laddie brought up in Crown Place. I knew that no one in Leith would appreciate his work, but I determined, if possible, to mount an exhibition of his, which would certainly draw wide attention to the Leith Festival. He had an exhibition at St Andrews that year, and I asked him whether at least some of the St Andrews show might be mounted in Leith, and what would be the cost. He was quite agreeable, provided I paid for transport and insurance. We managed this, and sure enough, the Leith

The Kirkgate Church - Phase 2

show was seen by a good many uncomprehending Leithers. In 1948, when I was chaplain to a club in Leith, which had no church connection and met in premises belonging to the Electricity Board, we received a group of young German women hoping to emigrate to Scotland to get free of the rigors of life in post-war Germany. We entertained them, arranged for overnight accommodation, and within a very short time they were all at work in the Western General Hospital, and we saw no more of them save for one, Winifred Seyberth, who attached herself to us, and she called on us frequently. I think now that Mary's ability to speak and understand German was the reason, for Winnie had not one word of English. After about a fortnight however, she had made astonishing progress, and had enough English to get by, but over the years following she was seemingly content with her form of Basic English, retaining an admixture of German words and phrases. She married Jimmy Beeby, and the marriage was successful, but Winnie wanted a baby. Unfortunately she had a miscarriage. She tried again, with the same result. She had seven miscarriages, and still no baby. As my brother Terry said, 'You'd think she was being given a message.' But Winnie wanted no messages: she wanted a baby - and at the eighth attempt she had a baby - who had cerebral palsy. That child, Paul, required endless attention and time spent on him, but he grew up and married a disabled girl.

Winnie was at pains to maintain contact with her family in Germany, and she and Jimmy made several visits there. She was very keen for Mary and me to meet her brother and his wife in Stuttgart, but for some years this could not be arranged. In the Kirkgate Church we had for some years been sending support to a family of refugees from Czechoslovakia, who were settled in Germany. We were advised by the Red Cross not to send money, so it was always clothing or blankets we sent. We always received a card of thanks ending with a wish for more. I thought it advisable to visit these refugees and assess their needs for myself. The Red Cross poured cold water on this idea. If this became popular among British helpers of refugees there would be all kinds of difficulties in administering and controlling this traffic. Mary and I decided to visit Winnie's brother in Stuttgart, then contact the Red Cross in Munich, and take it from there.

Having arranged things in advance as far as we could, we duly arrived in Stuttgart, where we got a taxi from the station to the hotel. On arriving at the hotel's address, however, there was no hotel to be seen. The taxi driver made inquiries and returned with the news that the hotel had moved a few days ago in a hurry. The city had been bombed in the war, and some buildings were only now being found to be unsafe. The new premises were not far away, and we had no complaints, for the service was very good. The tenement where Winnie's brother had a flat had been severely strafed, if the state of the walls was anything to go by.

The flat door was opened by Winnie's sister-in-law. Her husband greeted us, but after a little he had to go to work. There were no carpets on the floor. There was nothing to be seen in the bedroom but a bed and a chair. In the living room there was a table, two chairs, and a magnificent ebony sideboard which must have been extremely costly. They said they were lucky to have the house, and were determined not to go into debt. In their circumstances that sideboard was a great extravagance, but they were prepared to make do without what most people thought was necessary, until gradually they would furnish the house with items of the highest quality. In the meantime he was working as a labourer, for which there was an urgent need, and his wife was a nurse. They seemed very happy, and so they might well be, compared with what many others were enduring.

Stuttgart has long enjoyed a great reputation for printing, and we visited the premises of the Bible Society, and saw many fine samples of printed Scriptures. We then made our way to Munich, where we found the whole city centre in chaos, as the construction of an underground railway was in progress. We were fortunate to be present on the Feast of Corpus Christi, when the great procession took place on the Thursday after Trinity.

In an Interview with the Red Cross about our visit to our refugees we explained the circumstances of our visit, and they reluctantly agreed, and directed us to the rather remote village where they were staying. We boarded the train heading north, and when the ticket inspector saw our tickets he flew into an astonishing temper. It appeared we were on the wrong train. It was travelling the route we wanted, but this train was for first-class passengers only. We had missed the notice to that effect at Munich. We paid up. It was a simple mistake for foreigners to make. We found the refugees. They were living in a substantial house, and the husband, whom we did not see, had a job as a shoemaker in the nearest town, about six miles away. Their circumstances were not as bad as had been suggested to us, and I concluded that most if not all that we had been sending them, they had sold. The attitude of the Red Cross was justified, and we ceased our connection. There were many other good causes.

I had for some years been acting as chaplain to the Sea Cadets in Leith. This group had a wooden hut in the docks, where they met several times a week. It was run by a group of ex-naval officers. As soon as they entered their hut the boys had to use naval language. The floor became the deck, the walls were bulkheads, the lavatory became the heads and

The Kirkgate Church - Phase 2

so on. There was a strong effort to make the boys feel at sea. Classes were run teaching the elements of seamanship, and in summer they had the use of a small yacht. There was normally a queue of boys eager to join, but disaster struck one winter night, when some vandal set fire to their hut and it was completely destroyed. But in yet one more coincidence in lifetime's experience, one of the officers was a warder at Saughton Prison and, without promising anything, he suggested we need not worry too much. After a few days he turned up with a gang of workers from the prison who were only too pleased at this temporary respite from prison life. Materials appeared from nowhere, and the new premises were several degrees better than the old.

Out of the blue came an invitation to join a course for Sea Cadet chaplains. First-class travel was provided to Weymouth, and I responded smartly. On reaching Weymouth, I could see no one looking like a chaplain but there was quite a crowd of naval men in uniform who were boarding a bus, so I joined them. As they were all strangers to each other no one made any comment on my un-naval appearance. When we reached the drill square we all got off with our gear, and there was a roll-call. My name was not called and everyone looked at me. I said I had come in response to an invitation, but it seemed that someone had blundered. The chaplains' course was elsewhere, but as no one wished to be blamed for the mistake, I was told just to take the officers' course and say no more about it. I was quite happy to do this, and rather enjoyed the lectures. On Wednesday at lunch the officer in charge, a red-headed Irishman I suspected was to blame for the mix-up, said, 'This afternoon we shall be square-bashing, which will probably have little interest for you, so you could take time to see around Weymouth.' That suited me, and I did as suggested, but when I returned I was stopped at the dock gates by a policeman who demanded my identification. I had nothing to prove my identity, so I was arrested and shut in the police box while my captor referred my case to his sergeant, who heard my story and sent to the officer in charge of the course now in progress. The red-haired Irishman came running down, apologising for forgetting to give me the necessary chit. By and large in the Services, the chaplain is treated with much more respect than is the minister in civilian life.

The course for Sea Cadet chaplains took place every second year. It afforded an opportunity for chaplains from various ports to exchange news and ideas, but the lectures forming the official programme for the course were trite and boring. I attended two or three of these courses, and the last of these was a prestigious gathering at the Greenwich Naval College, where we had communion, followed by a dinner at a long mahogany table set with an impressive display of silver and crystal.

Everything Mixed with Mercy

That meal began with the naval grace - 'Thank God' - and ended with the port circulating steadily "the way of the sun".

The service of Holy Communion I shall never forget. It was conducted by a senior chaplain - a bearded, bumptious and overbearing type, whose personality and character were completely forgotten as he conducted that service with such dramatic force and timing as I have often looked for, but failed to experience, in other ministers.

After dinner, and over the port, this man asked for our opinion of the course, and one by one, in a variety of words, we all made the same answer . We were grateful and appreciative of the hospitality provided, but we had not learned anything we didn't already know. That finished it. There were no more courses for Sea Cadet chaplains, but we had all thoroughly enjoyed these get-togethers while they lasted.

The lack of public amenities in Leith, and the lack of information to the public of intended changes and developments induced the formation of Leith Civic Trust. Margaret Street and I, with a number of like-minded people aimed to keep a close eye on our situation. We pinpointed things that ought to be changed or improved, and as far as we could, we publicised our criticisms and aims for the future. Margaret Street paid a regular weekly visit to the window in Market Street where intended developments were displayed, with plans. This was the full extent of public information. An unforeseen difficulty was that time after time Margaret would see where immediate action by the Civic Trust was called for, and she would lodge the needful protest on behalf of the Civic Trust, without calling for a meeting or informing the Trust; so gradually Civic Trust business became in fact Margaret Street's business, and she was tireless in this work.

I myself was largely concerned with the fact that Edinburgh remained obstinately oblivious to the fact that in Leith, which she claimed was part of the city, there were two major amenities which were consistently neglected, and which, if properly upgraded and maintained, would add greatly to the city's attractiveness. One was Leith Walk, which Edinburgh regarded as beginning at the foot of Leith Street, and the other was the Water of Leith. The Walk was the widest, straightest street in the city. For three centuries this had been the direct route from the city to the port. In any European capital this would have been maintained as a boulevard, and developed. As such, it would be one of the main attractions of the city. I wrote to the Transport Department of the city suggesting that trees planted along the Walk would be an attractive feature to introduce. My letter was ignored. After some weeks I wrote again asking for the courtesy of a reply. I received a dismissive note saying that my suggestion was quite impractical, as there were far too many pipes and cables underground for any planting to be done. I let

The Kirkgate Church - Phase 2

the matter rest there as I had no time to mount a massive campaign. The other neglected amenity was the Water of Leith. In its seventeen mile course from the Pentland Hills to the harbour at Leith this was an attractive river until it entered the city, when it became progressively dirty and ugly. I took this up with the authorities, suggesting a clean-up, and the construction of a walkway along the river bank. I was told this was impossible as there was far too much in the way of industrial premises on the river bank. As for the filthy state of the river, if I could organise a party to clear rubbish from the water a skip would be provided to take it all away. The Civic Trust arranged for school children to clear the rubbish from the river, which they did with great enthusiasm, and the muck was all carted away, according to agreement. But a week or so later things were as bad as ever. The river had long been a convenient dump, and the habits of the public cannot be changed overnight.

A good deal of the trouble lay with the authority itself which, some years earlier had closed the outfall of the river into the Firth of Forth by constructing lock-gates which, when closed, kept the water at a constant level in the docks, but the river still flowed and had to be allowed passage through the new lock-gates. But the detritus that came down the river was now held back at what had been the harbour mouth. To deal with mounting sludge, which stank, it was promised that the river would be dredged regularly, but this did not happen. Dredging was very infrequent, because it was very expensive. A dredger was brought up from Hull only when it could visit Leith and several other ports so that the expense might be shared.

After many years trees have now appeared on Leith Walk[1], and there is a walkway along at least part of the Water of Leith, and the river is cleaner than it was.

When the G.P.O. Headquarters was moved to the new building at the West Port, Mary's hours were made flexible, and this enabled us to attend the Wednesday lunch-hour concerts in the Exhibition Gallery at the foot of the Mound, organised by Tertia Liebenthal. Our regular concert-going dates from then and has continued ever since. I joined the Overseas Club then as I thought it would be convenient to lunch there, but I seldom used the Club, and as all the members there in the middle of the day were apparently O.A.Ps I gave up membership after a few years.

In 1972 I celebrated my silver jubilee at the Kirkgate Church, and in these twenty-five years immense changes had taken place in Leith, and in my Parish. Owing to the Westminster Government's insistence in treating Leith as part of Edinburgh, and therefore not an industrial area and not entitled to the 30% development grant from the

---

[1] Trees have now (2005) been removed

Government, some businesses left the port for new locations where that vital grant would be available; others either shut down or were taken over by larger firms which soon closed the Leith branch of their business; and shipbuilding came to an end with the closure of Henry Robb. All this led to a massive decline in population. 80,000 at the end of the Second World War had by 1972 become 40,000. This affected churches, schools, and small local businesses. In the congregation an immediate problem for us was the realisation that our building was in need of extensive repairs. We had a survey made, and the report was that about £100,000 would be needed for necessary work to be done, and in those days before inflation that was an immense sum. The years had gradually affected the mortar of the 1880s, so that the large stones on the parapet of the roof were completely denuded of mortar and simply rested on each other. A severe gale might well dislodge them and cause a serious accident.

I put it to our office-bearers that we could not ignore these facts. We must either find £100,000 quickly, or agree to disperse. This was greeted with glum silence. I then said there was just one possible solution, and that would be for our congregation to join the congregation of South Leith. I referred them to the history of the Kirkgate congregation which they had had from me a few years ago. We had originated in a breakaway from South Leith in 1740, but had never moved more than about fifty yards from the old church. Many of our members were intermarried with members of South Leith. In the vastly changed circumstances of our day both congregations had difficulties albeit of different kinds. Why not rejoin South Leith?

There was no hearty agreement. Until recently the very idea would have been ridiculous and unthinkable. Before the Second World War, South Leith had had the largest congregation in Scotland, with around 5000 members, and even in the early post-war years Tom Brown, the South Leith minister, had told me that on one Sunday, in the winter of 1948-9 he had had to perform forty baptisms.

But South Leith had shared the disastrous post-war drain of the town's population, and another severe blow to that congregation had come with the steady decline, since the First World War, of shipbuilding in the port, the decline in the Merchant Navy, and the departure of wealthy ship owners and merchants from Leith even while their businesses still remained in the port. These well-to-do members of the congregation had almost automatically paid for the church's financial needs, while the poorer members had contributed next to nothing. After Tom Brown's death I had welcomed his successor, Jack Kellet from Dundee - welcomed him on behalf of all the ministers of Leith, but Jack was now trying to cope with what amounted to financial chaos in South Leith congregation. Jack Kellet's induction to South Leith was providential, for he was a very able businessman. He had come into the ministry from Standard Life Assurance, where he had a promising career and could have done very well for himself. In the Menzieshill housing scheme in Dundee he had started a congregation in a single room of his house, and built it up into a thriving congregation. He had now been in Leith for four years and was wrestling to bring the congregation to its financial senses.

Our office-bearers were still not keen. They were sure the Kirkgate congregation would be swallowed up in South Leith; the congregation would lose its identity, and we'd be no better off than if we had simply dispersed. I pointed out that what South Leith needed were members who would be ready to support their congregation with money and whatever talents and skills they had. What the Kirkgate Church lacked in numbers was more than compensated for by the need the congregation had always had to pay its way.

We could move over and into South Leith like a blood transfusion for a sickly patient. 'At least', said I, 'let's put out a feeler and see what

Last Communion at Kirkgate prior to progressing to South Leith

kind of response we might get.' This was agreed. We found South Leith very willing to discuss union. Jack Kellet and I got on well together. Office-bearers on each side knew each other as Leithers, and a form of union was agreed by Kirkgate on 14th May 1973, and by South Leith on 20th May. The Presbytery was not even consulted until all was already agreed. This was unprecedented. It took the wind out of the Presbytery's sails.

All previous attempts to make progress on church union in Leith had failed. The Presbytery congratulated us on this notable union, but the Kirkgate folk saw it as a reunion after an argument lasting 233 years.

9
SOUTH LEITH KIRK AND PARISH

At this point it will be as well to catch up a few loose ends before they are quite forgotten. 1960 was the quatercentenary of the Reformation in Scotland, and Mary and I joined a tour of towns in Europe notably connected with that sixteenth century upheaval. It was organised by the Scottish Reformation Society, with which I had had dealings from time to time. Members of the Society were what would nowadays be called conservative evangelicals, but they were pleasant folk with whom we got on well.

We took in visits to Paris, Geneva, Worms and Cologne. There was nothing unusual or unexpected in those places, but we visited Joan of Arc's birthplace at Domrémy. The cottage itself was, as expected, what we would call a single-end, but it looked rather later than Joan's time. To our surprise, however, there appeared to be no piped water in the village. There was a pond with cattle standing in the water, and women washing clothes in the same pool, a few yards away. There must have been a well for drinking water, but none could be seen. The last stop in the tour was at Bruges, where we had a meal in a restaurant, where the street door was wide open, and a huge dog came in and toured all the tables. Nobody turned a hair, and the dog was very polite, and after his inspection resumed his seat just outside the street door.

Being much involved with the dramatic club, I had a strong desire to visit the Abbey Theatre in Dublin, where so many outstanding plays had been produced. We hadn't been to the Free State before, so decided to make the Abbey theatre one visit in a general tour of Eire. Dublin, we felt, turned night into day. The General Post Office was open, and selling stamps at 11.30 p.m., and the house where we were putting up, never seemed to close the front door day or night. I don't remember the play we saw at the Abbey Theatre, but we visited Trinity College, known to all the artistic world at least, as housing the Book of Kells in its library. It is an illuminated copy of the Gospels, dating from the eighth century and considered to be the finest example of Christian art dating from so early a period.

Visiting several towns we found Cork to be the most memorable, for two or three reasons. We witnessed there a walking funeral. This used to be 'the thing' in Scotland, and I have told of my walking in my maternal grandfather's funeral in 1919. I remember my parents' sense of shock when they saw their first motorised funeral in Edinburgh. The unseemly haste to get rid of the body was scandalous. 'What's the world coming to?' was a widely heard comment. Cremation, of course, was also a jolt, but not as severe as the motorised hearses. Both my parents were cremated.

We thought the Cork funeral must have been for a well-known man, for the procession was long. The first half-dozen couples - all male - were solemn, and suitably dressed in black. Gradually however, the mourners seemed more relaxed, and the tail-end of the procession were conversing, and one or two with their pipes in their mouths. Well, as I suggested, it was at least memorable.

To my surprise we found a presbyterian church, which we attended on Sunday. Emerging after the service I heard some Scots accents, and spoke to a couple of men who were running a laundry in the town. They had come from Kirkcaldy some years before, and were doing very well, thank you. They introduced me to another 'Scotsman', also, I think from Kirkcaldy. He was a builder, and claimed never to have had an idle day since arriving in Cork. It seemed strange that there should have been this connection between Kirkcaldy and Cork, but there may have been reasons not mentioned to me.

I am reminded of a Jew who at breakfast dropped his toast to the ground, and it landed buttered side up. He had often dropped his toast, and it had always landed buttered side down. Why was this time different? He asked his rabbi for an explanation. The rabbi said he'd have to consult his brother rabbis. After a few days he said to the enquirer, 'We have considered your question, and we have all decided that on this occasion you must have buttered your toast on the wrong side.' There's nothing like a good education when confronted with these subtle problems.

The Boys' Brigade in Leith was a vibrant organisation, with keen competition between the companies, in football, swimming, athletics and company drill. The movement suffered a great deal through the dwindling population, but in 1968 the bad times were still in the future, and I decided to attend the B.B. Council meeting in Belfast. I attended as chaplain to the 12th Leith Coy. (the Gallant 12th. Each company in Leith had its own adjectival distinction).

I was also keen to travel to Ireland as I had heard disquieting rumours about Victor Miller, our organist at Kirkgate Church. He was manager of the Edinburgh branch of H.M. Stationery Office in Castle Street. Without warning he was sent to Belfast to investigate the affairs of the Stationery Office there, and after a while he sent me his resignation as organist, as he thought he'd be staying for the future in Northern Ireland. The B.B. Council at Queen's University went smoothly, and we visited Victor's wife, who told us the books at the Stationery Office in Belfast were in chaos, but what was much worse was that no-one in the office was in the least worried about their situation. Arthur was working late and early trying to bring order out of chaos. In fact we got word some months later that he had died - worried to death, in fact.

Mary had friends in Belfast, and we visited them. It was a mixed Roman Catholic and Protestant area, and the people we were visiting recommended us to see an R.C. procession due to take place in a few days' time; but we could not wait. The Protestants (Prodies) also had their processions. This fascination with processions in Ireland is something we in East Scotland just cannot understand, although in and around Glasgow, with far more first and second generation Irish immigrants, there is more sympathy and understanding. It all seems to stem from the Battle of the Boyne in 1690, in which neither side won, is traditionally counted a victory for Protestantism, and the Orange Lodges are determined never to let it be forgotten.

In South Leith Church, a girl came to us from Northern Ireland to train as a Deaconess. She was a nice lassie, daughter of a farmer north of Belfast, and intelligent. But there was something about her I felt needed explaining - something that prevented her opening up in conversation. I asked her if she liked the work. She said she did. 'Are you happy with the people you meet?' 'Oh yes.' Nothing more - just that. I said to her, 'I think I know what's wrong, here in Leith you don't find it easy to get on with people as you don't know who is Catholic, who is Protestant, and who is not at all religious.' 'Yes,' she said, 'until I came here I had never in my life knowingly spoken to a Roman Catholic.' This from an intelligent girl in her early twenties, was the statement of a massive problem for her. She didn't finish her course with us. I think she went home again.

We visited the Gibsons in Ballymena, where Bert had a thriving veterinary practice, married and with a family. His parents had followed him over from Twechar and were settled close by. This was in September 1968 - two months before the start of 'the troubles', during which our correspondence lapsed.

In the summer of 1970 we went to Orkney for a week. Having been to Shetland to see the Pitts and Fred Houston, we thought Orkney would give us a taste of the Northern Isles that were reputedly very different from Shetland. We went for a week only, as we didn't think there would be enough there to interest us for a fortnight. How wrong we were! Bill Cant had moved to Kirkwall from St Thomas Church in Leith. He was now minister at St Magnus Cathedral. We paid a visit to him at the manse, and I took a service for him in the Cathedral on the one Sunday we were there. We didn't yet have a car, but managed to get around fairly well in buses and on foot. We were surprised at the numerous Pictish relics - the standing stones of Stenness, the chambered cairn at Maes Howe, but there are numerous detailed histories of Orkney.

We put up at a hotel some miles from Kirkwall. On Midsummer Day I sat at a window at midnight reading a newspaper without any artificial light. There was nothing special in the news. I just wanted to test what I had often heard - that this could be done.

On one evening there was a wedding in the hotel. It really got going as we were getting ready for bed, so we waited up until the din might subside. Some time after midnight there was a lull, and we lay down, but after about twenty minutes things livened up again. That was how the night went - waves of jollification with short spells of silence. In the morning the landlord asked if we had slept all right, and I suggested he was joking. 'Oh,' said he, 'I forgot to tell you about the wedding, but it was a quiet affair. You ought to have come down and joined them. You'd have been most welcome. But of course I ought to have told you. I can only apologise.' He then explained that this was a local wedding, with the guests all from Kirkwall and round about. When wedding guests came from any of the other islands, the celebrations could go on for days. It is only possible to travel to the smaller islands twice a week or thereby, so wedding celebrations go on day and night, with brief intervals for a nap or a snack, until the boat comes in.

In September that year we paid a visit to Iona, which Mary had never seen. The weather was what we in the east of Scotland think is appalling, although in the west they accept it as worth enduring for the sake of the unequalled glory of the good days to come. We set off from Oban on a dull day, with a strong wind, and as we crossed Mull by bus the wind strengthened and the rain started. When we reached Fionnphort we found many people before us getting on board the little ferryboat for Iona. It filled up and set off across the Sound of Iona, leaving a group of us stranded in the rain. There was apparently just the one ferry boat, but a man with a rowing boat agreed to take us over, so we set foot on Iona and made our way to the restored Abbey, which was fairly well known to me from previous visits. Mary was not very moved, being rather concerned at being soaked to the skin.

We left for the return journey and got places on the boat, which was still an open rowing boat, but the wind was much stronger now, so that not only was spray coming over us, but solid green waves of sea drenched us as though we had been swimming, fully dressed. Of course the other passengers in the bus were in equal distress, and in the three hours it took to cross Mull in the heated bus, we all stripped off as much clothing as we judged the other passengers would stand for, and we arrived back in Oban dressed again in clothes that were still very damp, but nicely heated. The hotel people where we were to have dinner didn't turn a hair. All our wet gear was taken down to the basement where the central heating boiler did what we wanted done. I suppose this was a common enough occurrence on the west coast.

Bella Kesbi had been an *au pair* with Morag at Lathrisk, in Fife, improving her English and helping about the house. She was Jewish, but her parents having suffered much under the Hitler regime, had carefully never told her she was Jewish until just before she came to Scotland. She was now consumed with a passion for all things Jewish, and was determined to get entry to a kibbutz in Palestine, where she would learn Hebrew and become part of the urge to develop the potential of the Holy Land. Morag kept in touch with her (and still does), and in the 1970s Mary and I decided to visit Israel. We arranged with Bella, who had finished her six months in the kibbutz, and now had a job in the airport at Tel Aviv, that we would meet her at a bus station in Jerusalem. At Tel Aviv the bus for Jerusalem was filled with tourists like ourselves, and before we started off a young lady boarded the bus and gave us a lecture on how to behave in Israel, which we thought rather heavy-handed, as we were not football fans, and might have been able to give her a few hints on how to get on with the Palestinians. In Jerusalem we waited at the bus station, but Bella was not on the one o'clock bus. Having no bus timetable we were at a loss, but hung about, and at two o'clock Bella appeared from the airport bus. She apologised, but explained that the one o'clock bus was an Arab bus, so she could not take it. We asked why, and she said if she were seen on an Arab bus she would lose her job. We doubted this but she assured us that any consorting with Arabs was forbidden.

We had joined a Roman Catholic party for this tour, and found the people very pleasant, and the tour guide very competent. On the Sabbath the Old City of Jerusalem went dead. The streets were barred to traffic, and the effect of this silent area in the midst of a busy city was quite marked.

We did all the usual tourist things. As our group was Roman Catholic we walked the route of the Stations of the Cross - a narrow lane. We saw the Wailing Wall lined with penitents. We went down the road to Jericho, and I bathed in the Dead Sea, experiencing the strange difficulty of trying to swim in water much denser that the open sea. We visited the Garden of Gethsemane, the Pool of Siloam, the place at Sychar where Jesus spoke with the woman who had had five husbands, and was currently living with a 'bidie-in' - the woman to whom, of all people, he first indicated he was the Messiah. All of these places looked completely unlike anything I had imagined them to be. To me, the most surprising site was that of the Sermon on the Mount, which looked nothing like a mountain; it was like a stretch of rolling moor. Capernaum was a delightful place, with a view over the Sea of Galilee.

The Church of Scotland mission there was most attractive and the staff warmly welcoming. The Church in Jerusalem also had a strong flavour of home, with seats donated from all over Scotland.

Everything Mixed with Mercy

Another branch of the family now comes into the picture. Bessie, Mary's eldest sister, was a staunch campaigner for women's rights, and she became engaged to Benjy Miller, who was in the regular army. Before they could marry, Benjy was moved to the Far East. This was just after the First Great War, and Benjy was away for seventeen years. This came about as Benjy disliked travelling, so spent all his leaves in the Far East. Eventually he did fly home, where Bessie still waited for him. Bessie converted to Roman Catholicism, and they had two children - Francis and Margaret. Both children, like their parents, had strong opinions on a variety of subjects. Bessie favoured the Rudolf Steiner system of education. Benjy was a warrant officer, and after the war, with well over twenty years' service behind him, he joined the Civil Service and worked in the Charities Commission. It had always been assumed that Francis would follow his Dad in the Army, and accordingly, after his eighteenth birthday Francis came home and announced that he had joined up; but the smile was wiped from his father's face when he added that it was the Navy he had joined. But Francis was keen. In the Navy he volunteered for everything that was called for, and eventually he became a radio operator, and attained the rank of chief petty officer.

His sister Margaret trained as a nurse. She was best maid when Morag and David married, and thereafter nursed with the Queen Alexandra nurses, who provided nursing services for the Navy. As time went on, Margaret's nursing skills earned promotion until she in the nursing services ranked higher than Francis in the Royal Navy. This was no worry to anyone until they both were stationed in Malta. Margaret nursing at Mtarfa, where the staff nursed men from the Navy, and people from all over the island. Now Francis' ship berthed at Malta and Francis and Margaret almost inevitably met in public. This meant that Francis had to address his sister as 'Madam', which gave Francis something like a lump in his throat.

From Malta, Margaret sent us a pressing invitation to come to Malta for a holiday. Margaret was in charge of the hospital staff, and in her free time had nowhere else to go; so she bought a flat in Sliema, where she could retreat when not on duty. She wanted us to occupy the flat and make any suggestions that might occur to us for its improvement. We jumped at this, and when we arrived Margaret strongly advised us to drink plenty to promote perspiration. This would help us to keep comfortable in the hot weather. With this in mind she said she had left us some sherry in the flat. She had in fact left us a carboy full of sherry, with which we might easily have ruined our holiday; but we did drink off more than we'd ever done before, and perspired freely and were comfortable.

Malta was extremely interesting. The British were still welcome, and

South Leith Kirk and Parish

we were warmly received everywhere. Even travelling by bus was quite exciting as there seemed to be no traffic rules, and a picture of the Virgin Mary hanging in the interior of each bus didn't really reassure us; but we survived. We found a great variety of seafood in every restaurant. We took a ferry one afternoon to the little island of Gozo, where we walked around in a brilliant, very hot day. I went into a wine shop and asked for a drink. I was handed a full tumbler of white wine for which I was charged the equivalent of sixpence. When I expressed astonishment the shopkeeper said they had to sell the wine as cheaply as possible, as it would not keep and could not be exported.

In 1973 I became Moderator of Edinburgh Presbytery, and as this was also the year in which the Kirkgate Church joined with South Leith Parish Church, it was a busy time for me. It was only after a heated argument in Presbytery that I became Moderator. One group, led by Duncan Shaw, had voted me as Moderator in 1972, and there was a lengthy debate while I sat curled up in a corner in extreme embarrassment. However, it was all sweetness and light in 1973 when I took on the job. I had not looked forward to the Moderatorship, which would involve me in many committee meetings and other duties all over the city, and, unlike some who loved committees, I had always avoided as many of these as possible. It just happened that after twenty-six years in the Kirkgate Church I was the longest serving minister in the same parish in the Presbytery. It was assumed I had more experience in the work of the ministry than any other member of Presbytery. But unlike Tom Brown who had, as minister of South Leith, worn himself out with committee work added to his parish duties, I had never shone on any Presbytery committee. Instead, the Presbytery wags were now referring to me as 'Mr Leith'.

In fact, the union with South Leith made the Moderator's job much easier, as Jack Kellet as parish minister could see that my parish duties would be attended to when Presbytery calls intervened. The licensing of students took place in St Giles in those days. Nowadays this takes place in the church of the Moderator. I was well warned to remember to remove the microphone I would be using, which would be on a lanyard round my neck. In the event, I forgot, and coming down from the pulpit I almost strangled myself, which afforded a little light relief to the students being licensed. When I inducted Gilleasbuig Macmillan I was able to behave with more propriety - to my relief, for his father and I were fellow students at New College.

In South Leith, Jack Kellet and I quickly settled down. We organised ourselves into a team ministry - not a common arrangement then. Jack was parish minister, I was associate, and to our joint endeavours we added the assistant, and the deaconess. We didn't have any set rules, but we agreed that Jack would attend to urgent calls unless these came from members of the former Kirkgate Church. Hospital visits we shared, and I was surprised to discover, when I totalled up on one occasion, that we visited over thirty hospitals, nursing homes and old people's homes. Apart from these regular rounds the assistant was concerned with the youth and the deaconess with the women's organisations. We also had a list of about 400 sick or housebound people we tried to visit three or four times a year.

Every Friday we had a staff meeting, at which we reported on the past week's work, discussed cases presenting problems and discussed ideas or opinions we had. This followed the weekly vestry hour, taken by Jack or myself, when members of the congregation arranged with us for weddings or baptisms or brought forward family problems. The church halls were then in Duke Street - two busy streets away from the church, and here Jack would get involved with myself or the assistant in theological or ethical discussions, Jack was sweir to change his mind, and his most redoubtable adversary was Gavin Elliott, our assistant. These two would continue until eleven o'clock, when I would rise and make for the door, but Gavin and Jack became very close friends and remained so after Gavin was in a parish of his own.

Jack was a workaholic. He lived for it and was very efficient. His handwriting could cause him problems, and at staff meetings he would sometimes pass his diary round asking if anyone could read his notes. His answer to a call was always immediate, and he thought nothing of visiting at the Infirmary after ten o'clock at night, when he was scarcely welcomed by the staff. Walking home along East Hermitage Place one night a man, a few yards in front of him, suddenly jumped into the roadway and threw himself in front of an approaching bus. Jack at once jumped after him, grabbed him and yanked him to safety. That was typical. He was also impetuous in speech and would say things he later regretted; but this quick response to a situation endeared him to many in the congregation.

Apart from my share in visiting and preaching, my special role as Associate was never defined, but it was taken for granted that my ongoing concern would be the development of the congregation's relationship with the parish. This had always been a concern of mine in the Kirkgate Church. In Leith, if you had no church connection, but could claim your parents or grandparents had belonged to the South Leith congregation, you could claim membership and could call on the services of a minister. We never refused these calls, on the principle that he who is not against us is for us, and also that the parish congregation has a duty to the whole parish, and not merely to those who see eye to eye with us.

South Leith Kirk and Parish

Over the years, in researching for many articles, I had accumulated masses of notes on the history of the town, and these all had to be carefully filed, as I was constantly having to refer to them, as I gave addresses on Leith's history to clubs and societies all over Edinburgh. They all had to be different as, at least within Leith, the same people might turn up at more than one meeting. But I did use the same address for meetings where the audience was sure to be different from any others hearing me, for I spoke at Woman's Guilds, Rotary branches, Soroptimists, Probus Clubs etc. It was an exceptional week when I did not have to speak on Old Leith, apart from my Sunday work.

Sunday duties were of course much lighter in South Leith than they had ever been in the Kirkgate, where, apart from morning and evening services, preaching at each, I took the B.B. Bible Class at 10.a.m. once a month. After the morning service I had my regular Bible Class. Before the evening service there was a class for first communicants running for six weeks four times a year; and after the evening service there was the Youth Fellowship. By the end of the day I felt limp and drained. This eased off quite a bit during the 1960s, but Sundays were still quite heavy going. In South Leith there were three of us sharing the preaching, and the evening service was informal - a glorified discussion group, with a dozen or fifteen regular attenders, keen on this kind of gathering. In practice, with three ordained ministers, I only preached once or twice a month, and I was able to join the choir. If I weren't preaching I might be responsible for the prayers or reading the lessons and I was in the choir until my turn came round. The choir at that period was unusual in that it consisted of roughly equal numbers of men and women - six or seven of each. We met in the old Maltmen's Gallery, well above the congregation, which meant I had to sprint up the choir stairs, fortunately hidden from the congregation.

An unforeseen development from these arrangements at South Leith was that it soon became known that, on an odd Sunday when their minister was ill or called away unexpectedly, I might be available to take supply. I had also been on the Board of the National Bible Society for many years, and now I was asked to take services for the Society when they were hard pressed for agents to speak for the Society. All this meant that I was frequently away from South Leith at churches mainly in Fife, Angus and the Borders, as well as Edinburgh.

Neil Johnstone, my nephew, after a brilliant record at Fettes which he didn't much enjoy, being two years younger than the rest of his class, had spent a year in industry to grow a year older, and had now reached Trinity College, Cambridge, and we went there to see him in June week. We found Cambridge a much more attractive town than industrialised Oxford which we had visited a few years earlier. We went to see an open air performance of Shakespeare late one evening and shivered uncontrollably throughout the performance. Mary drove home from Cambridge, and I ended in Leith with a very sore back. When Dr Milne saw me he asked if I'd been sitting as a passenger on a long car journey, and warned me against doing the like again.

In Leith, St Thomas Church had closed and the congregation united with the Junction Road congregation. The St Thomas Church building was taken over by the Sikhs. All the Sikhs in Edinburgh were living in Leith since, naturally, like the Scots, when living in what to them was a foreign country, they liked to form their own community. Many of the Sikh men were driving buses, and had had a long argument with the town council for permission to wear their turbans while driving. They settled in very well as citizens, but their wives never left their houses and learned no English. I was chaplain to David Kilpatrick Junior Secondary School, where a number of Sikh children attended. They mixed well with the Scots youngsters, and from them learned what they naturally thought was English, but in fact was playground Scots. They were intelligent kids, and in class they were quick to put up their hands to answer questions. Their answers were given in the Scots they used in the playground, which reduced the rest of the class to convulsive laughter barely suppressed. But I handed it to the teachers. None of them batted an eyelid, and none tried to correct these Sikh bairns. Andrew Winton, the art teacher, and I got on well together. I visited the school regularly on Tuesdays, and we agreed that if I told the children a Bible story, he would get them to paint it on the following Friday. This produced some very interesting results, since not only the Sikhs, but many of the Scots children had no church connection, and were hearing these stories for the first time. Andrew said to me that two or three of those kids showed real artistic gifts, but would never get a chance to develop them, since as soon as they finished school they would be off to earn a living.

The Sikh women had never been seen in the community, and were quite unknown. This was why the men had taken the church, to establish a Sikh temple, which would also become the centre of social life. They went to work on the building, and after about a year they announced the formal opening and invited all the local ministers to attend. I appeared to be the only one to respond, and I found the former church transformed. The pews had all been removed, and the wide space completely covered with a beautiful carpet. The dais on which the communion table had stood was still there, and on it were seated what I took to be the equivalent body to a Presbyterian kirk session. The women were all seated round the walls, and the men - a great many men -were all seated on the carpet, cross-legged, and it was indicated to me that I should join them. I did so with some difficulty, not having sat cross-legged for many years past. Several speeches were made, but not a word in English. After fully three-quarters of an hour everybody suddenly stood up, and so did I, in agony, trying to keep my balance on legs that didn't seem to belong to me. A kind of servitor now came round issuing everyone with a paper serviette, on which he deposited a dollop of what looked like cold semolina, but there was no sugar in it. I hadn't nearly finished my dollop when suddenly everyone sat down again, and resuming the cross-legged position was even more painful than getting up. The service ended shortly afterwards, and we all made our way to what I took to be the hall next door, where we sat down at long tables for a meal. My only trouble here was that buckets of what I took to be cream were brought round and ladlefuls were added to the food on our plates; but it wasn't cream, it was yoghurt, which was the final shock of the afternoon. In this way I learned what it must have been like for the Sikh women trying to come to terms with life in Leith. This really was a triumph for the Sikh men. From then on the women came out to meet each other in their temple, and engage in various communal activities.

In this same year of 1976 Mary and I paid a visit to Twechar, celebrating the seventy-fifth anniversary of the building of the church there. We met one or two old friends, but after thirty years away from the village a great deal had changed and many people had died. Lord Whitelaw was there, and I was at considerable pains to avoid speaking to him. In the years following our departure for Leith, the bowling clubs of Twechar and Leith had met annually for a game in Twechar and Leith alternately, and one year, in Leith I had enquired for news of the horticultural society, only to be told it no longer existed. It had been strongly supported when we left, so this was quite shocking. I asked what had happened to the silver rose bowl given by Lord Whitelaw and was told the committee had sold it and it was jaloused[1] they had divided the proceeds among themselves. When I related this to Jean Innes, who had been our maid for the duration of our stay at Twechar, years later she was shocked and refused to believe it. I thought it quite typical of the committee concerned, but if Jean was right in refusing to believe the story, then someone among the bowlers was pulling my leg, and loaded with two versions of the facts I was nervous of meeting Lord Whitelaw, but I needn't have worried; his lordship was so closely attended to by the locals that, although we stood next to one another there was no chance of a private conversation.

It was at about this time that the affair of the North Carr Lightship took place. Frank Davidson, a captain in the Merchant navy, had had an accident. He fell down the hold and damaged his leg. He recovered

---

[1] jaloused - guessed

Everything Mixed with Mercy

to a degree, but was left with a permanent limp. He had been all round the world time and time again, but now he joined the Northern Lighthouse Board and visited all the lighthouses round the Scottish coast, interviewing the keepers and their families and noting any repairs needed.

The Lighthouse Board were then beginning gradually to convert the lighthouses to automatic functioning, and while the change was welcomed in Muckle Flugga and other remote spots, some people were not pleased when the North Carr Lightship off the coast of Fife was abandoned in favour of an automatic light. Captain James Hunter, a member of the congregation, had been master of the North Carr for some years before he retired, and he decided to have the ship preserved as a showpiece, to be berthed at Anstruther for the Fisheries Museum. He got me to join a committee along with Ronald Leask, to raise money to put this plan into operation. He reckoned we'd need £2000, and with much cajoling and pressing we finally got the necessary funds together. The lightship was brought down to Leith, and then taken to Anstruther - but not just as simply as that statement would imply. When we had the ship ready to be moved to Anstruther, we were told that Anstruther didn't want it!

Captain Hunter had never thought to ask permission to bring the lightship to rest in the harbour at Anstruther. The Fisheries Museum people said they couldn't afford to keep the ship. Even if it lay idle in the harbour it would need to be careened every year to free it from barnacles. We told them they could invite tourists and visitors to see round the ship at ten pence a time, and that would not only pay for careening but would make a profit for the museum. With reluctance the North Carr was allowed to remain in the outer harbour, where there was not much shelter, so after a year it moved to the inner harbour. For some years we were invited to the annual meeting of the Fisheries Museum, but that lapsed in time. The enterprise was never a success.

Captain Hunter, like many seamen, accustomed to restricted cabin space, was a meticulous man. His wife assured me he could never pass anything lying on the pavement - even a nail or a piece of string. He had an extensive collection of things dropped or thrown away, and kept in his garage, and everything so neatly arranged that it could come to hand in a couple of minutes. I once lost a nut from a silver candlestick. It was an unusual size and I could not come by a replacement anywhere. At his urgent request I gave him the candlestick one Sunday and he returned it the following week with the exact replacement. I found many seamen to be men of strong character, willing and able to turn their hands to anything, and never caving in to adverse circumstances. I visited an old ex-Royal Navy man in his nineties, who lived on his own.

He had moved to a new house in Pilrig on the top floor, four storeys up, with no lift. He looked after himself. He had joined the Navy in the 1890s and was paid sixpence a day. He had a uniform which was only worn on dress occasions. For the slops[1] to be worn for ordinar[2] he was given paper patterns and cloth and told to get himself dressed. They slept in hammocks, and at the start of their watch the third mate came round with a marlin spike belting each man still in his hammock. He had many almost incredible stories of the way things were done before the First World War.

With the advent of welding to replace riveting in shipbuilding, I knew two men each claiming to be the last welder in Leith- and there were other claimants to the same title. Ronald Leask, who was involved in the North Carr Lightship adventure, was a knowledgeable man. He became master of the 'Gardyloo' ship which carried Edinburgh sludge and sewage to be deposited at sea beyond the May Island, did a round trip by Inchcolm, The May, the Bass Rock and so back again. He normally took tourists and visitors of up to twenty, and entertained them with stories from the history of the Forth estuary, on which subject he was a recognised authority.

Benjy Miller, Bessie's husband, died in York in 1978. After the funeral we went down to Harrow, visiting Jimmy and Lilian Mackenzie, with whom we had always kept in touch. Jimmy was my nephew - Mary's sister Nellie's elder son. From there we made a short trip to Wales, where we had never been. We had not booked in at a hotel, and this being July we could not find any vacancy in Ludlow, but were recommended to try at a manor house a little way out of the town where it was rumoured a man was meaning to start a hotel. We duly called at the address given and got a warm welcome from the hotelier-to-be. He said he hadn't opened yet, so we were his first customers, and would we please make suggestions that might be of use to him. That was a very pleasant introduction to Wales, and next day we paid a visit to Aberystwyth. In a main street there, we heard not a word of English, to our immense satisfaction. I was just then taking up the cudgels for the use of Scots, and it was encouraging to hear Welsh in use as a colloquial speech.

Back home, things had been moving. I had conceived the idea of producing a connected account of how through the centuries Leithers had spent what leisure they had. As I wrote I realised that without financial backing I would never get any book published, for the appeal of my local history would be limited. As I finished the writing, however, I happened in conversation with Duncan Shaw to mention what I had been doing, and he asked me to consider publishing with the Edina Press. I thought this was an unusual request, and he went on to explain

---

[1] slops - loose fitting jacket or tunic   [2] ordinar - ordinary, plain

that the Edina Press was operated by four directors, of which he was one, another was John Gray, an Edinburgh lawyer I knew, and two others. They were concerned at the amount of academic material that was never published for lack of finance to pay for publication. They had engaged in publishing on a non-profit making basis, which would reduce costs considerably. There were snags, of course. Nothing of what the Edina Press published was ever reviewed, as the normal publishers, with much higher costs, objected. That didn't worry me: there was no need for reviews, as people in Leith would readily buy any book on Leith. Personal recommendation was all that was needed.

I put it to the Kirk Session that if they were prepared to meet the cost of publication of 'Old Leith at Leisure', they might well make a profit. With little reluctance they agreed, and duly made a profit. The following year I completed the story of 'Old Leith at Work', and again the Kirk Session had no reason to complain. It took another two years to complete 'Old Leith, the Caring Community', but this time the Kirk Session didn't want anything to do with it. It was now 1979, and the congregation was involved in raising money to demolish the Kirkgate Church and build halls for South Leith Church to replace the old halls in Duke Street. The cost of this enterprise was estimated at £70,000, but with the advent of inflation the final cost was £360,000. I published that third paperback myself and was not a loser by it. I had taken rather longer to write the 'Caring Community', as I had acceded to a request from Leith Hospital to write a history of the Hospital in Leith. This took some time to do, and emerged as a booklet, which the hospital had printed.

Some years later John Donald the Edinburgh publisher asked me to write a history of Leith. With some astonishment I told them I had already written the history of Leith. They said they knew about my three paperbacks, and I answered I would just be going over the same material again. They asked whether I had stopped taking any more interest in Leith, and of course I was still taking notes, so they told me to get on with it, and as I looked over old material I'd get new ideas on it. So I set to work again and 'The Life and Times of Leith' appeared in 1986.

On the brink of publication, I was told it would be advisable to get someone to write a foreword, so I suggested that I'd ask Gordon Donaldson, Professor of Scottish History at Edinburgh University, to write a foreword, as we had been good friends for a long time. 'No, no,' said the publisher, 'He won't do it. He has quarrelled with us - you'd better get someone else.' So I got Peter Heatly to do the job. He was well known as an Olympic diver. He was a Leith Academical, and his mother and mine were old friends. But I was intrigued, and approached

Gordon Donaldson in my well-known diplomatic manner. He said he was furious. John Donald owed him thousands of pounds, and he would never use them again, indeed he was sick of all publishers. I thought there was probably more to the story than that, and in due course I was able to put two and two together. The publisher said to me, 'We don't propose paying you any royalties - instead we shall pay you 25% of all profits.' This seemed fair enough to me, and a year after first publication I received a sizeable cheque. Drawing near to the second year's end I received a letter suggesting it was time for a second impression, and this went ahead, but I received no more money. I waited and waited, and at length I looked in at Thin's, the bookseller then in George Street, and found 'The Life and Times of Leith' still on sale, and it was in its fourth impression. I was furious. If they had made no more profit, why was the book now selling in its fourth impression? I did nothing. I felt a fool, but guessed there was probably something in the small print of our agreement that I had missed. This, I guessed, was where Gordon Donaldson had come to grief. Since then I have never knowingly had any more to do with John Donald, Publishers. The director of the firm I had most to do with was John Tuckwell, and he and I got on very well together. But shortly after my connection with the firm he left and set up his own publishing business, which appears to be doing well.

I shared the experience of many ministers in a city where I would be recognized and even greeted by people I didn't know. In Leith this was even more of a problem since I had spoken at so many meetings not connected with the congregation. Those who recognized me on a platform supposed that I must recognize them from the audience. One day a man accosted me in Duke Street. Later I learned his name was Beer - Willie Beer, I think. Some time later he published a handbook on the pubs of Edinburgh and Leith. When first he spoke to me he asked if I'd be interested in joining the Cape Club. I said I knew nothing about any Cape Club, but he reminded me that among the innumerable social clubs in Edinburgh in the eighteenth century, nearly all of which had long since disappeared, the Cape Club had recently been revived. The modern club had little to connect it with the original eighteenth century club, save the name. Membership was limited to one member from each Edinburgh district. They met once a month at a room in the Overseas Club for a drink and a blether and to arrange for their next excursion. Between these monthly meetings the members gathered in a city district with the local member as host, who would tell the others something about his district and take them to a local pub. Now the next meeting was to be in Leith, and he knew next to nothing about Leith, but knew that I was more knowledgeable about the port. Would I care to join the Club and take his place? I hummed and hawed a bit.

Everything Mixed with Mercy

I saw nothing wrong with the Cape Club, but in 1979 public opinion in Scotland was not yet prepared to accept ministers in public houses, although I remembered the Very Rev John Gray of Dunblane Cathedral had once informed the General Assembly that his house had always been a public house. But that was a joke: this was serious.

Willie Beer said they had one other reverend member in the duo - Donald Skinner from Gilmerton. I was interested. Donald Skinner was an unconventional minister. Originally an engineer, he had come into the church with a critical mind. Mining had ceased in Gilmerton, and unemployment was widespread. Donald cleared the church hall, managed to accommodate most of the organisations in the manse and converted the hall into an industrial training centre, where youngsters trained in various trades, using tradesmen in the congregation as instructors. Thereafter Donald took each boy in hand and claimed that 95% of his boys found jobs. I knew him, but never met him at any of the Cape Club meetings.

I agreed to join the club, and in due course they all came down to Leith and I showed them round Bernard Street and the Shore and more of the neighbourhood. We ended up at the Bridges Bar on the Shore, situated between the old Upper and Lower Drawbridges. It was an eighteenth century howff with a large open fire and settles instead of modern chairs. There were other customers in, including one or two ladies of the street. The place neighboured Leith's red light district. We all sat down with our drinks but a couple of minutes later one of the prostitutes, beside whom one of our members was sitting, leapt up with a scream and yelled she was being molested. Our member was deeply embarrassed, as we all were, but he said the girl had had her hand in his pocket. We all left with Leith under a cloud as it were. I never knew the Cape Club to come back to the port.

Living and working in the port where I had lived and been to school, I came across reminders of the past. Leaving Leith in 1931 and returning in 1947, the university and Watten and Twechar lay between the present and the past. One day I visited an old lady in the South Leith congregation - a Miss Jamieson - who was living in our old flat at 233 Leith Walk. I used regularly to slide down the banister to the ground, but now the banister was studded to prevent that special thrill. I did not recognize the house itself, although it was the same, with the same number of rooms, but it did not feel like home any more. Something had gone out of the place and the atmosphere was quite different from what I remembered. Adding to the dismal air was a scaffolding round the tenement. Edinburgh Corporation had become very keen on cleaning old stonework in the city. Some of this work was very successful, but other stones were not improved and took on a piebald appearance. Leith Walk was in this latter category. When I visited the old house scaffolding had been there for several months and no work had been done for weeks as the money for that year was finished and no more progress would be made before the following April.

That same year at the reception in Trinity House following the Seamen's Service I recognized a man at the far end of the room and at the same time he recognized me. We had last seen each other fifty years ago in the same class at school. After all that time we were each recognizable. This was Captain Tom Blaikie, recently retired and now living in Edinburgh at Lauder Road in the Grange. There was something peculiarly satisfactory and reassuring about this encounter, and we exchanged addresses but took the matter no further.

For a long time I had nursed the idea of visiting Greece as another of the Bible countries I had not seen. These visits to the Middle East helped me to preach with a little heightened authority. SAGA, then in its young days, advertised a tour to the area I was keen to visit, and we decided to go, although we had hitherto avoided joining these tours where you had no idea what your holiday companions might be like. If that was snobbish, so be it. Come to think of it, the trip to Israel with a group of Roman Catholics had turned out very happily, so we signed up, and joined with two or three from Edinburgh who left with us from the Waverley. Unfortunately the railways were having some kind of go-slow, in line with frequent practice, and we arrived at King's Cross just in time to miss our connection for Stansted, from which airport our flight was due to take off at 5.00am. This was one of the inconvenient arrangements made by SAGA to keep the cost down. Others of our party from other parts turned up even later than us. We looked all round King's Cross to see where we might spend the rest of the night, but every shelter was closed or closing except a waiting-room, where there was not any seating apart from around the walls. Even there, however, we could not settle, for presently a group of prostitutes came in and made enough noise to prevent us sleeping. After a while the police came in and moved them on, but they were all back again in little more than a quarter of an hour, and after a while the police were in again, and this pantomime was repeated until we caught an early train for Stansted, where we boarded the plane just in time for take-off. The group who had been in time for the plane were all Londoners, who fulfilled my worst snobbish fears. They sang and sang, and mostly sang 'Tie a yellow ribbon round the Old Oak Tree.' As the holiday progressed we found that they generally came to life after midnight, by which time they had had enough to drink and a bit more to make them happy. They were good-natured, but just a bit overbearing. We hit it off rather better with a banker and a schoolmaster from the north of England.

Everything Mixed with Mercy

We were centred in a village several miles north of Athens, where the houses and our hotel were all on stilts - not for fear of floods, but of earthquakes. It was autumn, and the folk were gathering olives, which were collected by beating the tree branches with sticks, which brought the olives down. Several houses in the village were only half built. No work was done on them during the week, but at the weekends a little progress was sometimes made. People from the village worked in Athens, but they almost all had a bit of land in and around the village - a family possession which was never given up. There they could build a house for their retirement. There was no hurry: retirement was a long way ahead.

I spoke to the courier on our bus, asking how the problem of unemployment was dealt with in Greece. 'We have no unemployment in Greece' she said. What she meant was that the Government pays no unemployment benefit. In other words the problem of unemployment is solved by ignoring it. The unemployed are looked after by their families, and if that is not possible they emigrate. We did the usual tourist visits to the Parthenon, Delphi, Corinth. We took a sail among the Greek islands, enjoying the brilliant sunshine and fresh, breezy warmth. The food was good, and I particularly remember four of us at one table being served a sucking-pig - the whole animal, head, tail and four legs on one large ashet. It tasted good, but we fykie folk from Scotland approached the beast with some diffidence, as well as a knife and fork.

The hotel staff were very co-operative, and in the evenings they gave us an exhibition of Greek line-dancing, encouraging us to join in. The one disappointment was the church - the Greek Orthodox Church. We went to church, the village church, on Sunday morning, prepared to understand nothing of the language, but interested to watch the service proceeding. But the church interior was very dark, everyone was standing and remained standing, and no one addressed a word to us. Knowing no English, these locals were probably too embarrassed to make any approach.

Back home, in the course of a hard winter we woke at two o'clock one morning to the sound of rushing water. To our horror water was pouring through the roof of our bedroom. I leaped out of bed and ran to the attic bedroom, which had been Donald's room before he married. A pipe had burst in the roof there, and the cistern was emptying itself. I ran downstairs and found the water swamping the books in the study, and it was also pouring, cascading, on to my mother's bed. She had died in that bed a few years previously. I phoned the water company, and they arrived quite speedily. They found the manhole on the pavement but it was frozen so hard they could not move it. Jonto, our cat, was just a few months old, and pranced around at this un-looked-for diversion, while I, still in nothing but pyjamas, was just a helpless bystander, ready to be of help. The men turned the water off. I made tea, and we went to the attic, where there were three single beds. We lay down, but now I found I could not stop shivering. I shivered uncontrollably through the rest of the night, unable to sleep. Mary was not much better, and I was surprised to find that neither of us suffered any ill effects from the hours of non-stop shivering. In fact, Dr Milne said shivering was nature's way of keeping up body temperature.

The damage, of course, was extensive. Furniture dried out eventually, but we had no central heating and many books were beyond recovery. But one good result was the installation of a new bathroom suite, with a shower. That was the first shower we had ever had, and I have had very few baths ever since.

Mary had for years been yearning to see her brother Walter, whom she remembered as a teenager at home before he immigrated to Canada. For some years after he went off there was no word from him, but one day in the early 1930s Mary had a long letter from him, and from then on they corresponded quite regularly, although at rather lengthy intervals. Walter married an English girl during the great depression when he had no money to support a wife; but Lil did not look for support. She was quite a remarkable character, cut off from her family in England as Walter was from his folk in Scotland. She became a splendid partner for Walter and wrote Mary racy letters, and when we decided to go for a holiday with them in Vancouver we looked forward to meeting both Walter and Lil.

On the plane crossing I asked Mary if she thought she'd recognize Walter after more than fifty years, but she had no doubts. I produced some haggis, which I thought would be appropriate as a gift, but the Customs man at the airport confiscated it. I told him that at least he could look forward to a good supper that evening, and he blew his top as though I had been trying to poison him. When we got through with our luggage, there was Walter, the image of his father - fully six feet and broadly built. There was naturally an emotional reunion, and he and Lil took us to Burnaby, a suburb. The house looked rather small, and we wondered where we would be able to sleep, when Walter took us downstairs to an extensive bedroom which was to be ours for a week. The house, in fact, stood on rising ground, falling away to the rear, and Walter had built this basement with a view over the garden. I marvelled at Walter's ability, but he shrugged it off, saying this kind of thing was common. In fact, we had an early example of it a day or two later when, on returning one evening from the town, we found a house at the corner of the block where Walter and Lil lived had been

Everything Mixed with Mercy

demolished. We hadn't seen any furniture being removed that morning. I thought I must just have failed to notice any upheaval. I mentioned the extraordinary matter to Walter. He didn't know what those people had done about their furniture, but he knew they were having another house built on the site of their present house. 'They should be in in about a fortnight' he concluded. This would be a frame house - quite unfamiliar to us in Scotland.

A couple of days after our arrival Walter announced he'd had a phone call - an urgent summons to a job in Alberta, about 500 miles east of Vancouver. 'I thought you had retired?' I said. 'So I have, but they keep sending for me for special jobs.' He started packing, and I noticed he was putting together some heavy clothing. This was September, and it was warm here in Burnaby. He said it would be freezing in Alberta, where winter would have started, and he'd be away for three or four days. When he'd gone to the airport I asked Lil what sort of a job he did. She said he was a bridge inspector, and was well-known and was sent for to examine bridges far and near. He had a very unusual talent which had been the making of him. He was able, just by looking, to detect flaws, misalignment, weaknesses beginning to develop. He was able to warn companies to bring in surveyors long before anyone else spotted the trouble.

Lil was a born story-teller. I knew from indications in her letters to Mary that there must be a great deal she could tell us about her life with Walter. She was slow to start, not really knowing me, and aware that I was a minister; but once she started she gave us a spell-binding account of their early adventures and sufferings in the great Canadian depression years between the wars. Unemployment was widespread, money and food were scarce, and some folk were actually starving. She and Walter relied on each other and survived until he finally got a job and they gradually bettered their lot. I urged Lil to write down the story she had been telling us, and she agreed it might be done, but a busy life fills the time and we get old and forgetful. Lil ended her days in an old people's home, and the story was never written, to my lasting regret.

On Sunday morning Walter said they normally went out to breakfast; so we four sat down about nine o'clock in a nearby restaurant, well-filled with customers I presumed to be neighbours. After this we drove about 150 miles up the Fraser River to a place called Maple Ridge. To my complete confusion the address of the house we were visiting was 11097 Lockwood Street. I couldn't see any street, and the house was built in a clearing in the forest. Here lived Howard and Dianne Penfold and their two children. Dianne was the daughter of Walter and Lil. Howard, I understood, was a school janitor, though I didn't see any

The Kirkgate Church - Phase 2

school, or indeed any other buildings or houses. Their children were students. The girl was Jamie (still more confusion) and is now a G.P. in Moncton, New Brunswick. The boy, whose name I have forgotten, was at University on a sports scholarship, but we didn't meet him. We have kept in touch with Jamie. The house at Maple Ridge we found of considerable interest, being entirely built of timber.

Lil and Walter's son Larry lived with his wife Irene in North Vancouver. He was a plumber and heating engineer, and they had two boys. Our second week in Canada we spent with them. Larry had much to say that was interesting, but we didn't see their two boys, then still at school. Larry had a brother Stephen, unmarried, and a bit of a mystery. We didn't hear what he did for a living but he seemed to move around. We met him one day and he took us to a night club which was merely a late-night restaurant with some dancing.

Street traffic in Vancouver flowed along very smoothly with no hold-ups. The bus driver chatted away with the passengers, and there were few cars parked in the streets. Also there were no awkward turns or road junctions at narrow angles. The street formed a network with all crossings at right angles. As Larry explained, Vancouver had come into existence and grown with the motor car, so there was no parking problem. Part of the original Vancouver was retained and preserved and was interesting to walk through, but there isn't much of it. Anything over fifty years old is really old, and a hundred years old is definitely antique in Canada. We were strongly advised not to miss visiting the island of Victoria, just off the west coast. We'd find that in fact it was an English island with the population almost entirely English, with beautiful extensive public gardens. No doubt this is all true, but the day we had decided to make the trip turned out to be very foggy and very damp. We went over by the ferry hoping for improvement, but we saw little or nothing except the famous underwater garden which is constructed under the sea and we viewed it -from a covered way. It really was impressive.

Larry took us for dinner in a large restaurant on several floors, and the top floor, where we dined, was a circular restaurant, slowly turning to give most impressive views of the city by night. In all Canadian restaurants you are served with coffee before you have had time to order anything, and all through the meal your cup is replenished. In the evening, when you order dinner, the waiter provides a doggie bag, which seemed odd to us, until we saw the size of the portions they see fit to serve - far beyond our capacity. We soon acquired the habit at a meal of ordering just one course, and afterwards judging our capacity for any more.

A couple in South Leith, when they heard we were going to British

Columbia, asked if we could please pay a visit to relatives of theirs who lived about 150 miles north of Vancouver. We travelled north by train, along a very spectacular coastal route analogous to our West Highland line from Fort William to Mallaig, but on a much larger scale. After an enthralling journey we were met at the terminal station by our hosts, who, like the Penfolds at Maple Ridge, lived in a timber house built in a forest clearing. The man had worked on the railway for many years before recently retiring. In the house there were many, many dolls, of all kinds and sizes - a very interesting collection, but, many miles from the nearest neighbour, who would ever see this quite bizarre collection? The lady explained. A group of half a dozen ladies living far apart from each other were each interested in various types of doll, and bought additions to their collection whenever they saw something worth buying when on an infrequent visit to town. Each lady had some special skill - dressmaking, painting, repairing broken or chipped limbs, and through the cold, dark, lonely winter they met together and worked on each other's dolls. It was a splendid pastime and got them through the winter nicely.

On our return to Vancouver, we discovered that we had been on the last run that train would do. Not enough passengers were using that line to make it pay. The line would still be used for freight, but we had been among the last passengers.

Larry and Irene have a daughter whom we didn't meet. She is a teacher in a school in Alaska. That northern land has a winter lasting eight months in the year. This was her first experience of Alaska, and she had contracted to serve there for one year only. We heard later from Larry, however, that his daughter came home for summer holidays and said she loved the place and the people, and insisted on going back. Larry keeps us up to date with an annual account of his family's doings and as he has written no more about his daughter, she is presumably still teaching in Alaska.

Things were now moving fast in Leith. The Kirkgate Church was about to be demolished, and the work was now in hand. The pews of the old church were much lighter in colour than the South Leith pews, and under the direction of Willie Bald, a Master of Works with Edinburgh Corporation, the South Leith pews in the nave were scrapped and the Kirkgate pews fitted. This change made a surprising difference to the Parish Church interior. The pulpit steps and the stone balustrade round the dais in the Kirkgate Church ended up in the kitchen and garden of Old Lathrisk House, where Morag and David were settled; the capital of one of the pillars is now on the patio of our garden in St Andrews, although in 1981 we had not yet gone to live there. The organ of the Kirkgate Church was more of a problem, as no other church

The Kirkgate Church - Phase 2

wished to buy a complete pipe organ, although we offered it free, apart from the cost of transport. However, one of the girls in the Kirkgate congregation had recently married the organist at the Methodist Central Hall at Tollcross in Edinburgh, and he readily bought four of the organ stops, to enlarge the range of his organ.

This work now going ahead smoothly, Mary and I had to prepare for another trip abroad, this time to the United States. As secretary to the Scottish Church Society I had been in correspondence with Professor Haws of Old Dominion University in Norfolk, Virginia. On a trip to this country he had become fascinated with Scotland and its history and was eager to establish a chair in Scottish History at Old Dominion University. When his intention became known, the Scots, and those of Scots descent in Norfolk got the idea of having a Scots week. So now we were invited to take part in a conference on Scottish History, to be followed by a Scots week.

We were to fly from Heathrow to New York, and from there, by another plane to Norfolk, Virginia. We arranged to catch a shuttle flight from Glasgow to Heathrow at 7 a.m. so asked the staff at the Glasgow Airport Hotel to waken us at 6.30, which they failed to do. Fortunately I have always been an early riser, so we reached the plane for the shuttle flight, to find what seemed like hundreds of other folk all aiming for the shuttle flight. Mary and I were the last to be allowed on the plane, leaving many others stranded, and at Heathrow we boarded the New York plane without any hassle. This was 29th March 1974 - a day for us to remember.

On arrival at Kennedy Airport we went to find our connection, but were told it hadn't arrived yet. We waited - and waited - There were others travelling with us from Scotland for the conference, whom we had met at Heathrow, and after a very long wait I asked for information. What was wrong? Why the delay? They couldn't tell me. It could have been the weather, or engine trouble. They said they ought to have been informed, but advised us to move to La Guardia Airport, where we might pick up a plane for Norfolk. We did that, but the La Guardia people were no help. No planes for Norfolk. We then transferred to a much smaller airport, where we finally got a plane to take us to our destination, where we arrived about midnight, and were met by our host Bud Watson. He congratulated us on our arrival, and I thought his tone needlessly enthusiastic, and told him of our frustration in trying to get a connection from New York. He was silent. Then, 'Didn't you know?' 'Know what?' 'Someone shot at the President today. Fortunately they missed, but everything came to a halt. The only news we have had all day was repeated accounts of the attempted assassination.' He added, 'I must also congratulate you on your safe arrival. You got

South Leith Parish Church Quincentenary, 19th June, 1983
left to right: The Reverend A Gordon McGillivray, Clerk to the Presbytery of Edinburgh, the Right Reverend J Fraser McLuskey, Moderator of the General Assembly of the Church of Scotland, the Reverend Jack Kellet, Parish Minister of South Leith, the Reverend Dennis Connor, RC priest of St Mary Star of the Sea, Leith, the Reverend Dr J S Marshall, Associate Minister, South Leith Parish Church

that small plane because it is a small aircraft company with a very bad reputation for safety.'

Mrs Watson was awaiting us and offered a meal, but all we wanted was a cup of tea, which speedily appeared; but to our horror it was iced tea, which was normal in Virginia, but it was soon heated, and we went to bed happy. In the morning we were asked if we'd like creased wheat for breakfast, and ready for new experiences we agreed. It turned out to be semolina without any sugar. These culinary surprises, were capped by a boiled egg served in a cup. The Watsons had never heard of an egg-cup, and just smashed the egg in the cup.

Having studied the map, I knew the way to the university, not much more than half a mile away. I was only a few yards along the road, however, when a passing car pulled up and the driver asked if he could be of any help. I said I was heading for the university and reckoned I knew the way. He drove off, but a little further on another driver

The Kirkgate Church - Phase 2

pulled up and we went through the same pantomime, after which I turned right and managed to reach my goal with no more trouble. I was reminded of Edna Ferber in her reminiscences saying that she was fond of walking, but was arrested in Los Angeles for walking, or, as the police put it, acting suspiciously. A neighbour of ours in Leith retired and shortly afterwards lost his wife. He went to Canada to visit his son and his family, toying with the idea of making his home there. He returned a few weeks later complaining that nobody ever walked anywhere over there, and he couldn't be doing with that.

Bud Watson was in advertising, and his wife gave lectures on English to Navy personnel; many of them completed school with the haziest knowledge of the language. On Sunday they invited us to church. Morning service was at eleven o'clock, as with us, but before that, Sunday school was at ten o'clock. The Watsons' two children, about eight and ten years old, had their junior school. For adults there were two schools; one run-of-the-mill, dealing with straightforward exposition of the Scriptures, and the other dealing with various questions of Moral Philosophy and Christian Ethics, taken by a professor from the university. These classes were all well attended.

For the eleven o'clock service we were each handed an order of service and told not to throw it away afterwards, but to hold on to it. One of the hymns was sung to the tune of 'God Save the Queen', but I don't know what it was called in Virginia. I thought it rather a lugubrious hymn tune. The highlight of the service, however, had nothing to do with the worship of God. The minister and his wife were celebrating their wedding anniversary or birthday or what have you. I didn't catch what occasion it was, but the two of them stood in the centre of the dais and kissed and embraced each other at long length, to the applause of the whole congregation except Mary and me, who remained strictly spectators.

As far as worship was concerned, the high point of the service was the admission of some twenty youngsters, male and female, to full membership of the church. I found this impressive, and at the same time rather worrying. Remembering the half dozen or so we might see at a similar service in Scotland, I said to the minister afterwards, 'How do you get all these youngsters joining?' 'That's the school year,' he said. 'You mean they are drafted in here automatically?' 'Does that not worry you?' I pursued, and he was silent for a bit; then, 'Look, I've only been with this congregation three weeks. This procedure over joining the church is an old tradition here; it will take a long time to change it.' We left it at that.

Outside, the Watsons took us to a nearby soft drinks restaurant, where we handed over our Orders of Service to prove our church attendance and were given a free drink. If we are worried about church attendance in Scotland why can't we experiment with some form of blackmail like this?

Norfolk harbour is said to be the largest natural harbour in the world, and is quite well known in South Leith to both Royal Navy and Merchant Navy men. There was an American aircraft carrier berthed in the harbour, and while the public were banned from going on board Mrs Watson got permission to let us walk around. The ship is immense, with ample deck accommodation for 'planes. Below we looked in at what I can only describe as the operations room. A great range of dials controls operations all over the ship, and nothing there looks remotely maritime.

The city of Norfolk itself was certainly geared to Scottish week. The mayor, or whatever the American equivalent is called, laid on a sumptuous lunch for our party, and we walked all round the centre of the city and viewed the statue of General McArthur. There was no apartheid on the South African model, but there was certainly a distinct divide between white and black. On our way into town from the Watsons' home, we suddenly came to a large block of flats built of cheap, ugly bricks and without gardens. These flats were black houses. In Scotland we read about blacks in America entering the professions and making names for themselves in sports, but such blacks are exceptional. The vast majority have basic education and fill poorly paid domestic jobs and the like. Mrs Watson had been brought up in Alabama and there had always been black servants in the house, and in Virginia the Watsons had a black servant, who did not live in but had long been attached to the family.

There was a procession one day which we found rather comical. I should judge that few if any of the marchers had ever been to Scotland, but they all probably had Scots ancestors and they had arranged themselves into clans, each clan headed by its chief, bearing the clan crest and motto. About half of these names I had never heard of, and among the music they marched to was 'God Save the Queen! There must have been some significance in that tune for them as they used it both as a hymn and a march. I never discovered why they were so fond of it.

Then there was the ball, where we enjoyed ourselves very much, and of course the Scottish guests were asked - pressed - to dance a Scottish reel. I was relieved at this, as I had been taught the eightsome reel in the Boy Scouts in preparation for our attendance at the World Scout Jamboree at Birkenhead in 1929. Since then it had been difficult to find any casual group in Scotland who knew the steps and their sequence. But this time, for some reason we were superb. The only jarring incident

The Kirkgate Church - Phase 2

was a man lying on the floor at our feet. I was very annoyed. In all our time in America I had never yet seen a drunk, but sooner of later it was bound to happen, I thought.

We paid an interesting visit to Williamsburg. Americans are immensely proud of Williamsburg, and indeed they ought to be. This town, dating from the Colonial era of the seventeenth century, has been carefully preserved as it was 350 years ago, and all the inhabitants wear the costumes worn by their ancestors. The details of antiquity make for interesting, even absorbing sightseeing, but always there is the inescapable awareness that this is a kind of play that is being enacted day by day. In Britain our stately homes are preserved and admired, but the American aim is to make the visitor forget he is a visitor and persuade him to become part of the 17th century community

When we arrived in Virginia at the beginning of April the trees were leafless and no flowers were showing in the Watsons' garden. A fortnight later, as were leaving, the trees were flourishing, in full leaf, and the few bulbs we saw were fading. The temperature, too, was climbing to the nineties Fahrenheit. 'That was the spring,' the Watsons said, 'it normally lasts a fortnight.' Apart from the normal seasonal change, however, Norfolk had had no rain for the past two years, and water had become a major problem. Watering the garden was forbidden. Drinking water came from bottles, and the neighbours were all digging wells in their gardens, for water was available thirty feet down. Bud Watson was helping the man next door to dig a well, and once we had gone they would be starting on a well in the Watsons' garden. There was some urgency about this work as the summer was just starting and there was still no sign of rain. Everyone with a garden well had a ticket on the front gate saying that their well was their own and was not a drain on the town's resources.

We took the plane back to New York without any untoward incident, but when we left the plane we got a shock. It was freezing. We had left Norfolk in summer heat, but spring in New York felt like winter in Scotland and our heavy clothes were in our heavy luggage and not accessible. Our flight home was from Kennedy airport, which was a good distance across the city. We had to stand for half an hour in a queue in the open air waiting for an airport bus. We had a comfortable flight home and got off at Prestwick on a beautiful sunny spring day, mild and fresh.

Back home the following Sunday I was telling the choir something of our experiences, when Stephen Shepherd interrupted me. Stephen is a Maths teacher at Currie High School, and he said, 'My father saw you.' 'Your father?' said I. 'How come?' 'He's a photographer with the B.B.C. He was on an assignment with a reporter to cover the Scots Week at Norfolk. He was at the Ball and saw you dancing the Eightsome, so he got down on the floor to photograph your footwork, for that's something the Americans are interested to see.' So I had to revise my ideas of drunkenness in America.

About a month after our return from America, the foundation stone of the new church halls was laid, and the daunting prospect of raising about four times the original estimate for the work now faced the congregation. We had some lawyers in the congregation, and through them Jack Kellet acquired a huge list of funds that might have money tied up for specific purposes. The hope was that some of that kind of money might be released for our use. The hope was slender, but Jack set to and wrote no less than 4000 separate letters, and money began trickling in. I never heard how much came in by this means. All I heard from Jack was that little or nothing came from local firms, but some surprising responses arrived from far away. There was even one contribution from India!

The completed Halls were opened the following year by the Duke of Edinburgh. At the opening of the halls while we were waiting for more and more people to gather, he said to me, 'Is there a loo anywhere?' I directed him and off he went. Returning, he said 'I always take the opportunity when it occurs, I never know when the next chance may come.' In the church I showed him the two King James communion cups with the London hallmark of 1617. He was very interested and examined the royal arms and said he was puzzled about some detail on the arms. As the congregation was sitting watching us, we couldn't continue the conversation, but I have often wondered what it was that puzzled him.

After the halls were opened, Jack received an invitation to spend the weekend at Balmoral and preach at Crathie Kirk. This was quite stunning. Jack was not a republican, but his attitude to the Royal Family had always been cool and non-committal - not unlike my own view. He had asked the Duke of Edinburgh to officiate at the opening because he saw it as due and appropriate for such a historic church with such a close-knit relationship with the town and parish of Leith. Well, off he went, and duly returned on the way to becoming a royalist. He had had a warm welcome, conversation with the Queen and Duke, and preached (I presume) satisfactorily. The only untoward incident occurred when having a meal at the Castle. As he rose from the table he stood on one of the corgis who let the world know he was being attacked, but it all ended happily.

In the autumn we had a visit from the Sealed Knot, who went through a re-enactment of the Siege of Leith in 1560. The French troops of Mary of Guise were occupying Leith, and were attacked and besieged

The Kirkgate Church - Phase 2

by the English. The Sealed Knot is a company of enthusiasts who go around Britain acting out famous historic battles. They dress in period costume and as far as possible bear antique arms. To my critical eye, they are youngsters who have never grown up, like adults who go train-spotting or who play with toy trains. The irony of their efforts on the Links was, that it has recently been discovered that the fighting in 1560 did not take place on the ground the Sealed Knot had occupied. Stuart Harris, the Edinburgh City Architect, and I, had got a copy of the Petworth Map and photographed it. This map had been drawn by an English army officer after the ending of hostilities, and before the English army moved back south. It clearly shows that the two hillocks on the Links, traditionally thought to have been emplacements for field cannon, were nothing of the kind, the guns being sited elsewhere.

Celebrating the quincentenary of the Church in 1983, I wrote a historic pageant depicting memorable events in the Church's history, and this was acted out appropriately in the Church. 'The Church in the Midst', over which I had been sweating for many months, was also published by the Edina Press in time for the quincentenary.

Hardly were the quincentenary celebrations over when I received notice from the Church Offices at 121 George Street that I was now retired and would, instead of stipend, receive a pension from the Aged and Infirm Ministers Fund. This was not unexpected, but I had kept it at the back of my mind. In 1939 I had been ordained *ad vitam aut culpam* - ordained, that is, for life, or until such time as I might from some misdemeanour or culpable activity be deprived of my ordained status and dismissed the ministry. This had always been the accepted status of a minister, but two developments had altered things for me. First, when I got the Kirkgate Church to join with South Leith Parish Church, I forfeited my standing as a parish minister and became an associate minister. This was a novelty at the time, but is now quite common. There are now a fair number of associate ministers in the Church of Scotland. The other development affecting me was that the General Assembly passed a law requiring all ministers to retire at the age of seventy. Too many ministers were hanging on to their parishes and stipends long past the time when they were fit and able for the job. This was having a disastrous effect on the congregations affected. When I became an associate minister I automatically forfeited my right to lifelong parish ministry.

Realising this, I also realised that I could not be put out of the manse, as South Leith had no need of it. A house to live in when retired was a major headache for most ministers, as under the old system they could live in the manse until death, and few had had the resources to buy a house for retirement and rent it.

When I told the Kirk Session of my new standing as a retired minister, they said they did not think I was fit to retire - they could not see anything physically or mentally wrong with me. They made a proposal. I would remain a minister in South Leith, and they would pay me half the stipend, while I'd receive the Aged and Infirm Ministers grant which would provide the rest of my pay. The underlying assumption, never mentioned between us, was that I would do only half the normal work of the ministry, but of course that was impossible to decide on. I just carried on as usual.

10
LAST YEARS IN SOUTH LEITH 1988 - 1990

Maybe it was just as well that the Irish lassie didn't stay on with us, for it occurred to us that Good Friday was the one day in the year when mass was not celebrated, and we felt we ought to make use of this fact. The Roman Catholic Church stood just about fifty yards from South Leith Parish Church, but our contacts with the priest there were flimsy. This was not from any hostility, but from the fact that every two or three years the priest was changed, so there was hardly time for close relationships to be established.

After the Reformation there were no Roman Catholics in Leith apart from the family of the Duke of Gordon in the late seventeenth century. At the turn of the nineteenth century, during the French wars, Britain and Ireland were united, and with an acute shortage of men, Irish labour was used to build the Martello Tower (The 'Tally Tooer') as part of the country's defences against the French. At the same period, during the French Revolution, the Church there suffered persecution, and in an effort to survive the 'troubles' a priest established an Order called the Oblates of Mary Immaculate (O.M.I.) which carried on in Italy until the advent of Napoleon allowed them back into France. But the Oblates were a missionary Order, and soon crossed the Atlantic and made considerable headway in Canada.

In the meantime there was a gradual, but steady increase in the number of Roman Catholics in Leith, The end of the Napoleonic War brought great industrial depression. Schemes like the Radical Road and the Forth and Clyde Canal provided work for the unemployed. Then Leith's independence and the coming of the railways brought great demand for labour. This was supplied by massive immigration from the Irish potato famine in 1847, and a similar potato famine in the Gaelic speaking Highlands at the same period.

Parliament at Westminster had passed an Act for Catholic Emancipation. All the Trade Incorporations had vehemently opposed emancipation and petitioned Parliament against it, but in fact, on a personal level Protestants and Roman Catholics in Leith got on quite well together. There was no Roman Catholic church but from time to time a room was hired in Constitution Street and a priest would come from Edinburgh to celebrate mass. Then at some time in the 1850s the Leith Roman Catholics acquired possession of Balmerino House and grounds in the Kirkgate and established a school there, and in time built a church. Where the money for all this came from was never made known. There were no wealthy Roman Catholics in the district, and the

Roman Church had no money to spare, and there was much sympathy for the plight of starving incomers from Ireland and the north-west Highlands. The new church was built in what had been the garden of Balmerino House.

From 1859, when the new church was opened, the priests supplying the charge were all members of the Order of Oblates of Mary Immaculate (O.M.I.) This meant that Leith, in fact, was regarded as a mission station, and the priests did not settle as in a normal parish. They were regarded as being on active service, liable to be moved to any other place where the need for a priest was more urgent.

David Thorburn, minister of the Free Church in South Leith, lived in Charlotte Street, and his elder son, John, in his old age, wrote:

'I remember being taken to the lofts at the back of Charlotte Street to see the laying of the foundation stone of the Roman Catholic Chapel from one of the windows. The procession marched round the ground, consecrating it, when halfway round the mitre fell off the head of the Bishop, and there was a hubbub, all retraced their steps and began the service over again.'

If the congregation became warmly attached to their priest they could ask to have his period with them extended, as happens in the Methodist Church, and this happened occasionally. In August 1982, Father Michael Fitzpatrick, O.M.I, died in Leith at the age of 98. On his ordination in 1921 Father Fitzpatrick came to Leith and soon had a great reputation as a preacher and pastor, and founder of a thriving Boys' Club. He remained for five years. The next eighteen years he spent in Ireland, London and Wales, before returning to Leith in 1944. The rest of his life was spent in the port, where he remained in retirement, known to all and sundry, and the mingled affability and earnestness of his nature commended him as a friend to those of other Christian denominations, and indeed to those of no fixed faith. He was one of the outstanding Oblate Fathers and a Christian reconciler whose presence in Leith was a blessing to all.

We suggested to the priest that on the evening of Good Friday any who were interested from South Leith Parish Church might join with the members of St Mary's Star of the Sea (Stella Maris) for the service of Stations of the Cross. He would conduct the service just as he normally did, and the South Leith clergy and members would attend as visitors. The priest (Sean Hynes) was delighted. So about forty of us from South Leith attended. There are fourteen Stations of the Cross, marking incidents on Christ's journey from Pilate's Hall to Calvary, and in the church there were fourteen paintings depicting these incidents - all of them badly oxidised and in need of restoring. At each picture a prayer was said, with responses. After the service, we were all welcomed to the R.C. hall, where one end of the hall was fitted up as a bar, although I saw no alcohol on offer. This was in the old Balmerino House, as was the priests' presbytery.

This annual pilgrimage to the Stations of the Cross continued with roughly the same number attending, but our people found it increasingly boring. Having started it, however, it was difficult to stop. We felt, however, the answer was not to walk away, but to become more familiar with them and their ways. They recognized our difficulty, and readily agreed to having a joint Songs of Praise in South Leith Parish Church in the autumn. I was quite surprised at the number of hymns they knew. I spoke briefly about the hymns we sang, and we ended with tea and biscuits in our hall. The next useful development was when the Roman Catholics installed a 'cry chapel'. This was achieved by closing off the west end of their church behind a perspex screen, providing a small room where mothers with infants and toddlers could attend church, leaving their children to be looked after. The kids could make as much noise as they liked and would not be heard in the church, and the mothers could see if their youngsters were becoming obstreperous and could go to them in the cry chapel. This all worked very well, and our people thought they could use a similar idea in the Parish Church, which, indeed, we did achieve some years later. I now met Anna Franchi, the organist at St Mary's Star of the Sea. She lived in Easter Road, was the Infant Mistress at Holy Cross Primary School, and thought it would be a good idea for our two choirs to rehearse Mendelssohn's *Elijah*. I was happy with this, and we set up rehearsals with a piano in their cry chapel. But it didn't come off. Attendance at rehearsals was too irregular, but we felt it was a good thing to have tried.

The priests didn't preach in the Parish Church, but both Jack Kellet and I preached at St. Mary's more than once in my time. In the vestry before I went to start the service, the priest said to me 'When you go in, Dr Marshall, you don't have to genuflect. We all know you don't do that, so don't worry about it.' I was only preaching and the priest was taking the rest of the service. In the pulpit I began with the invocation 'In the name of the Father and of the Son and of the Holy Spirit' to which the whole congregation responded loudly 'Amen'! This never happened in the Church of Scotland, although I had always thought it ought to. I was taken aback, but quite thrilled. It was a complete contrast to the Nazarene Church in Twechar, where the numerous Neil family went to sleep when I announced the text. The congregation now in front of me were saying 'Go ahead; we're listening.'

I was now chairman of the National Bible Society, and was asked to attend a Bible Society conference at Mannheim, with Andrew Doig, our general secretary. We arrived at Turnhouse in good time, with our seats booked, and tickets in hand, only to be told that the plane was fully booked and there was no room for us. We argued, of course. Why had our booking been accepted if there were no seats available? We were not speaking to the party responsible, and there was no time to sort things out before take-off. Then fortune smiled. A man standing beside us said he could take us to London in another airline. He would get us to Gatwick for no extra charge. We said we had a connection to get at Heathrow, but he intimated that was no problem as there was a bus connecting the two airports. We travelled gratefully, but on arriving at Heathrow found the whole place in chaos. Early that morning, in pursuit of some claim, the staff had decided to go slow. With frightening speed the place was a shambles, as no planes were accepted or allowed away, and thousands of people were hanging about in complete ignorance of the cause of all this. After about an hour, however, things started moving again, but the tailback for planes was so long that we were separated and hemmed in more and more tightly in the queue hoping to get on the plane for Frankfurt. Suddenly I felt an attack of claustrophobia, and fought my way out to a nearby wall where I could breathe. This was a situation in which I could feel the build-up to an epileptic fit, even after all those years. After a bit, I saw Andrew Doig leaning against the wall a few yards away. I asked if he was all right, and he said he had had to get out of the crowd as he had had a turn of claustrophobia - which greatly relieved me. We reached Frankfurt about midnight and got a train, even at that hour, for Mannheim. At Mannheim, after one a.m. we got a taxi for our hotel. The door was closed, but a light shone through a chink. We knocked, the door opened and two waiters welcomed us and asked if we'd like a full dinner or perhaps just a cup of tea. We were astonished at this activity at this hour. 'We heard on the radio of the trouble at Heathrow, so realised you'd be late.' We went to bed, realising this level of service would not be available in Scotland.

Jimmy Brown, an assistant with us, belonged to Kirkcaldy, and had a lively interest in the arts. He went off to the Rhineland and began working with the German Evangelical Church at Bochum. He was involved with young people, and met Heike Lengenfeld, who was being ordained as the first woman minister in the Evangelical Church. They decided to marry and Jimmy sent a strong invitation to Jack and/or me to attend the wedding. As Mary had enough German to get by in conversation, we went over as part of our summer holiday. Jimmy had organised digs for us, and we settled in for several days. The wedding was conducted in two languages; Jimmy took the vows in German and Heike in English. The lessons and prayers and hymns switched from

Last Years in South Leith 1988 - 1990

one language to the other. At the reception only German was heard, for only Jimmy's close relatives had made the journey. One man was pointed out to me as having fluent English, and I said to him, 'I'm told you speak English?' 'Oh ay.' said he in a strong Scots accent, and it turned out he had taught in Kirkcaldy for a year.

On the Sunday, the church attendance was poor - worse than in Scotland, and this was the more marked, as the whole town of Bochum was divided into four and one church building allocated to each quarter. But there was more to church life than appeared at the morning service. In the afternoon Jimmy took us on a tour of the churches. Each congregation had its own orchestra, and on this Sunday they were all performing. We heard a splendid programme in one church, and at the end of it we were invited into the church hall for afternoon tea, after which the concert was resumed, with the music provided by a succession of soloists. There was no time to visit the other congregations.

The next day, Mary attended a meeting of the Woman's Guild (or its equivalent - a women's meeting) while I explored more of the town. We then made our way to the Rhine and joined a cruise up the river. I hadn't been on the Rhine since the school trip in 1931. Going ashore for brief spells at various towns, my abiding memory of Cologne is of a piano and violin outside the cathedral offering classical music to the passing crowds.

It was on this cruise that we met Murray and Marie Lambden on their honeymoon. They came from the Isle of Man, and I was intrigued to hear that his favoured sport was walking - not the walking we are all adept at and take for granted, but the athletic form of locomotion - strictly heel and toe. We have kept in touch ever since, and went on holiday to the Isle of Man and found it a delightful place.

Lord Murray, chairman of the Leith Museum Trustees, said to me on one occasion, 'Edinburgh's attitude to Leith has completely changed in the last twenty years or so.' This is true, Edinburgh used to see the port as full of whingers, always asking for what could not be given, now the same place is a money-spinner and well worth listening to. Edinburgh never understood Leith, never realised the reality of the strong and close community spirit of the port, which in many ways was still a large village. A recent report described Edinburgh as the city in Britain where the fewest smiles were to be seen. Leith, again, has often been described as the Glasgow of the east. Coming down from Edinburgh by bus in silence, most of the Edinburgh passengers get off at Pilrig, and are replaced by Leithers who look round for any friends or neighbours, and start conversations in which anyone is welcome to take part.

Golden Wedding, 1989 at Donald's House, with James' brother Terry and Sister Isabel

Diamond Wedding at Lathrisk, Freuchie, September 1999, with some of the family

Grandmother Isabella Cormack
1855 - 1926

This portrait was known to the grandchildren as "Grannie when she was a boy".

Her hair had been cut to 'cure a fever'

Mother
Isabella Cameron
Cormack Scott in
1966

Wife Mary in 1958

Everything Mixed with Mercy

Daughter Morag in 2000

Morag's Daughter Josephine in 2000

Mary's daughter Morag's daughter Jo's daughter Katie aged 14 in 2003

Last Years in South Leith 1988 - 1990

There are salubrious areas east and west of the old town, which consists entirely of tenements. Leithers like tenement life. It has a special quality. When I returned to Leith in 1947 I met an old friend in the street. He was an old classmate from Leith Academy. I asked where he was living, and he said, 'You know where I live.' He was a professional man in Edinburgh, but was still in the tenement flat where he had been born. I pointed out that he had for years been earning a salary at least five times the amount of my stipend. He could have been living in the Edinburgh New Town. 'Why would I do that?' he countered, 'I've lived in that stair all my life. I know everyone in the stair and they know me.' However, a year or two later the Corporation knocked his tenement down, to develop the site, and my friend moved to the Edinburgh New Town. I met him again. 'You were quite right,' he said, 'there are advantages now that I didn't have in Leith.' 'But you're not smiling,' said I. 'No neighbour has called.' he said. 'Nobody wants to know me.'

Another angle on Leith's peculiarity from Edinburgh's point of view was brought home to me when I called at the Transport Department in Edinburgh to make some enquiry. 'Before I answer your query' said the man in charge at the office, 'would you mind answering a question that bothers everyone in this office? Why is it that everyone in Leith talks about Edinburgh as if it were another place? Leith has been part of Edinburgh since 1920. Edinburgh consists of a cluster of what once were separate villages. People in Corstorphine, Morningside, Newington, Portobello, don't talk about going to Edinburgh. This eccentricity belongs to Leith only.' I agreed that it was a mystery. The time was not appropriate for a lecture, but four centuries of antagonism between the city and the port leave their mark.

When, at the Duke of Edinburgh's instigation, money was found to clean up the Royal Mile, modernising the interior of the tenements while carefully preserving the ancient street faces - Leithers assumed that the port, as part of the city since 1920, would share in this enlightened attitude to the historic buildings still with us. That was naive: Leith was part of Edinburgh when it suited government to stress the fact; but when financial help was at issue, Leith was not at all the same place as Edinburgh. The Westminster government shared the outlook of Edinburgh Corporation, and Edinburgh did not like that at all. Those were hard times, business was in the doldrums, and the Westminster Parliament passed an act to encourage industrial development - a 40% development grant. But Edinburgh, said Westminster, was not an industrial city, despite Leith being part of the city, so did not qualify for the grant.

This was a body blow to Leith. One after another, firms packed up and left for Bathgate, Linlithgow, Glasgow - any place where the

Everything Mixed with Mercy

Government grant would be available for expansion - and many workers followed. At the end of the Second World War the population of Leith was around 80,000, but it diminished to half that number and continued to fall. So in 1964 the city corporation finally decided to do something for Leith. The state of the Kirkgate would be attended to. This news thrilled the port. The Kirkgate (locally known as 'The Channel') was at the heart of the old town - mostly small shops run by 'characters' like Hungry Erchie, attracting customers from Edinburgh to the offal butcher and other shops where prices were lower than in the city. Immediately off the Kirkgate in St Anthony Street, William Younger's mother brewed ale in her kitchen, and the great brewery grew from that small beginning. In Giles Street at the corner, 'The Big Sixes' - two huge white 6s on a blue painted wall - was well known over a wide area. Here everything was in sacks - oatmeal, lentils, sugar, flour, as in the nineteenth century, and poor people could buy what they needed in one or two ounces or spoonfuls. This not only suited the customer, but also greatly enhanced the profit on each sack of goods sold. The shopkeeper had got the idea while on holiday in Germany before the First War.

Opposite the Parish Kirk and Kirkyard stood Trinity House, the old Hospital of the Incorporation of Mariners, the wealthiest of the trade incorporations, and the only one to survive practically unchanged after the act of 1848 abolishing the privileged incorporations, and the Mariners were still paying a hundred pensions a week to their aged, sick or disabled members. Next to the Churchyard stood the Gaiety Theatre, considered to be the finest small theatre in Scotland. All this area was 'attended to' by Edinburgh, by the simple process of destroying the Kirkgate and its adjoining streets - demolishing everything except the Church and Churchyard, and Trinity House. In place of the old and historic came the new, in the shape of a new housing scheme, and a shopping complex at the Foot of the Walk called the New Kirkgate - a final slap in the face to the traditionalists. Once the shock of the changes had died down, old men were proud to detail to me what they remembered of the Kirkgate in what they thought of as the glory days. They would begin at the Big Pipes, an eighteenth century pub at the foot of the east side of the Kirkgate and mention every shop or other building right up to the Foot of the Walk, then down the other side to the corner of Tolbooth Wynd. This narrative took a long time, for it included mention of the shopkeepers, with tales of their sayings and doings.

Graham Wood, my grandson, was now a student at Edinburgh University. He had from his early days suffered a number of allergies but with self discipline had pretty well coped with them but lived in a flat on his own, to avoid the food others took for granted. He played the jazz trumpet and rehearsed with a like-minded group. On his way back to the flat late one night after a rehearsal, he was jumped on in King's Stables Road, beaten up and left lying unconscious until being picked up and taken to the Infirmary. He was a resilient young man, however, and was persuaded by a pal of his, a fellow musician, to go busking with him in Princes Street one summer afternoon. In three or four hours on this ploy, he made £20, and wondered how long this might last, as he was spending so much time at classes with no income.

He was reading for a degree in Arabic and Turkish, and in his final year he went to Damascus for a course in colloquial Arabic. From that ancient city he sent a warm invitation to Mary and me to spend a holiday there. We jumped at the chance. Damascus figures largely in the Bible, and has been extensively written about. Obtaining a visa was not a routine exercise. We applied from Edinburgh, about a month before our intended departure, and the Syrian Consulate in London promised repeatedly to post it - but didn't. Two or three days before departure we travelled to Harrow Weald and put up with Jimmy and Lilian Mackenzie. Jimmy had newly retired from the Metropolitan Police and we called with him at the Syrian Consulate, where we were told they collected applications from 10 a.m. till noon, and gave out visas between 2 and 3 p.m. Our application had been with them for two or three weeks, and it was only after waiting over an hour that the man responsible showed up. He at last arrived and gave us the visa from a drawer full of visas.

Since I kept a diary of this holiday, my memory of it has stimulated me to write at some length, too much for inclusion in the main narrative but perhaps worthy of inclusion as an appendix, 'Damasus Diary'. At this point I'll confine my report to our visits to "The Street Called Straight".

We set off to find the Christian quarter. The maps were not reliable in detail, but we knew we must travel from the north-west of the city, where we stayed, to the south-east end. We walked through a maze of back-streets and alleys and ancient buildings, and finally had to take a taxi. During our walk we saw a Muslim funeral. First came a minibus with the chief women mourners, all hooded; then the coffin, draped with an embroidered green mortcloth and borne on the shoulders of eight men; then the procession of mourners, walking - those who had made the pilgrimage to Mecca in their white skull caps. Khalid, a friend of Graham's, later explained that they were either on their way from the house of mourning to the mosque, or else from the mosque to the graveyard. Walking was normal, unless the distance was too great. All this took place along a very narrow, very busy street.

'The Street called Straight' is about half a mile long, and bisects the area enclosed by the old town wall. Very narrow in parts, the width varies considerably, and it is lined by little shops and houses. These buildings are two or three stories high, with a flat roof where the washing hangs behind the parapet or railing. Various crafts and trades are carried on in these little shops, which have often no front but are open to the street. Through all this, donkeys, cars, and even school buses somehow manage to find their way, pedestrians giving way as necessary.

Towards the further end of this street we turned right to find the Church of St Mary. We could find no way in, but Graham spoke to a man, who told a boy of about nine years to guide us. He led us to a door set in a high wall, where he banged, and presently it was opened by a woman. The boy refused the tip Mary offered him, and on passing through the doorway we found ourselves in a paved yard surrounding the church.

Inside, the church was unforgettably beautiful. Walls, ceiling and pillars were all white. Icons innumerable, a centre aisle, a small communion table, and two pulpits, one on each side, each against a pillar. Access was by spiral staircases round the pillars to the pulpits about fifteen feet from the ground. Brass candlesticks eight feet high, and four flower arrangements - two at the table and two flanking the entrance at the back of the church. A wedding was due to take place at four o'clock that afternoon, and an intricate arrangement of white ribbon stretching from a central point in the gallery down to each pew formed a kind of canopy for the bride right down the central aisle.

We looked for St Paul's Chapel, erected on the old city wall at the place where traditionally St Paul was let down in a basket to escape his enemies. Approaching from the opposite end of the Christian quarter, we tried to thread our way through the old town and got lost in a warren of very narrow wynds, each about eight feet wide. Eventually we found ourselves in Straight Street, and the rest was easy. This chapel of St Paul is fascinating, bare, and empty of pews, there are two marble wall plaques showing Paul's conversion on the road to Damascus, and his being lowered over the city wall in a basket, and icons representing Paul, Barnabas, Ananias etc., etc.

In the yard behind the chapel is an orphanage, and the youngsters were having games supervised by their teachers, and the noise was on a par with the noise Scottish children make in the same circumstances.

Back in South Leith Parish I turned my attention to what had increasingly been my concern in recent months, which was the recovery and proper use of the Scots language. For years past I had watched the slow but inevitable decline of Gaelic. The tragedy here was that while a

Last Years in South Leith 1988 - 1990

century ago in my grandparents' day they had done their best to kill off their language, the Gaels were now frantically trying to recover it, but I judged the rot had spread too far, and there would be no recovery. An enthusiastic and determined group had for long been selling the idea of a renewed Gaelic and had received financial backing to the extent of several million pounds. Despite this kind of backing the number of Gaelic speakers was declining year by year - and the over-riding, vital statistic was the number of Gaelic speakers. My father's parents, both Gaelic speakers, had refused to teach their children the language, saying that if they were known to be teuchters - Gaelic-speakers - they would never get on in the world. This was true in that the lowland and English population did rather despise the uncouth, countrified northerner, but instead of accepting this judgement the Gaels should have stood up for their language and used it colloquially from day to day. This they failed to do in an English-speaking community.

Gaelic literature and poetry is still being added to, but this is the work of scholars, who form a kind of language club, in which the members share the same hobby. This has no impact on the community. If the language is to survive it must be used by the public at large. This has happened in North Wales and in Norway. In the Irish Free State the scholars, enthusiastic for the preservation of Erse, have succeeded in having Erse included in the schools' curriculum as a compulsory subject, but school-leavers very soon forget almost all they learned through the lack of use in everyday life.

In South Leith congregation a husband and wife became keen to learn Gaelic, and began attending classes. At first things went well, but after about two years they became despondent, and said they felt they could never get any further, as they had no Gaelic-speaking friend to converse with. On the other hand, in his memoirs, Angus Graham, 7th Duke of Montrose, tells how, as a boy being brought up on the Island of Arran, he became interested in Gaelic through hearing it spoken by the islanders. He learned a little of the language from them, and thereafter, wherever he went in the world - and he was far travelled - he sought out Gaelic-speakers and made a point of conversing with them, and always adding a little to his knowledge of the language.

For over thirty years I was a Board member with the National Bible Society of Scotland (now the Scottish Bible Society). Our business was largely to do with languages, and our translators produced many languages in writing for the first time. This exercise, of course, was to provide the Bible, or at least portions of Scripture so that the people using that language could be communicated with even without the presence of a missionary. A language does not need writing to survive. Many people in the third world live in communities remote from the

Everything Mixed with Mercy

rest of the world. They all have their own languages: but if and when they make contact with other people using other languages the pristine language inevitably adds new words, and the people acquire different ways of seeing things and looking at the bigger world. This is what happened to Gaelic. Originally the language of a people cut off from contact with the rest of the country by the lack of roads, their language, their view of the world, their culture were markedly different from the lowlands. In the modern world, Gaelic can never be the everyday language of the community.

To my deep concern, the Scots language seemed to be heading along the same road as Gaelic had gone. In my youth Scots was frowned on by teachers, employers, all those in authority, and while Scots was used in the street, it was a poor, emasculated version of the language. Today there are those who claim that Scots is not a language but a dialect of English, in which English words are mis-spelt, mis-pronounced, and English grammar and syntax mangled. There is no denying a great many words and phrases have inevitably been added to what might be called basic Scots. This happens in all languages as world circumstances change, new inventions and discoveries appear. Language, in its nature, is for ever changing and developing. Local communities have their own words and pronunciations. Local accents say a lot to the rest of the country. All this can be readily acknowledged, but in Scots there are many words peculiar to Scotland, many idioms very expressive of truths or angles on the world quite unknown in English. This sets Scots up as more than and different from a dialect of English.

It is surely worth striving to preserve this surviving language. There are dialects within Scots, as in Ayrshire and Fife, and Doric, spoken in Buchan and Aberdeenshire, is the most pronounced and vigorous variety of Scots, because the northeast is mostly an agricultural area less influenced by English infiltration and the culture of the big cities. Glasgow has its so-called 'Glesca Patter', which hardly amounts to a dialect. It has a very limited vocabulary and is intended to be funny. A Doric festival is now held every autumn, and at one of these a man complained to me about visitors from the south who regarded Doric as a joke. This was insulting, for Doric is the everyday language of everyone in the area, young and old, rich and poor.

Many interested people are trying to establish Scots as a literary medium of expression in today's world, but there are problems. In the late seventeenth century English and Scots were separate languages, and in neither tongue were there any strict rules for spelling, grammar and syntax. As a large percentage of the population was illiterate this had not mattered much, but with the beginning of the eighteenth century these needful rules were introduced in England. This did not happen in Scotland, as it seems to have been assumed that with the Union of the Parliaments in 1707, and the English population being around ten times as big as the Scottish population, the pressure must be on the Scots to learn English rather than the other way about, and nothing was ever done to set this matter right, so that today writers in Scots are still a law unto themselves, although the Scots Language Society is trying to set these matters right.

All this having been on my mind for some time, I was thrilled when in 1983 William Lorimer's New Testament in Scots was published. This was the culmination of twenty years' work by Lorimer, who was Professor of Greek at St Andrews University. In Scotland this was a publishing sensation, and indeed it was a *tour de force*. Translated from the original Greek of the New Testament, it was presented in a form of Scots never before seen in print. Words, phrases and idioms from all the airts of Scotland, following the supposed variations in speech of different New Testament characters - it provided a hugely exciting symphony, as it were, of our language. But there were difficulties. Nobody understood all the words, culled from many districts. Some idioms and phrases, genuinely Scottish in their feel, were unfamiliar. These were no great difficulties for private reading and access to a Scots dictionary. As Hugh McDiarmid, the poet and fervent Scottish Nationalist, once said, 'If people don't understand what I say or write, it's up to them to find out, and so learn something'. Reading in public was a different matter. Many who were fluent enough Scots speakers read the language with difficulty.

In church I began reading the New Testament lessons in Scots, and this was welcomed enthusiastically by the middle-aged and elderly. Younger people had had less experience of the language in daily life than their parents. As time passed I occasionally preached in Scots, at St Andrews-tide and at services for the elderly, which the disabled attended in wheelchairs. One Sunday, after a service which had been taken in Scots, an American couple came to the vestry. They were from a mid-western state and had never before been in Scotland. I began to sympathise with them on their unexpected introduction to Scots. They said they were very happy to have had the experience, and said that while they didn't understand all the words, they were able to understand what I was driving at, and I realised that they felt as I did listening to a public address in Paris.

From time to time I'd ask our assistant to read the lesson in Scots. Every assistant was familiar with Scots as used in conversation, but faced with the printed page they were taken aback with the spelling and needed a week's notice to be able to read fluently. I attended a service conducted by a well-known Edinburgh minister who was a very effective preacher. On this occasion he read the New Testament from Lorimer. It was not a success. He was obviously dealing with an unfamiliar language and had several mispronunciations. Again, one of our assistants, hailing from Lossiemouth, read Scots very effectively, and in the vestry after the service I congratulated him, but mentioned two or three words he had mispronounced. He denied this, said he had known and used these words all his life. I apologised, said we had a different pronunciation in Leith, and we left it at that.

I now got the idea of translating the Old Testament into Scots. It would not compare with Lorimer's work, for I could not work from the original Hebrew and Aramaic; it would be a rendering of English into Scots, and I knew it would take many years, as the work could only be pursued in my spare time. I began by translating the Old Testament passages read in church. Before long I realised this could only be a kind of introduction to the work, as very little of the Old Testament is ever read in public. It was also soon apparent that I'd have to compile my own dictionary of English into Scots. There were several good versions of Scots into English, but English into Scots was not well served, so I began compiling my own card index, which has become very useful.

It became obvious that most of the congregation liked to hear Scots spoken and read but that was as far as it went with them; but a much smaller group became enthusiastic. Two or three primary school teachers told me on different occasions that they would very much like to teach Primary 7 to read and speak Scots, but there was very little material available. I told them there was masses of poetry being written in Scots, but they said that sort of thing was useless for teaching. What was needed was a good collection of stories in Scots. I promised to do what I could, and have written some Old Testament stories in Scots for children.

A young couple in South Leith asked me to marry them in Scots, and I agreed to do that. I needed help. Fortunately David Ogston of St John's Church, Perth, had recently published a marriage service in Scots in the Church's 'Life and Work' magazine, and something along those lines would suit South Leith. I had also heard of the Rev Dr Joyce Collie, of Strathdon in Aberdeenshire, a friend of Johnny Mack, an associate minister at Premnay, and a good friend of mine. Dr Collie had for years worked in Edinburgh with the Scottish National Dictionary Association before entering the ministry of the Church of Scotland. She was widely known in Aberdeenshire for her use of Scots. At the remote village of Strathdon all the services were conducted in Scots, and this attracted sizeable congregations to hear her. I travelled to Strathdon to consult her, but found she was ill and in Aberdeen Infirmary. I found her there, told my story, and was rewarded with her keen interest. She offered to

Last Years in South Leith 1988 - 1990

sketch out a service in Scots. I said there was still a week or two before the wedding, but she began writing straight away. With material from David Ogston and Dr Collie I put together a suitable marriage service in Scots, but the girl then said her mother now wanted the service in English, as many of the guests would be lost with a Scots service. I told the lassie to ignore her mother, who was needlessly nervous. 'It's your wedding', I told her, 'not your mother's'. We carried on with the Scots wedding, with the two principals well rehearsed in their responses. It was all a great success, and the guests all thrilled and very happy to have had the experience.

David Wood's sister, Lyndesay, was married and living in Qatar, where her husband worked, but they were proposing to retire and live in Cyprus, where they were having a house built. When it was reported that the house was ready for entry, Mary and I were asked whether we'd care to go on holiday to Cyprus, occupy the new house and make suggestions for any improvements or alterations that might occur to us. We gladly accepted this chance - Mary anticipating a relaxed time where warm summer weather could be guaranteed, and I very keen to visit Cyprus, which bulked so largely in Paul's life.

It was cheaper to fly on a plane arriving at Paphos around midnight, and I arranged for a taxi to meet us, and all went smoothly thus far. The house was at the village of Chloraka, which the driver said he knew. I said the house was one of a group of newly built houses, which the driver said he didn't know but anticipated no difficulty in finding once we arrived at the village. The snag was that everything was in total darkness. There were no streetlights. We couldn't even see a street, but after much prowling about the driver said we had arrived. He produced a torch, which gave us enough light to see the house at the end of a row of half-built residences. Ours was the only one that looked reasonably complete in the torchlight, and to reach the door with our cases we walked through a heap of builder's rubble. Fortunately, electric light and power in the house was working, but we paid little attention to anything. We were both dead tired and went straight to bed with the comforting thought that everything would be all right in the morning.

In the morning almost everything was all right. The house was lovely, with a verandah at the back where we could sunbathe and have meals. The one snag was my shoes, which I found encased in concrete. When we arrived in the dark the previous night I removed my shoes on entering the house as I realised I had walked through mud, which was adhering. This was one of the things that 'would be all right in the morning'. In fact, it was concrete which had presumably been lying and slowly setting since work finished the previous afternoon. Fortunately I was able to chip the concrete from my shoes without too much trouble.

Ours was the only house completed in a row of eight or ten being built, and the immediate surroundings were what was to be expected on a building site. A high wall ran parallel to the houses and about eight yards clear of the buildings. This wall had all kinds of plants growing on its face, and each evening, about sunset a man appeared with a hose and sprayed the wall thoroughly. I understood he in fact was the owner of the site and in this way could keep an eye on the workers' progress.

We were on the fringe of the village, and from our house a ten minute walk took us down to the beach. The road, however, was just a track, which ended in a stony fifty yards, difficult to cross. The beach was on a little bay - a sun-trap, secluded and warm. As Mary couldn't swim, and had always been very nervous of the water, this was a new experience for her. We spent all day in and out of the water. Not another soul appeared all day, which was perhaps not surprising, considering the difficulty of the approach to the beach. A bonus to that day's enjoyment was that on the way home we found the road was bordered by fig trees bearing ripe, luscious figs.

The villagers were very friendly and keen to converse, the only difficulty being that none of them had any English. We were urged to speak to one woman who, we understood, could speak English. The break-through on this front came on Sunday, when we went to church. In Greece we had found the church a dismal, dark place where everyone had to stand through the service, and the Scriptures were read in an old, traditional language no one understood any more. Here in Chloraka the church was a modern building in very light limestone, with large windows and seats for everyone. A fair number of children were at the service, and I found their behaviour quite remarkable. They were restless, of course, left their seats and ran around the aisles and in and out the doors of the church, which were left open.

But they were quiet; they talked and laughed, but there was no screaming or shouting and the congregation just seemed to take them for granted.

A man in the congregation spoke to us - in English. It turned out he was the local school headmaster, and he explained the service as it went on, and afterwards sat with us on a bench in the square outside the church and told us about the village. The church was indeed modern - Greek Orthodox, like that one in Greece, but here a different spirit possessed the people. The old church, still standing on the other side of the square, looked dark and grim, and the people had over years raised money, to build this new church, of which they were very proud. The village school was a primary school, and in their teens the children were bussed to Paphos. We had been unable to find a bus when we wanted it, but now we joined the school bus. This was not allowed, but the driver said he would take us to the outskirts of the town and drop us there. As this arrangement was illegal we were not charged any fare, and our presence on the school bus kept the children quiet, and we used this bus several times.

Paphos we found rather disappointing. Sites connected with Paul and Barnabas are pointed out, but the town itself has no distinctive character. Hotels and shops, as in many other towns, and some interesting traders in small workshops - and, of course, the eternal sunshine. This, for some people, all adds up to a perfect holiday location. We met a Welsh couple who spent some months here every year, being retired. The dependable weather here attracted them, but they hadn't given up their Welsh home. Somewhat to my surprise I now realised that cloudless skies day after day, week after week was monotonous. The unpredictability of the weather in Scotland is interesting, given good health, and of course is a conversational gambit when strangers meet.

However there was more to Cyprus than we had yet discovered. We went on a bus tour of the island, which included a trip up a mountain road. At something over 5000 feet the bus stopped and we stepped out to view the countryside. We didn't linger. It was desperately cold, and we were dressed for the tropical heat at sea level. It was on this same trip that we learned that the Turkish occupation of the north end of the island, of which we had heard but had seen nothing, prevented the bus touring that part of Cyprus. H V Morton once said that if he were able to choose anywhere in the world to live it would probably be Cyprus for its climate, but it takes more than climate to make an earthly paradise.

Dr Donald Davidson, minister at Queen's Park Church in Glasgow, in 1928 received a call from South Leith Parish Church, and on leaving his Glasgow charge he published a book, entitled 'Afterthoughts', which consisted of excerpts from sermons he had preached at Queen's Park. How this was done was never explained, for he preached extempore - i.e. without notes. He also cast aside the normal pulpit style of address and spoke in a conversational tone. He came from the West in his mid-thirties with a great reputation, and on being interviewed by the vacancy committee, said "I hope I may be able to fill your church, but I certainly could never fill your manse", and he refused to live in it.

The house that was the manse had never been built as such. It belonged originally to the Thorburn family - well-known as wholesale tea merchants in a very prosperous line of business, drawing customers from all over Edinburgh New Town. The family lived over the shop at the corner of Laurie Street. But Mr Thorburn, owner of the business, became the father of eighteen children from two successive wives. As this numerous brood could not be accommodated over the shop, a house with twenty rooms was built beside the stagecoach road from Edinburgh to London - an area developed as Hermitage Place. Here the family grew up, married and scattered. The old man married a third time, but the lady only said 'yes' on condition that there were to be no more children. One of the sons, David, entered the ministry in the second charge of South Leith, and at the Disruption he left the parish ministry and joined the Free Church. South Leith did not have a manse. The old manse had become ruinous in the late seventeenth century, and from that period the ministers had been paid money in lieu of a rent. David Thorburn's house was the largest private house in Leith, and he gave it to the Parish Church he had left, to be used as a manse. Since Donald Davidson refused to live in it, it has now become a hotel.

Now that I was seventy-seven years old I found myself in a similar situation to Donald Davidson. Mary and I were free to continue at 4 Claremont Park for as long as we liked; but just two of us in a twelve-roomed house with a garden of a third of an acre. As my daughter put it, 'If you don't leave now, one of these days you'll be carried out feet first.' There was a house waiting for us in St Andrews with six rooms, a kitchen, central heating and a quarter-acre garden. Why did I hesitate? Leith was holding me; the town so long ignored by Edinburgh, so long enduring poverty and unemployment, yet a community so closely bound together in pride of place and warm neighbourliness. Leith had as it were become part of me. So what was I leaving? What abiding memories would settle with me as long as I lived? I cannot list them all, but they crowd into my mind. From men and women in the Kirkgate congregation and South Leith, and the community at large, I learned patience, perseverance and dedication to a good end. These and other virtues in them I observed and learned many a much-needed lesson.

The Leith I was leaving, however, bore little resemblance to the town I grew up in. It is now a vibrant part of the City of Edinburgh. The long years of depression are now historical, and I have become a visitor.

EPILOGUE

Today there is a great shortage of ministers, and even with so many parishes linked and so many church buildings sold off, the shortage of ordained men and women is still acute. But entering the ministry is not easy. The candidate has to be interviewed by a Board, and that is a stumbling block to many an aspiring applicant, and rejected applicants are apt to think it is easier to go through the eye of a needle than for a would-be minister to pass the Board. Some are too old, having retired from another profession, some are judged as not being 'up to the job' or physically disabled. Epileptics don't get the length of the Board, knowing that they wouldn't stand a chance. In my day there was no Board. There was a Bible exam and a general conversation. I was naive, of course, not realising that you can't have fits in public places without the news penetrating far and wide with no one saying a word. Epilepsy was a mystery; doctors were baffled and the Church felt stymied, as many people thought St Paul had been epileptic. I was rejected three times as an applicant for missionary service. In war-time I was rejected by the Army; I was not allowed a driving licence. So the rules were set for my daily living and I had to conform.

As a youngster I was not 'kirk greedy', but Church and Sunday School were routine on Sundays, and it was only as I entered my teens that from time to time I was away at weekends camping or hiking. It was the advent of John Shedden from Glasgow as colleague and successor to 'Jimmie' Law, our minister, that suddenly brought the church alive to me. He was a powerful preacher who dealt with issues that were beginning to trouble me, and I felt it a personal loss when he died of war wounds from the First World War.

Who are we? Where have we come from, and where are we going? I could never see any sense in the atheist's belief that the universe started with a big bang and would end in a big hole. The stories in Genesis of Creation and the Fall I also found quite unhelpful, and at that time I was reading through the Bible as an exercise, as I didn't like arguing about what I had never read. I got some shocks. I found more than one version of the same story; Jacob and others had several wives; there were several examples of what we call ethnic cleansing. The *lex talionis* - an eye for an eye, a tooth for a tooth, also made me pause, and of course in the New Testament the Virgin Birth, the miracles and the Resurrection were all problems, to which could be added the Apostles' Creed. Far from driving me into agnosticism, these problems fascinated me. I could not brush them aside as of no account. They were real questions, apparently unanswerable; yet people had been living for centuries without any answers.

The Bible itself was a problem. It was said to be 'true', but the parts that would not fit into this were ignored, and very little of Scripture was ever read in public. The Church also, despite saints and martyrs and heroes, also had a dreadful record of persecution and all kinds of sin, from the apex of the hierarchy down to the groundlings. In fact it became clear to me that Christian faith could not be based on either the Bible or the Church. The Bible was an anthology of various books written by poets, philosophers, historians, storytellers - writers of many generations, through hundreds of years. These writers were all human, liable to error. People said they were inspired by God, so that what they recorded was perfectly true and free from error. But how could they be divinely inspired to produce two or more versions of the same happening? It was surely obvious that what we were reading in two different versions of how the first Israelite king was appointed, were two accounts by different authors using information they had from different sources.

The New Testament highlights another mystery. How can we describe or explain a spiritual experience? The Old Testament has examples of this, as in the story of Jacob's wrestling with God at Peniel; the boy Samuel discovering God calling him; Isaiah's awareness of God's presence in the temple. The New Testament tells of the angel's visit

Epilogue

to the pregnant Mary, the raising of Lazarus, the transfiguration, the resurrection, the miracles. These narratives are sometimes ambiguous, but they were real happenings, real experiences, but how can they best be put into words? It is the experience that matters, and it is on spiritual experience that our real religion is founded. The difficulties in describing or explaining them don't alter the reality of the experience.

I have spent many years among theologians and historians, and the ideas they throw up can be challenging and disturbing; but nothing alters or detracts from my ongoing experience of God in my life, day and daily. This is not a virtue; it does not make me in any sense better than anyone else. Faith is a gift from God; some have it, others don't. I don't know why. Nobody knows anything about heaven or the future life; we can only make pictures as in The Pilgrim's Progress - an attempt to describe what we are ignorant of. What we have is faith, and that is what our religion is built on. The Church is the organisation Christians have devised from the earliest centuries, to spread the faith, to support each other in times of trial or persecution, to strengthen one another's faith, to offer comfort and reassurance in grief, disappointment or trauma. But the Church is not divine; it is a human organisation, liable to error, open to adopt new methods and this has characterised it over the centuries. Our religion does not consist in our churchgoing; our religion stems from, and is founded on our spiritual awareness of God with us day by day. To those with faith this is a real experience, but always indescribable. The saints are those with a more vivid experience of God, who have made better attempts than the rest of us at describing that experience.

Christianity has spread remarkably in the world, multiplying from the twelve disciples to billions of believers today, and still growing more rapidly than ever before in the Third World. Even so, Christians amount to a small percentage of the world's population, and it should be noticed that Jesus anticipated his followers would never amount to more than a small minority in the world, as in the parable of the yeast. Christianity would not dominate the world by numbers, but by influence - and so it has come about.

There are few atheists or agnostics in the world. Most people are religious - by name at least, although they are not Christian. How significant is that for us? When I was young the Church was still sending missionaries 'to convert the heathen', and I recall attending General Assemblies in my teens on Foreign Mission nights, when in a packed house and a highly charged emotional atmosphere missionaries were dedicated to the work. That has all changed. Missionaries now go to serve and even become members of churches where their grandparents went to convert the heathen, and to gain new understanding of other faiths, for there are insights, and understanding of truth not much considered within Christianity.

There is the question of life itself. Is the divine purpose in creation completely fulfilled in human life and activity? Domestic and farm animals and the vast proliferation of wild animals all have life, and the birds of the air, the fish of the sea and the creepie-crawlie inhabitants of the earth all share life in some form or other. To a degree they live off each other, and we raise animals and birds specifically for food. So what is the significance of these variable forms of life? Were all these, and all the plant life that to a degree makes and sustains the universe, all created for us? We have to assume the Creator is real, but certainly not human. The Fount and Origin of the universe must be transcendent in mind, beyond gender and ageless. We may assume that God shares our way of thinking, approves our ideas of right and wrong, good and evil, beauty and ugliness, memory and conscience, time and eternity, because we were born with these attributes; but all these are aspects of faith, as is our expectation of a life beyond death.

These thoughts and expectations we Christians share in some degree with those of other faiths, but in Jesus Christ we are aware of a spiritual genius whose teaching and actions offer us inspiration and guidance. We assume rather too much in thinking human life is the sole purpose of creation. There are mysteries still beyond us, for example in the migration of birds and fish, in the intelligence of working dogs and horses, and those living close to animals would not deny them a kind of personality. There is a fellowship of life among the creatures of God.

On this philosophic and theological basis I have lived for over fifty years as a minister of the Church of Scotland. In that half-century public attitudes have changed markedly, especially in matters of faith and morality. Young couples coming to be married, nowadays, more often than not, have been living together. I have never refused such a request. People living together with the firm intention of being married eventually, are in quite a different category from those living together with no intention of marriage. The Church would be well advised to retreat to the pre-Reformation position, in which the Church blessed the betrothal, and the wedding followed when convenient.

Another difficulty today is the number of people leaving the Church because they do not see the Church as relevant to daily life. This way of thinking arises because people think only of what the Church does for them; but the Church only has meaning and relevance in daily life in and through the active membership. The greatest need of the Church in this country today, and of Christian marriage, is commitment.

DAMASCUS DIARY (1985)

Saturday morning, Heathrow 6.30 a.m. Plane for Paris at 7.30. Turbulent flight. An hour at Charles de Gaulle airport before flying to Damascus. We left Paris almost half an hour late and arrived at Damascus more than half an hour early. All this time gained was lost by the long procedure over getting through Damascus airport. Passports were examined; then 100 U.S. dollars were collected from each person entering the country. We had been warned about this charge. No other currency was acceptable. The man in front of us offered Canadian dollars, which were rejected. One of the dollars I had collected in Edinburgh had been torn and mended with a piece of sellotape. This caused quite a sensation. The two men behind the counter each examined the dollar bill closely, then summoned a third man, presumably their superior, who finally allowed the faulty bill to be accepted. Our passports were then examined again and entry forms issued to be filled in with many items of information including the names of my father and mother. We then collected our baggage and the cases were opened and inspected.

Graham was sharing a flat with Gordon Dobie, who had been a fellow student at Edinburgh, and they were now dying for some British news to read; but the newspapers I had brought were confiscated. A French magazine - Jour de France - was gone through page by page, and finally allowed through. Graham later told us that all foreign news items relating to Syria are always deleted before foreign papers are sold in Syria. Fortunately some other newspapers in our bags were overlooked. It was now pitch dark, but Graham got us on to the airport bus to the city. Over one third of the population of the country now live in Damascus. The city has grown rapidly in the past twenty years and now counts three million inhabitants from a total population of eight million.

The flat, on the fourth (top) storey of a block, was in the prestigious diplomatic area. The flat itself is gimcrack, the plumbing not far from the primitive, and there seemed to be a layer of dust over everything outside; but the President lived just around the corner (although I'm told a new palace was being built for him). Armed soldiers were on duty at all street corners and other important points. Not surprisingly there was no vandalism.

Many of the pavements were occupied by parked cars, so that pedestrians have to use the roadway, but the traffic is sympathetic. In the local High Street - shopping area - iron stanchions three feet high were set in the ground at the kerb, to prevent parking, so that shoppers can get access to the shops.

Everything Mixed with Mercy

We had dinner in a local restaurant - Graham, Gordon Dobie, his flatmate, Mary and me. Quite a small place - half a dozen tables, and everything bare, clean, and over-bright, with innumerable electric lights. Catering was *table d'hôte* - take it or leave it. This is universal in the city, except for the one or two very prestigious hotels. First, several plates of vegetables and salad were put on the table. One was a paste made from aubergine and oil; another was a mush of chickpeas; a third was a red and spicy mess - a hot red pepper to be approached with caution. A pile of what looked like very large, thin potato scones was placed alongside. This is Arab bread - *khobz* - a kind of unleavened, tasteless and tough article. Instead of handling knife and fork, these flapjacks are torn to pieces and used for scooping up the salad mush, and so eaten. I strongly disliked this *khobz*, and after two trials in different restaurants I gave it a miss thereafter. This course was followed by a large ashet of mutton chunks which had been roasted on a spit, served with roasted onions. This was good. For drink we were offered 7-up, Pepsi-cola, or water. We all chose water. Tap water here is drinkable, sweet and very good. Restaurants usually offer bottled water. Two more dishes of salad were served with the meat. This meal cost the equivalent of £1.80p each - astonishingly cheap.

Shops opened late in the forenoon - 10 a.m. or so. They closed from 1 till 5 p.m., and opened again till late evening.

Next morning was cool - in the sixties Fahrenheit. Sunday 10th November - Remembrance Sunday at home, but not here. Graham went off to get milk, but forgot to take empty bottles with him. The shopkeeper refused to let him have bottles; instead he took the cap from two bottles of milk and emptied the milk into a plastic bag! Bottles are scarce. A bottle of milk costs 3 lira (the Syrian pound), which equals 35p in our money, but 2 lira (25p) is a deposit on the bottle. The milk itself costs 10p a bottle - a half litre - roughly one pint. Graham assured us that if you buy petrol by the litre instead of having it hosed directly into your tank, the garage man will pour the petrol into a plastic bag, because of the shortage of petrol tins.

We three went to the local market - *suq* (Arabic spelling) or *souk* (English). This is a fascinating place - a narrow street, partly asphalted, partly bare earth. On each side hundreds of little shops/ booths, each with a six to eight feet frontage, and electric light. Vast quantities of vegetables and fruit. Tradesmen at work in the middle of their shop floor, making and repairing furniture, tailoring, baking, cobbling. The street is partly roofed over with corrugated iron as a protection against the sun. The roadway was extremely congested with pedestrians, stalls set up in the middle of the road, and through all this passed donkeys with saddle-bags containing immense bundles of vegetables, trolleys

Damascus Diary (1985)

and even motor cars nosing aside the crowds. Huge, misshapen tomatoes were on sale, badly marked, but tasting delicious - great red apples, bread fruit, aubergines, pomegranates, bananas, oranges. Hawkers bawling, children everywhere; everyone seemingly happy.

Many of the women were completely hooded - completely enveloped in black, nylon-type material. Through these black veils, however, they can see quite well. The main disadvantage to the wearer I imagine, is the stifling heat in warm weather. Other women had their hoods folded back to leave their faces exposed, but they could cover up at once if necessary.

In the afternoon, a party developed in the flat. Our immediate neighbours, two German students, Ulrich and Willy, dropped in for a chat, and then five Syrian students - Khalid and four girls - arrived. The girls, aged around 19 or 20, were all pretty, dark, lively and animated talkers. Graceful posture, beautiful manners. They talked, sang, drank tea and ate cakes until ten minutes to six o'clock, when they stood up, said goodbye, and departed with their escort.

Syrian girls are normally married at about 19 years of age. A girl usually marries a man of around 40, who is chosen for her by her family. Men seldom marry earlier; by then they have a settled job and income. Their place in life is settled. The couple usually meet for the first time at the marriage, and the girl brings a dowry. But a well-educated, pretty, personable girl, will bring a smaller dowry, as her intelligence, education and appearance are all valuable assets. Syrian girls are as romantically minded as their Western counterparts, dreaming of handsome husbands, but they are completely conformed to the system of their society and to its conventions. If unmarried girls go out, they must be home by six o'clock - dusk. There are no students' residences. The only women to live in such freedom are prostitutes. These four girls all live with their parents at home.

Monday morning we called at the British Embassy for mail. The man at the door didn't let us in; he handed out the bundle of mail he had collected at the Post Office and we sorted through it. We next paid a call on the house agent who had arranged accommodation for the students. He had a beautiful, ground-floor office with a fountain playing in the middle of the tiled floor, an aquarium and comfortable chairs for clients. This gent fancied himself as a comedian and indulged in a little horseplay with Graham and me.

We walked into the town centre and visited the *suq*. Nothing special here and like similar places in Jerusalem and Athens - the usual clamjamfrey of little booths and people, with donkeys and cars inching through the main alleys. The *suq* leads straight into the great Mosque where the head of John the Baptist is enshrined.

Lunch in a little restaurant on a main street in the city centre. Food quite uninteresting - the eternal *khobz* and salad. Back at the flat, Mary had a sudden violent attack of dysentery and retired to bed. Graham and Gordon went to a film at 9 p.m. - part of a film festival. Posters advertised this festival but the programme was not announced, and the boys say that it was probably being argued over, and that this was typical of the Syrian way of doing things. They had no idea what film they would see, and this remained the state of things all through the week-long festival. They went on several evenings. Sometimes it was good; sometimes very much the other way.

I had congratulated myself on having escaped the dysentery, but at 3.30 a.m. I had to run to the bathroom. Everything was in total darkness, for when the boys came home and switched on the light there was a short circuit affecting the whole flat. There are frequent power-cuts here. Gordon says the Government orders these cuts - normally every afternoon during the hours of siesta. The current saved is sold to Iraq - all grist to the mill, for there is a desperate shortage of money in Syria. Fortunately, Ulrich next door was once an electrician and he repaired our lights in the morning.

This was a very warm day, but Mary stayed in bed while I sat about reading and sunbathing on the verandah, Graham did his washing, went to change books at the library in the American Cultural Centre, and cooked the evening meal. He also bought us dysentery pills, although Mary had some with her, which she was rapidly gobbling up. Gordon has set himself the massive task of copying out a book in longhand. It seems the book is very important for him, and unobtainable in Britain, so he has borrowed a copy here and has got his head down to the job.

Wednesday 13th November. All in good health and spirits this morning. Got a taxi downtown and visited a shop specialising in tapes of classical music. Lady in charge (aged 35?) spoke excellent English. I got two tapes of Mozart Flute Quartets and two of the Bach Violin Sonatas. Graham got Strauss' 'Also Sprach Zarathustra' - 20 Lira each for these and 25L for longer tapes. This is about one-fifth of the price in Britain. Apparently the copyright laws are ignored here. I'd be back. Graham had about 130 tapes - pop and classical.

Lunch at a better restaurant next day, and no ill effects. Home again about 3.45 and soon joined by Khalid and friend, an Eritrean working here as press officer for the Eritrean Freedom Movement, Ulrich, and an American, Susan Carter - a student from Washington D.C. Intelligent and knowledgeable on the Middle East, about which she has written articles in U.S. and has edited some magazine there. Here

Damascus Diary (1985)

for nine months to improve her Arabic, loves the place (unlike Graham and Gordon), and attends the classes the boys are taking at the local institute for teaching Arabic to foreign students. She wears a wedding ring, but no husband in sight. A pleasant, civilised lass who thinks of taking this flat when the boys leave.

We changed money at a back-street money-changer, who gave us 16 Lira per £1 sterling. The official rate today is 10L per £1 stg. As in Israel, no-one changes money at the bank.

We decided to get tickets for a day-long trip to Palmyra by car, with chauffeur and guide, and lunch at the Meridian Hotel there. These trips are organised by the Karnack Bus Co., who also run the long distance buses in the country. The business of getting tickets was a prime example of the Syrian way of doing things. The Karnack agency is in the city centre and we made our way there, only to be told we must go to the bus station to get tickets. This was a fair distance away, so we got a taxi. At the bus station we fixed everything and were handing over the money when a discrepancy became evident, for the girl at the counter was asking much less than we were offering. It then appeared that in her brand of Syrian - or English - 'bus' and 'car' was covered by the same word. What we should be asking for was the 'American Car'. We were directed to the main office of the company - a four-storey building where all the finances of the company are handled. We made enquiry at various rooms on various floors of this building, always being passed on to someone else. Eventually a man passing from one room to another saw us dithering on the landing. He asked if he could help and we explained our case. Ah yes, we were in the wrong place. He politely took us down in the lift and out to the street, where he directed us round the corner. Round the corner we found ourselves at the place where we had started. This time another girl was behind the counter, and we got the tickets without any more trouble. Graham said this kind of thing happened again and again to him and Gordon.

Transport in Syria was cheap; petrol there was half the price it was in Britain, and the municipal bus service was seemingly good, but we were unfamiliar with the routes, and at the rush hour all the buses were packed to suffocation. I saw one bus running along with four or five would-be passengers clinging to the rail at the entrance, trying to struggle on board. At a bus stop, I counted over twenty passengers alighting and the interior still looked as packed as it had been before. Graham said he had seen passengers leaving by the windows as it was impossible to get to the exits when the bus stopped.

We now began looking for a book on flower arranging, dealing with Syrian flowers - at Mary's instigation. While most shops were closed in the afternoon for the siesta break, bookshops mostly remained open.

But every shop said either 'No flower books' or 'No English books', but persisting, we found a splendid place in the Cham Hotel block which was devoted to French and English books, and Mary found what she wanted - 'A history of Flower Arranging' by an American woman, for 50L (about £3 at our back-street exchange rate) as against the U.K. price of £3.95p.

Off before eight on Saturday morning, we mingled with children going to school. Classes ran from 8 a.m. to 1 p.m. six days a week, with Friday off. Christian schools had Sunday off. There are no organised games that I could see, but basketball was popular. Education is compulsory up to the age of twelve, when Primary School finishes after a six-year course, Preparatory School follows for three years, and then Secondary School for a further three years. University follows. According to the marks gained at school scholars are drafted to the various university courses. There seems to be no choice. The highest passers do the medical course; the next highest bracket go to engineering, and the rest appear to be given a freer choice of which course to follow. This arrangement presumably reflects the dire need of the country for more highly qualified personnel.

All boys do 2 years national service. This may be done at age 18, but if proceeding to the university they go as graduates to train as officers. There seems to be no idea of trying to select 'officer material'. No doubt there is a shortage; but officers don't actually fight - they just tell the other ranks what to do. Gordon and Graham assured me this is a fact.

The 'American car' turned out to be a large one, high slung, with wide windows for viewing, with room for eight passengers and the driver. We started from the British Embassy with the driver and a courier. The driver, with a huge spade beard and a European-style white checked cap, was overjoyed to learn we were Scottish. He announced himself as a Protestant Presbyterian. His great-grandmother was a Stornoway woman who married a Syrian, and he was very proud of the connection. On learning I was a Presbyterian minister he insisted on calling me 'Excellency' thereafter.

A three-hour drive took us to Palmyra. The desert road system was impressive and must have been a very expensive project. We passed a group of Bedouin. About a quarter of a mile from the road their black tents and animals were plain to see, as well as a couple of lorries. The courier said about 20,000 Bedouin still moved around the Syrian Desert, and they were not poor. They made yoghurt from ewe-milk and sold it. They owned their lorries and were well-dressed, but they stuck to the nomadic life. I read somewhere that in Saudi Arabia the nomads are gradually settling down as farmers, but in Syria this did not appear to be so.

Damascus Diary (1985)

I cannot understand how so many sheep and goats could survive on so little. We saw many herds in the desert, where nothing but sparse tufts of the coarsest grass are to be seen, and for miles on end nothing but sand and not a blade of grass. Here and there were pools of stagnant water, for there is occasional rain, but nothing grows around the water, for the earth is quite infertile. Yet the desert has its own resources. We saw a phosphorus mine, which yields ingredients for fertilisers, and in the area adjacent to the Iraq border oil has recently been discovered, which promises a better future for this struggling country.

Palmyra was originally Tadmor, and is so named on the map of Syria. The Greeks renamed it because of the innumerable palms growing there. This is the great oasis in the desert between Iraq and the Mediterranean. Here from ancient times the caravan routes travelling east and west, and north and south all met, and here the Romans built a town of 30,000 inhabitants. To date (1985) 40% of this Roman town had been excavated, and the work went on as money became available. The Poles worked here excavating for twelve years, but their financial resources dried up. The University of Chicago was then sending a party over every year, but no one knew at the end of one year's work whether money would be available the next year. Because of the summer heat and the rains in the early part of the year, work was only possible for about two months each year - March-April or September-October.

We were conducted through the local museum, the ancient city, the Temple of Bel (Baal) and the necropolis both above and below ground. The courier gave us a view of the Roman town from a nearby height, and pointed out the 'Praetorian Way' - the straight road running from end to end of the town. This, he said, was the common practice in Roman town-planning. Roman roads were always straight, and even towns did not affect the overall direction of the roads. The built-up area was developed on either side of the road - the Praetorian Way - the road along which emperors, generals, magistrates and other leaders and officials travelled with their following. This was locally 'The Street called Straight' - as in the old city of Damascus. The modern equivalent would be 'High Street' or 'Main Street'.

Back in Damascus that evening we saw another film - 'Heat and Dust' at the Cham cinema downtown - and so to bed. ('Cham', by the way, is the local name for Damascus.)

Heavy rain started while we were at lunch in the city so we ended the day at the flat.

Any bus journey in the city costs 1L - 5p in U.K. Tickets are purchased at machines in packets of five for 2½L. For ½L you may travel any distance which must be a considerable benefit for city workers.

Everything Mixed with Mercy

Graham was seedy one day and stayed at home, so Mary and I set out for the National Archaeological Museum. There is some splendid material here - a reconstruction of a tomb from the Palmyra necropolis - a Jewish synagogue with walls and ceiling completely covered with mosaic and frescos, and a magnificent hall or room panelled from floor to ceiling in richly carved wood, the ceiling and central cupola painted and with stained glass windows. The rest of the collection is set out in cases, most of them showing finds from one particular archaeological site. An Islamic section of the museum is being prepared, but is not yet open to the public.

Lunch in a nearby hotel - a good meal, but *table d'hôte*, like every other restaurant we visited - rice and spinach with a salad, followed by hamburgers and chips. Very ordinary, but we were relieved to be eating something we felt we could depend on not to start up our sickness again. Chips were served in minute portions - four or five each. There must be a shortage. The only sweet offered was custard, which we refused. Mary had had it the day before and did not wish to repeat it.

With his history of allergies Graham had problems with the food here and the poor standards of hygiene; but with caution, he was managing. We bought a bottle of milk - roughly a pint. This cost 35p, but as there is a 25p deposit on the bottle, the milk is cheap - 10p a pint, approximately. When emptied these bottles of milk look revoltingly dirty and they cannot be easily cleaned as they have narrow necks, like our lemonade bottles. Water was cut off about eight o'clock this evening, with no warning. We managed supper from water left in the kettle. The water came on again around 5 a.m., but this was going to happen daily until further notice: Khalid said this was because there was a shortage. The rains which ought to have fallen at the end of September failed this year. Presumably an announcement was made in the local press and radio, but we were unaware of it.

We went by taxi to a Shiite mosque about fifteen miles from the city centre. This was the only Iranian mosque in Damascus. It is a place of breathtaking beauty, still being built, as it had been for many years. They were now working on a second minaret. The completed minaret was covered with brilliant mosaics and enamelled tiles. Inside the building the walls and ceiling were covered with millions of little lozenges of mirror-glass - even the pillars. This dazzling effect is relieved by the brilliant colours of the carpets and enamelled tiles on a kind of wainscot. This would be garish and vulgar on a domestic scale in our country of muted sunshine and duller conditions, but here in this land of brilliant sun and little or no green vegetation and miles of entirely barren land, the effect is superb.

We are a conspicuous group in Damascus - men with fair hair and blue

Damascus Diary (1985)

eyes, and the lady's dress plainly European - targets for enterprising salesmen in the *suq*. As a haggler I'm a flop; I just pay the price asked, or move on. Mary and Graham are different. Mary had one purchase reduced from 90L to 50L, and Graham beats down taxi-drivers by asking for an estimate in advance. There are taximeters in the cabs, but drivers are allowed to add an apparently unspecified percentage to meet rising costs. This makes a kind of fencing match of the business, and without the language I am helpless.

At the flat Gordon was preparing a curry, so with Khalid, we ate a hearty meal at 10.30 p.m.

Reverting to the Army here, we saw two soldiers walking along the street hand in hand. Mary saw a bored sentry playing with his automatic rifle, tossing it up and catching it again; and I saw an officer in full regimentals lounging on the front steps of one of the Government ministries.

Thursday morning we called first at the Ministry of Emigration to get an exit visa. There was the usual complicated exercise of traipsing around from one queue to the next. Finally we were told to come back on Saturday to collect the visa, tomorrow being Friday, when the office would be shut.

On Friday we realised we had not eaten fish since our arrival here, so Graham said we could get fish in the Christian quarter, especially on Friday. After prowling around we found a place which provided a fish unknown to us. Plenty of bone, but the flesh sweet and toothsome. After lunch, strolling by the Barada river, Mary found a large glass and pottery shop. There was no building; the whole stock of earthenware and glass containers from small phials to huge carboys was laid out in the open on the banks of the Barada. This was impressive, for that stock could not be removed overnight and set out in the morning. Yet theft is unknown.

I took the bags of rubbish downstairs from the flat this evening. City rubbish is collected daily - or rather nightly. The collection begins about 11 p.m. and I heard the scaffies passing along our street on several nights from about 12:30 to 1 a.m. No bins are used. Everything is put into plastic bags and left on the pavement.

Mary and I went on another Karnak tour this morning. The road north has been driven through the hills in long and wide cuttings, laying bare the solid limestone. This, in turn is used for building the city. The whole of Damascus is stone-built - not a brick to be seen. The harder limestone is used for building, the softer variety for floors and pavements.

By the roadside, as it drives further and further into the desert, there are many large villas, and many still building, as we saw in Greece. They are first-class jobs of original and beautiful design. These are erected by Syrians who have jobs in the oil business in the Persian Gulf. Having made money, they build their dream homes here in the desert and live here, as and when they can.

On the way to Maloula we were shown over a very old convent, built on the summit of a high hill, approached by many hairpin bends, and finally up several long flights of stairs.

Maloula, one of three villages where Aramaic is still spoken, is an impressive place. The priest in charge assured us his church dates from before the fourth century A.D. The communion table looks like a solid block of stone, about three feet square on top. This altar, he said, is identical with the pagan altars of the period. The surface is not flat, but bevelled towards the centre. The one difference from the pagan altar is that whereas in the pagan altar there was a central hole through which the blood of the sacrifices drained away, this Christian altar has no hole, as no sacrifices were offered by Christians. This, said the priest, was the way in which Christians carried on worship during the centuries of persecution. Only when the emperor Constantine became Christian, and Christianity became the official religion of the Roman Empire - only then did the altar acquire a flat top and become a communion table. It is at least a good story.

Our guide also took us through a remarkable fissure in a mountain nearby. Centuries ago the mountain was split right through by an earthquake, and the two halves of the mountain, being solid limestone, have remained in position, only a few feet separating them. A stream now flows at the base of this fissure, and walking along the verge one can look up through the very narrow crack where the sun never shines. It is a cold place even on a hot sunny day. In the walls of this fissure are many caves in which people lived in many times of danger, and were never discovered.

Returning to the city, we had lunch at the prestigious Cham Palace Hotel. The restaurant is on the top (15th) floor, which is a panoramic revolving floor with. a magnificent view over the city. The cost of the meal matched the fact that this is the top eating-place in Damascus (in both senses) but it was a first class meal and we enjoyed the luxury.

The afternoon had to be given over to packing, and in the evening we went with Gordon and Graham to see a film at the Cham Cinema - part of the current film festival. A crowd, mostly of students of various nationalities, was gathered on the pavement outside the cinema. All the lights were blazing, but a man came along and told us there would be no film that evening. No explanation, just no film. Mary and I took

Damascus Diary (1985)

a taxi back to the flat, read, and went to bed. Graham and Gordon returned much later. With friends they had gone to a pub which refused to sell them any beer, because the next day was the birthday of Mohammed. This was the reason for the cinema's closure too. We missed the news, not reading the local press or attending the mosque or hearing local radio.

We got the airport bus at nine o'clock in the morning. The bus started with a full load, but apart from ourselves, there seemed only to be another two air passengers; the others were workers on various sites who were dropped off along the road. A number were airport employees.

Unexpectedly we had to pay the equivalent of about £1.50p as a last-minute tax for leaving the country. Graham said we were lucky; any Syrian leaving must pay 1000L (approx £100 sterling). When the plane did take off, there was a full complement of passengers - especially Syrians and French. France still has interests in the country after her long occupation of Syria as a Protectorate - the same period during which Britain had Palestine as a Protectorate.

While we waited to board the plane I spoke to a man from a Lebanese town who was bound for Paris to visit his brother. He said no planes were entering or leaving Beirut, so he had driven to Damascus to get a plane - a 2½ hour drive. About the continuing war there he shrugged his shoulders. The argument between the Druze and the Shiites gets more and more complicated. He said he did not understand it any more, and claimed that the ordinary Lebanese citizen was equally bemused. People just kept their heads down and hoped for the best. I had a wad of Syrian notes and found a branch of the Commercial Bank of Syria at the airport; but the man there refused to change my notes for any other currency - not even the U.S. dollars they insisted on my bringing with me into the country. As I doubted whether Syrian money would be acceptable in Paris I was despondent, but Graham had 38 U.S. dollars which he willingly parted with. I handed him my money and told him to keep the change, if any. (There would be just a little).

The homeward flight was uneventful, but the alteration of the time by three hours, returning to London ensured our being pretty well exhausted: but Jimmy and Lilian thought of everything, provided everything and smoothed our way to supper and bed.